James C. McClelland

CITIZENS FOR THE FATHERLAND
Education, Educators, and Pedagogical Ideals in Eighteenth Century Russia

J. L. BLACK

with a translation of
BOOK ON THE DUTIES OF MAN AND CITIZEN
(St. Petersburg, 1783)

EAST EUROPEAN QUARTERLY, BOULDER
DISTRIBUTED BY COLUMBIA UNIVERSITY PRESS
NEW YORK

1979

EAST EUROPEAN MONOGRAPHS, NO. LIII

by the same author

Nicholas Karamzin and Russian Society in the Nineteenth Century, Toronto: University of Toronto Press, 1975. xvi, 264 pp.

Essays on Karamzin: Russian Man-of-Letters, Political Thinker, Historian, 1766–1826, The Hague: Mouton, 1975. Slavistic printing and reprintings, no. 309. 232 pp.

J. L. Black is Associate Professor of History at Carleton University, Ottawa, and Associate Editor of *Canadian Slavonic Papers/Revue Canadienne des Slavistes.*

Printed in the United States of America

EAST EUROPEAN MONOGRAPHS

The *East European Monographs* comprise scholarly books on the history and civilization of Eastern Europe. They are published by the *East European Quarterly* in the belief that these studies contribute substantially to the knowledge of the area and serve to stimulate scholarship and research.

1. *Political Ideas and the Enlightenment in the Romanian Principalities, 1750-1831.* By Vlad Georgescu. 1971.
2. *America, Italy and the Birth of Yugoslavia, 1917-1919.* By Dragan R. Zivojinovic. 1972.
3. *Jewish Nobles and Geniuses in Modern Hungary.* By William O. McCagg, Jr. 1972.
4. *Mixail Soloxov in Yugoslavia: Reception and Literary Impact.* By Robert F. Price. 1973.
5. *The Historical and National Thought of Nicolae Iorga.* By William O. Oldson. 1973.
6. *Guide to Polish Libraries and Archives.* By Richard C. Lewanski. 1974.
7. *Vienna Broadcasts to Slovakia, 1938-1939: A Case Study in Subversion.* By Henry Delfiner. 1974.
8. *The 1917 Revolution in Latvia.* By Andrew Ezergailis. 1974.
9. *The Ukraine in the United Nations Organization: A Study in Soviet Foreign Policy. 1944-1950.* By Konstantin Sawczuk. 1975.
10. *The Bosnian Church: A New Interpretation.* By John V. A. Fine, Jr., 1975.
11. *Intellectual and Social Developments in the Habsburg Empire from Maria Theresa to World War I.* Edited by Stanley B. Winters and Joseph Held. 1975.
12. *Ljudevit Gaj and the Illyrian Movement.* By Elinor Murray Despalatovic. 1975.
13. *Tolerance and Movements of Religious Dissent in Eastern Europe.* Edited by Bela K. Kiraly. 1975.
14. *The Parish Republic: Hlinka's Slovak People's Party, 1939-1945.* By Yeshayahu Jelinek. 1976.
15. *The Russian Annexation of Bessarabia, 1774-1828.* By George F. Jewsbury. 1976.
16. *Modern Hungarian Historiography.* By Steven Bela Vardy. 1976.
17. *Values and Community in Multi-National Yugoslavia.* By Gary K. Bertsch. 1976.
18. *The Greek Socialist Movement and the First World War: the Road to Unity.* By George B. Leon. 1976.

19. *The Radical Left in the Hungarian Revolution of 1848.* By Laszlo Deme. 1976.
20. *Hungary between Wilson and Lenin: The Hungarian Revolution of 1918–1919 and the Big Three.* By Peter Pastor. 1976.
21. *The Crises of France's East-Central European Diplomacy, 1933–1938.* By Anthony J. Komjathy. 1976.
22. *Polish Politics and National Reform, 1775–1788.* By Daniel Stone. 1976.
23. *The Habsburg Empire in World War I.* Robert A. Kann, Bela K. Kiraly, and Paula S. Fichtner, eds. 1977.
24. *The Slovenes and Yugoslavism, 1890–1914.* By Carole Rogel. 1977.
25. *German-Hungarian Relations and the Swabian Problem.* By Thomas Spira. 1977.
26. *The Metamorphosis of a Social Class in Hungary During the Reign of Young Franz Joseph.* By Peter I. Hidas. 1977.
27. *Tax Reform in Eighteenth Century Lombardy.* By Daniel M. Klang. 1977.
28. *Tradition versus Revolution: Russia and the Balkans in 1917.* By Robert H. Johnston. 1977.
29. *Winter into Spring: The Czechoslovak Press and the Reform Movement 1963–1968.* By Frank L. Kaplan. 1977.
30. *The Catholic Church and the Soviet Government, 1939–1949.* By Dennis J. Dunn. 1977.
31. *The Hungarian Labor Service System, 1939–1945.* By Randolph L. Braham. 1977.
32. *Consciousness and History: Nationalist Critics of Greek Society 1897–1914.* By Gerasimos Augustinos. 1977.
33. *Emigration in Polish Social and Political Thought, 1870–1914.* By Benjamin P. Murdzek. 1977.
34. *Serbian Poetry and Milutin Bojic.* By Mihailo Dordevic. 1977.
35. *The Baranya Dispute: Diplomacy in the Vortex of Ideologies, 1918–1921.* By Leslie C. Tihany. 1978.
36. *The United States in Prague, 1945–1948.* By Walter Ullmann. 1978.
37. *Rush to the Alps: The Evolution of Vacationing in Switzerland.* By Paul P. Bernard. 1978.
38. *Transportation in Eastern Europe: Empirical Findings.* By Bogdan Mieczkowski. 1978.
39. *The Polish Underground State: A Guide to the Underground, 1939–1945.* By Stefan Korbonski. 1978.
40. *The Hungarian Revolution of 1956 in Retrospect.* Edited by Bela K. Kiraly and Paul Jonas. 1978.
41. *Boleslaw Limanowski (1835–1935): A Study in Socialism and Nationalism.* By Kazimiera Janina Cottam. 1978.
42. *The Lingering Shadow of Nazism: The Austrian Independent Party Movement Since 1945.* By Max E. Riedlsperger. 1978.
43. *The Catholic Church, Dissent and Nationality in Soviet Lithuania.* By V. Stanley Vardys. 1978.

44. *The Development of Parliamentary Government in Serbia.* By Alex N. Dragnich. 1978.
45. *Divide and Conquer: German Efforts to Conclude a Separate Peace, 1914–1918.* By L. L. Farrar, Jr. 1978.
46. *The Prague Slav Congress of 1848.* By Lawrence D. Orton. 1978.
47. *The Nobility and the Making of the Hussite Revolution.* By John M. Klassen. 1978.
48. *The Cultural Limits of Revolutionary Politics: Change and Continuity in Socialist Czechoslovakia.* By David W. Paul. 1979.
49. *On the Border of War and Peace: Polish Intelligence and Diplomacy in 1937–1939 and the Origins of the Ultra Secret.* By Richard A. Woytak. 1979.
50. *Bear and Foxes: The International Relations of the East European States 1965–1969.* By Ronald Haly Linden. 1979.
51. *Czechoslovakia: The Heritage of Ages Past.* Edited by Ivan Volgyes and Hans Brisch. 1979.
52. *Prime Minister Gyula Andrássy's Influence on Habsburg Foreign Policy.* By János Decsy. 1979.
53. *Citizens for the Fatherland: Education, Educators, and Pedagogical Ideals in Eighteenth Century Russia.* By J. L. Black. 1979.

to Melba Jernigan, Babs and Alison Flood, and Maryking

Contents

Acknowledgements

A number of people and institutions have contributed to this study in a variety of ways. Laurentian University, Carleton University, and the Canada Council have provided monies for travel, research, typing and other related work over the years since 1972 when the project first got under way. I am grateful, too, to the inter-library loan staffs at the Lenin Library in Moscow, Helsinki University Library, Laurentian, and Carleton for their perseverance in finding material for me. The Russian and East European Research Center at the University of Illinois, Champaign-Urbana and Yale University served me in good stead, as did the McGill University Library, where the microfiche versions of nearly all the eighteenth-century texts cited herein can be found. David R. Jones, director of the Russian Research Center of Nova Scotia, Cambridge Station, N.S., was kind enough to allow me access to his useful collection on military education. The first, and much different manuscript was read by Professor K. A. Papmehl of the University of Western Ontario, and he made suggestions that set me on a more practical path. Professor Paul Dukes, University of Aberdeen, contributed in much the same way. Mrs. Jackie Hunt read the final manuscript and made many useful suggestions about style. For all this help, I offer sincerely felt thanks.

Preface

As the reader will soon discover, the greater part of this work deals with Catherinian Russia. The main purpose of the information about earlier periods is to demonstrate the continuity of pedagogical thought and practice in Imperial Russia. Rather than examine the minutiae of institutional development and curriculums, I have chosen to emphasize the principles upon which they were founded. Furthermore, since educational planning on the part of the government in St. Petersburg is the focal point, certain patterns of schooling indigenous to non-Great Russian areas are alluded to only insofar as they affect the central question.

Moreover, the book features ideas of individuals and groups of people who made direct or near direct contributions to projects initiated by their monarchs. Therefore, the otherwise important writings of several well-known proponents of education and enlightenment, notably A. N. Radishchev, are granted but cursory attention.

Since this is a general overview intended mainly for students of Russian history and of education in eighteenth-century Europe, its footnotes include all relevant English-language sources along with the specific Russian-language references.

All titles of eighteenth-century works are printed here as they appeared in the original.

J.L.B.
Ottawa, 1978

Introduction

not very well-written in that main point are not focused or sharply made. some are question-ionable

Throughout the eighteenth century, the Russian monarchy and its adherents outwardly patterned their lives after their royal and noble counterparts in Western Europe. Russia's intellectual life mirrored that of the West even more. The apparent turn away from an isolationist tradition was no accident, for Peter I legislated the term "Muscovite" out of official nomenclature and abandoned the ancient capital, Moscow, for a new site on the Neva. Nevertheless, for all of the western gilt of St. Petersburg, Peter's "window on the West," the essence of Muscovite social and political tradition remained and sustained Russian autocracy until 1917.

Peter? Cath? Russian rulers continued to regard themselves as the possessors of ? God's divine sanction, with unique rights of testament which gave them both the responsibilities and the powers of paternalistic overlords. In the eighteenth century, they even had the right to select their own successors, no matter the chosen one's lineal connection to the throne. An obsequious church and a total absence of public political forums assured that Russians were still ruled by autocratic tsars even though Europeans might have found some comfort in the fact that that title was replaced by the less chilling one of Emperor.

The nature of absolutism in Russia is still a matter of debate among both Soviet and Western scholars, and there is a school of thought which sees absolutism in Russia as an innovation of Peter the Great. At least he tried to bring order to Muscovy's monarchical system, which was governed by a political philosophy that defined only loosely the source and degree of a ruler's authority. The uniqueness of absolutism in Russia, whether or not it commenced in the century of Peter and Catherine, is that it was to change very little in theory and practice over the subsequent two hundred years. Although one of its main institutional props, serfdom, was abolished in law by 1861, the role and character of its other components—bureaucracy, army, clergy, and service nobility—did not undergo many modifications after the eighteenth century. Indeed, it was in the eighteenth century that Russia's estates were given some definition. Centralization had been one of the consistent ambitions of Muscovite princes, and it was a starting point for most policies undertaken by the government of Imperial Russia. At the opening of the century, monarchies in Western Europe were very powerful, but none of them had at hand quite so strong a theology as that which supported the Russian ruler. And few of them had a bureaucracy as chaotic and ineffective as the Russian one. As the century progressed, the Russian state slowly grew more secular and efficient, and Orthodox leaders became less vital to the state apparatus than they had once been. But the paternalistic notions about the ruler's prerogatives in the field of ideas, which Orthodox leaders had finally accepted and then advocated in the seventeenth century, remained and were even strengthened.

The reality of the birth and accession to power of most eighteenth-century Russian monarchs tended to contradict the myths which were so important to their claims for legitimacy. Church and state-sponsored legends which justified monarchical omnipotence were often shaken by real crises at court. The predominance of foreigners and the quite alien visage of St. Petersburg unavoidably dented further the aura of sanctity which had surrounded Muscovite autocrats. Nevertheless, the office of monarchy was strong enough to allow rulers of foreign birth to withstand the intense xenophobia which permeated Russian society after the 1740s and even stable enough to make it possible for women to govern an empire in which they had been regarded as lesser beings.

One factor in their favour was the ability of most rulers to tie themselves to Russian national sentiment. In spite of their predilection for things foreign, Peter I, Elizabeth I, and Catherine II each became symbols of Russian greatness and patriotism. This was partly a result of their remarkable accomplishments in foreign affairs and their talents for "divide and conquer" at home. The birth of a nationalist belle-lettrism and the subservience of the illiterate and superstitious peasantry to church dogma also helped, as did the fact that the gentry needed a stable monarchy in order to strengthen its own claims to privilege. It may be, too, that the case put by Michael Cherniavsky is the correct one; that is, that the notion of a sovereign emperor in which all power resides was so well established in Russia by the eighteenth century that "a German woman could fill the position" without presenting a challenge to the sanctity of absolutism.[1] Whatever the case may be, the rulers of Russia also took specific cultural actions which contributed significantly to their own success. One of these was the policy initiated by Peter I and re-instituted by Catherine II of employing education as a means of creating a loyal and useful citizenry.

In most of Europe, educational theories and schools of all sorts were usually the result of individual experiments in pedagogical techniques. The founders of such schools had a variety of motives and their accomplishments were uneven. Kings and governments were also involved in education, sometimes on a small scale like Madame de Maintenon's programme for young ladies at the court of Louis XIV, and sometimes in larger projects like those sponsored by Maria Theresa and Joseph II of Austria. In Russia, it was the emperor and the emperor alone who initiated serious educational activity, and in this development Peter the Great's initiatives played a consummate role.[2]

Peter's educational system was designed primarily to train technically proficient servants of the state. This was no simple task, for before him there had been no secular school system in Russia. The Church long had a monopoly on whatever education had existed and it had been used to train men to occupy the place in the world to which "God" had assigned them.[3] After a long hiatus in educational development following Peter's death, Catherine II widened the school's function. She assigned to her educators the dual task of providing skilled technicians for state service and training an unfailingly loyal citizen body. She intended her subjects to be consumed with acceptable religious and moral beliefs, and fully cognizant of the benefits of autocracy.

Peter's attempts to hasten Muscovy's transition from a medieval, religious culture to a modern secular one, a process through which most West European nations had been going for two centuries, amounted to revolution. Struggle between advocates of change and those who wished to cling to the past remained a characteristic of Russian society for the duration of the century.

The progressive eighteenth-century Russian monarchs, above all Peter and Catherine II, recognized that their state desperately needed a literate populace. But autocracy also required an unquestioning populace. Constantly faced with this dilemma, the state characteristically reacted by prohibiting any scepticism, whether social, political or religious, no matter the cost to Russia's practical needs. Free and open enquiry was anathema to the Russian state and its right arm, the Orthodox Church, so just as it was everywhere else myth was a more vital and dynamic force than reality in the evolution of Russian national feeling. The history of Russian education then is in the first instance a history of a state monopoly. Thus, an examination of the state's presumptions about the purpose of education will help explain the nature of the state itself and the society which it encompassed.

The twists and turns of the fledgling educational system in eighteenth-century Russia have already been the object of monographic description in Russian, although very little further study has been undertaken since that completed in the nineteenth century.[4] D. A. Tolstoi, M. I. Demkov, A. S. Voronov, S. V. Rozhdestvensky, M. Vladimirsky-Budanov, N. P. Cherepnin, and others from the last century have left us both general and statistical information of value. Memoirs and correspondence of persons who designed and participated in eighteenth-century schools, for better or worse, also exist in reasonable abundance. These, along with various official publications, laws, and school reports, all provide a wealth of scattered material on Imperial Russia's embryo programmes. In English, Marc Raeff, K. A. Papmehl, and Nicholas Hans have singled out specific aspects of eighteenth-century Russian schools for study in periodical literature, but the widely-used general works on Russian education by Hans and W.H.E. Johnson touch upon that era in only a very cursory manner. Recently, two dissertations, one by Max J. Okenfuss on the first half of the century, the other by George Epp on Catherinian education provide us with an overview of the entire century.[5]

The purpose of the present effort is to survey and illustrate the attitudes of the Russian state, specifically its rulers, and a myriad of educators towards the function of schools. The actual institutions and curricula will be looked at only insofar as they shed light on the central problem, that is, the designated place of formal schooling in Imperial Russian society.

Russian noblemen retained throughout the century a faith in their obligation to serve the state. Even those personae who have been often categorized as liberal critics of the state and its paternal society, among them Pososhkov, Novikov, and Fonvizin, were basically adherents of the German *Aufklärung* in that they did not challenge autocracy so long as its rulers fulfilled an obligation to govern in the best interest of the governed. They had no quarrel with the assumption that subjects in their turn, especially educated noblemen, should obey and give dedicated service to their rulers.

Although formal study of *Aufklärung* was not really integrated into Russian education until the founding of the University of Moscow in 1755, its basic precepts were very much part of petrine ideology. For that reason, and in spite of the onslaught of French *philosophe* culture by mid-century, there was a consistency to Russian notions on pedagogy that endured for the entire century. And those notions will be the object of the present study.

As the classic demonstration of Catherinian ambitions for her schools, the textbook, *On the Duties of Man and Citizen (O dolzhnostiakh cheloveka i grazhdanina kniga,* St. Petersburg, 1783), which was made compulsory reading for national public schools in 1786, has been translated by Elizabeth Gorky of Laurentian University, Sudbury, and is included with this text.

* * *

In order to fit into a larger context the attempts by Russian rulers to find the best means for training their subjects to be good citizens, even a skimpy overview of events and peoples involved in such undertakings in Europe during the eighteenth century may prove valuable.

In every European country there was mixed concern with the nature and purpose of education. Nowhere was there an established public schooling programme which suited all educators and statesmen, or which was yet able to meet the needs of rapidly modernizing nation-states. The variety of theoretical and practical pedagogical conclusions reached, and the general weakness of school systems before the French Revolution, indicate that in this area Russia did not lag far behind Western Europe.

Poland's Committee for National Education which was founded in 1773 was Europe's first state educational authority, and was formed just in time to witness the slow absorption of that ill-fated nation by Prussia, Austria, and Russia.[6] Although the stimulus towards school reform in Poland was undoubtedly a common panic felt after the First Partition of 1772, it was contemporary to a general move, throughout Europe, in the direction of the national and the practical in schools. The philosophical milieu for most of the century was dominated by Classicism which emphasized order, balance, and simplicity. It was widely touted by the *philosophes* who concentrated on reason and analysis. In their attempts to emulate the ancient Greek search for a systematic interpretation of reality and the Roman view of civilization as an organized, cooperative enterprise, eighteenth-century neo-classicists showed a concern for the family, the role of women, and the mutual obligations of rulers and subjects. They thought in terms of the state as an organic whole, the components of which should all contribute to its welfare. Their emphasis upon good citizenship was translated into practical policy by statesmen who were concerned with the encompassing nature of the warfare which was the constant arbiter of relations between states in the eighteenth century. They recognized the need for new technology and bureaucratic centralization if they were to survive further such conflicts. Schools were seen as incubators for the country's future warriors, civil servants, and technocrats. The usual attention paid to Latin in schools was rapidly either replaced or accompanied in continental Europe by the vernacular; and secular, moral education tended to take over from instruction dominated by religion. Special schools for the nobility and reliance upon private tutors helped widen the gulf between the upper and middle classes. Moreover, as the century progressed, there developed within aristocratic circles the conviction that their sons should be educated to govern, and that other classes of people should be trained specifically to obey. The growth of political idealism and its formulation in principles behind political institutions during the second half of the century brought an intransigence to the political philosophies of Europe. And that helped shape people's attitudes towards the purpose of schools and the type of citizens they were expected both to serve and produce.

In the Germanies there was a tradition of active educational programmes which stemmed from the religious debates of the Reformation and the need to establish schools in support of particular religious creeds. By the eighteenth century, the German aristocracy was being taught modern utilitarian subjects, with less emphasis on Latin and religion, and they had their own fashionable boarding schools where they could learn things deemed suitable for upper society. Languages, modern politics, history, geography, genealogy and some of the natural sciences were given special attention, and knowledge of the law was regarded as indispensable to future rulers and officials. Mathematics, rhetoric, and courses in the social graces were also considered important. Part of the young aristocrat's education was the Grand Tour. Separation of the nobility from even the upper middle classes increased during the eighteenth century, and the emphasis on class distinction often resulted in the use of private tutors in wealthy homes until the young nobleman was able to attend university.

The peasant in the Germanies received little in the way of education, though most states offered free teaching in the villages. In practice, attendance in village schools was irregular and the quality of teaching poor. The provincial gentleman tended to begin his education with the village schoolmaster and continued it at a grammar school in the nearest town. Few advanced beyond that level.

In the towns, grammar schools continued to teach classical learning and religion, and the private tutor reigned supreme. The *Aufklärung* placed emphasis upon education but not very many people below the

upper middle classes actually benefited from it. J. P. Basedow
(1724–1790) introduced utilitarian principles to German pedagogy in
the 1770s. Basedow's work in Prussia followed closely that of La
Chalotais in France, and his publications on curriculum and methodology incorporated the ideas of Amos Comenius, John Locke, and
J.-J. Rousseau. Assisted in part by money from Russia's Catherine II,
he set up in 1774 a model school, the *Philanthropinum*, at Dessau. It
failed because of weaknesses in Basedow's own character, but his
teachers transformed the school system in Prussia. Influenced also by
Rousseau's naturalistic approach to education, Basedow's followers
made the instilling of patriotism into students one of the main purposes
of schooling in Prussia. In 1762, the university conference in Moscow
called for the translation into Russian of Basedow's syntax of German
grammar. It was used by M. I. Agentov as a basis for teaching German
to young Russians.[7]

   A *Realschule* was founded in Berlin in 1747, and it became the model
for schools of practical training for the middle classes who did not go
to the aristocrat oriented universities. Frederick William I had established elementary school programmes as early as the 1720s, and they
remained unchanged until the passing of a *Landschul-reglement* in
1763, which made schooling compulsory. Prussian kings constantly
called for practical programmes, but hoped only that the schools
would produce contented citizens, trained in religion and morals, who
would not be interested in challenging the status quo. Frederick the
Great expanded the school system for youngsters, but maintained the
utilitarian motivation for it established by his father. Secularization
and centralization were his main contributions to the edification of his
subjects.

   Whatever the monarchical ambitions for schools were, German and
Prussian education in practice owed much to Immanuel Kant
(1724–1804). Advocating education for citizenship, he emphasized the
creation of good persons as opposed to simply useful citizens. Kant
read Rousseau's *Émile* and *Le Contrat sociale* and took from them the
idea that moral development was far more important to man and his
society in the long-run than was purely technical training. In the 1760s
he wrote that students must be taught to think for themselves, so that
they could use reason to combat wrong doing. "Man must be educated
to be good," he said, adding that the initial move in that direction
should come from parents. A number of Kant's former students became prominent in Prussian education. Like Locke and Fénelon, who
were to play an important part in the formation of the educational

ideas held by Russia's empress Catherine II, Kant included discipline and moral training in education with a view to forming the student's character. He did not approve of Basedow's insistence upon state control, but he was enthusiastic about the *Philanthropinum* and wrote a very favourable evaluation of it.[8]

It was in the area of higher education that the German states excelled, for it was there that secularism was more firmly entrenched and new ideas could be absorbed and spread to peoples of other nations, including the large number of Russians who travelled to Europe and studied in German universities. The higher institutions gained most of their students from state schools (*Fürstenschulen*), several of which were founded as early as the sixteenth century.

The state schools were expected to provide civil servants for the state and novitiates for the church, so they concentrated on Latin and on religious matters. Each town of any importance had a grammar school as well, run by the town council. For the peasants there were *Volksschulen,* which accomplished little more than the rudiments of reading, writing and memorization of the catechism. There had also developed in the seventeenth century special schools, *Ritterakademien,* for the sons of the ruling class. Here the young aristocrat learned to imitate the customs of French upper society, and gained little in the way of knowledge. But Leibniz saw great potential in them and the eventual establishment of such institutions in Russia may well have stemmed from his enthusiasm for their principles if not for their practice.

New ideas which stressed efficiency and modernization seeped into the upper schooling system with the founding of a university at Halle, Prussia, in 1694. It was at Halle that the Pietist conception of the state as an institution responsible for its subjects' welfare was best disseminated. The university was dominated by A. H. Francke, who insisted that the purpose of schooling was to prepare young Germans for public life by instilling in them practical skills, a sense of morality, and the idea of responsibility. Instruction in the German language, appeals to freedom for research and of ideas, and rationalism characterized this development. Textbooks by Christian Wolff and the notions of Leibniz brought a spirit of criticism to German academia. The useful, the rational, and the practical were the catchwords of education as it was espoused at Halle, Leipzig, and Marburg. These ideas were to make a great impression on Russia's Peter the Great, who conversed and corresponded with Leibniz. "The Prussian spirit of efficient practical organization," is what W. H. Bruford calls it in his book on eighteenth-century Germany.[9]

At the University of Göttingen, where a great deal of research was done on Russian antiquity and from whence professors of history came to the Russian Academy of Sciences and universities, there was more emphasis placed on the learning process as something distinct from instruction. Because Göttingen was in Hanover and so ruled by a king who lived far away in England after 1714, politics were relatively unimportant there. Thus, the university, which was founded in 1734, was reasonably unrestricted in matters of freedom of speech and enlightenment. It was through these institutions and others that German principalities became the centers for and exporters of university education. There was no doubt, however, that their purpose was to train men to serve the state efficiently and loyally.

In France, which had a tradition of centralization in most political and intellectual activity, the problem of education was far less complicated. Organized school systems existed before the eighteenth century, and the University of Paris had been strengthened considerably at the turn of the century by Charles Rollin (1661–1741). One of France's most important educators, Rollin insisted that the purpose of teaching was to create, "bons chrétiens, bons fils, bons pères, et bons citoyens."[10]

From the sixteenth century until the 1760s, education in France was a monopoly of the Jesuits. By the middle of the eighteenth century, however, religious and political issues and the rationalism engendered by the *philosophes* brought the Order into disrepute. A series of decisions by various parlements of France, and a royal edict expelled them from that country in 1764. That left an educational vacuum which called for immediate filling. Writings by Helvétius and Condillac attracted attention to a more pragmatic type of education than that offered for so long by the Jesuits. In fact, education had long since been a matter for considerable discussion, but the disappearance of the Jesuits from the scene stimulated an outpouring of plans for instructing France's youth. Louis-René de Caradeuc de la Chalotais (1701–1785) campaigned for complete state control of education for the purpose of creating a suitable citizenry for France. He supported a secular education, with emphasis upon French instead of Latin, recent history instead of the Classics, and a more systematic teaching of religion. La Chalotais had an ally in Diderot, who was to bring his own ideas on education to Russia personally in the 1770s. But they differed sharply on their assumptions about who should receive the benefits of education. La Chalotais and many others like him were convinced that too much education was bad for those who were fated to perform the necessary menial tasks in society.

It was in France too that the idea that education might provide the means for creating a new, more moral generation of citizens first became popular. Pedagogues called for moral training in schools, filled curricula with didactic readings, lessons in ethics, and moralistic handbooks.[11] Increased emphasis upon practical subjects naturally followed, and so did the notion that education could bring a basic uniformity to society. These new axioms gained wide currency in Europe.

Émile, ou l'éducation was published by Rousseau in 1762 and raised the question of the role of children in education. The importance of childhood as a crucial formative stage in life received wider recognition as *Émile* became the most fashionable book to read in Europe. But the issue had been raised earlier by John Locke, who had stressed the formation of good habits in children in his *Some Thoughts Concerning Education* (1693). In their original languages and in translation, these two books remained for a long time the most widely-read works on education in Europe. Locke insisted that the earliest years of a child's training were by far the most important ones, for they saw the formation of his later demeanour. His *Essay Concerning Human Understanding* (1690) had advanced the idea that the mind was a *tabula rasa,* or a completely blank mechanism, on which the environment and experience worked and created the educated man. This notion was taken up by the historian David Hume, the utilitarian Jeremy Bentham, and the French *philosophes* of the 1760s, whose rationalism became the framework for most intellectual activity of the times. C. A. Helvétius, (1715–1771) in particular, saw the importance of the human as opposed to the physical environment as the proper context for educational development. One of the products of eighteenth-century rationalism was the conviction that the governing classes could be educated from youth to govern. Morality, too, was placed among the sciences by Locke, and by Helvétius, as something "capable of demonstration."[12] Such assumptions were picked up in diluted forms by Russians, among them Feofan Prokopovich during the first decades of the eighteenth century and by Ivan Betskoi in its latter years.

Reform and experiment characterized the school system in Britain as well. In the early years of the century there existed grammar and public school programmes which allowed a fairly widespread cross-section of the middle class and gentry to achieve a basic education. Elementary education for the poor had not progressed since the seventeenth century, and was limited to Charity schools and Sunday Schools run by groups of subscribers, or to the workhouses of the large parishes. Privately endowed schools increased rapidly in the next century, and so did those for which tuition was necessary, but there was little coordination between them. Illiteracy was the lot of the majority, but for the ambitious a reasonably available teaching apparatus existed.[13]

As early as the 1750s, reformers like William Gilpin and David Manson advocated that schooling be closely related to society and that the authoritarianism of existing schools be abrogated. Gilpin demanded that schools instill some kind of moral principles into their students, and that youngsters be swayed towards the "love of order, law and liberty."[14] He saw that the needs of the community should take precedence in curricula over the traditional field of concentration, the Classics. Like Gilpin, Manson rejected such things as corporal punishments and advocated that students master the English language and its literature before anything else. He also sponsored moral education to the extent that he insisted that "virtue is preferable to learning."

Émile was translated into English several times in the 1760s and made a lasting impression upon English educational ideals.[15] The private tutor became the rage throughout Britain's upper classes, as parents tried to emulate the young Émile's education for their own children. Above all else, Rousseau's writing put the child at the centre of the learning process and showed the folly of trying to produce young carbon copies of all that was useless and extravagant in society. But Rousseau had his British and Scottish opponents who espoused the rigid indoctrination of youngsters in the established traditions. Arguments over whether or not the child was naturally wicked or virtuous were commonplace among those who tried to work out some basic philosophy of pedagogy. Such discussions were to have their counterparts in Russia.

Eighteenth-century English educators pondered the purpose of education and most reached conclusions like those of David Williams, who wrote in the 1770s that education was the act of forming a man on rational principles, enabling him to enter the community and become a good citizen.[16] Nevertheless, education in Britain remained somewhat haphazard and in the hands of private individuals and groups.

Among all the European examples to which Russians could turn for guidance, the Austrian Empire of Maria Theresa and Joseph II was to provide the most appealing model. Jesuit schools long held sway there as they had in France, and only a few *Ritterakademien,* established by Charles VI (1685–1740), broke their monopoly on the instruction of Austria's youth, but they were attended only by aristocrats. Some change had been initiated in 1749 when Gerard van Swieten was asked by Maria Theresa to reform the medical school and then the other faculties of the University of Vienna. When the Jesuit Order was dissolved by Pope Clement XIV in 1773, depriving schools of their traditional teachers, the Austrian monarchy had to look for new means to educate its subjects. An immediate consequence was the issuing of the famous edict, *Allgemeine Schul-Ordnung* in 1774, which called for the complete coordination of schooling facilities into a national, centralized system. It was written by the Prussian educator, Abbot J. I. Felbiger, who had been invited to Vienna by Maria Theresa. His associate, the Serbian pedagogue, Theodor Iankovich (later Mirievski, or de Mirievo) was to go to Russia in the 1780s to serve as Catherine II's chief adviser on education.[17] *Volksschulen* were organized for elementary instruction, and in Austria they provided a unique, even pleasurable learning experience. Competent teaching, emphasis upon equality of opportunity, and moderate rules made these schools the envy of Europe.

Joseph II, who became co-regent in 1765 and was emperor 1780 to 1790, had an obsession with creating "respectable moral citizens," and Austrian schools were designed to impart ethics, religious instruction, and patriotic loyalty. His most helpful ally in this endeavour was Joseph von Sonnenfels (1732–1817) who had expressed the opinion in 1767 that the role of education was to make citizens out of individuals. Good citizens, he said, were men educated to love their ruler and to respect his laws. Von Sonnenfels was appointed to the chair for political and administrative economics at the University of Vienna in 1763, where one of his students was Iankovich. In 1779, von Sonnenfels became a member, and then vice-president, of Austria's Commission on Education and Censorship (*Studien- und Zensur-Hofkommission*) and worked hard at achieving the educative ends he had called for earlier.[18] Thus, the cameralist philosophy which dominated Austrian political and economic thought came to include the centralization and control of ideas. Schools took on a firmly utilitarian rationale which called for strict adherence to prescribed textbooks (*Handbücher*) and standardization of pedagogical method. From this school system were to come the Austrian Empire's soldiers and bureaucrats.

Russians were aware of all the changes and new ideas in the field of education in Europe, for representatives of its young aristocracy studied in Europe throughout the century. Rulers consciously undertook to examine the organization of schools in the West. The process began in 1697 when Peter I sent Peter Postnikov to England to study medicine and the means whereby young Englishmen were educated.

Postnikov became the first Russian physician. Fifty other students were sent to England, Italy, and Holland in that year. His instruction to them, however, insisted that they acquire technical knowledge only. Any general learning had to be on their own time and as a result of their own inclination.[19] Thirty more were despatched to Western Europe in 1716.

Catherine II was the next monarch to send an official delegation to England for educational reasons. In 1764, she sent a group to seek information on universities and schools. According to Gladys Scott Thompson, the commission produced a comprehensive survey of a wide stratum of schools in Great Britain.[20] There is no evidence to suggest that Catherine took much heed of the report, but she did send students to study in English and Scottish institutions.

Peter also began the practice of directing young noblemen specifically to Leyden, when four students journeyed there in 1719. Catherine II ordered several other groups there in the 1760s. All in all, one hundred and twenty Russians were to register at Leyden during the eighteenth century. Nicholas Hans has printed a chart on each of these students, indicating the skills which they eventually brought back to Russia.[21]

M. V. Lomonosov, who became Russia's greatest academic, was sent with others to the University of Marburg in 1737, where they studied under Christian Wolff.[22] Peter III ordered S. E. Desnitsky and I. A. Tret'iakov to Glasgow University in Scotland in 1761, where they remained for six years. They were both appointed to Chairs of Law in Moscow in 1768 and brought with them the ideas of Adam Smith and of the Scottish enlightenment.[23] Catherine continued the practice and chose six of her Corps of Pages, and six others, to go to Leipzig for a liberal education in 1765. Among these was the future juridical expert and author of the first major literary assault on Russian society, Alexander Radishchev.[24]

The university at Leipzig was a major intellectual centre in Germany, and there the young Russians came into contact with a great variety of ideas. Their curriculum included a good deal of history and law, and they were able to listen to famous men of other disciplines. C. F. Gellert, the moral philosopher, lectured to them and his works were later used as textbooks in Russia's *pensions*. The writings of the French *philosophes* were eagerly read by the Russians who were particularly attentive to Rousseau and to the *Encyclopédie* of Diderot and d'Alembert. Helvétius also had considerable influence on Radishchev and his friends, and it was from him and the Marquis de Condorcet that they and later Russian students in Europe picked up the notion that education was the primary agency of social progress — "educational meliorism" as S. E. Ballinger calls it. Helvétius's *De l'Esprit* (1758) was banned in France, but his Russian pupils knew the work well and were taken with its theme that morality could be taught in the same way that other subjects could be disseminated to children.[25]

Other Russians studied at Oxford, Cambridge and Edinburgh, at Halle and Göttingen, and in various institutions in France.[26] Some, like Lomonosov, returned home very well educated. Others came back to Russia with a zest for luxury and vices, but no education whatsoever. And nationally-conscious Russians of the latter quarter of the century wrote of the futility of education in Europe. Denis Fonvizin, N. I. Novikov, Princess E. Dashkova, I. N. Boltin, and others were all to warn their readers of the dangers of a foreign education, although they worried about it on different grounds. The point to be made, however, is that there were plenty of Russian witnesses to the unfolding of pedagogical theory and practice in Western Europe. The extent to which these ideas were applied to Russia, both by foreigners and by Russians who studied in Europe, remains to be seen.

I

The Seventeenth Century:
Some Preliminary Ideas

But earlier he implies that utilitarian ed. ideas had an a-religious tone·

The conception of education as a means of creating loyal and acqui-
escent subjects of the state and faithful followers of Orthodoxy originated long before the eighteenth century. There were a number of
attempts by individuals, especially within the Church, to establish
patterns of instruction which would at least keep young Russians
within the fold of Orthodoxy. Indeed, if one wished to do so he could
find evidence of educational projects as far back in Russian history as
the time of Vladimir I. But, although no real visionary had appeared
who thought in terms of systematic educative programmes even as late
as the seventeenth century, there were scattered endeavours on the part
of quite a few progressive men who collectively brought to Muscovy a
limited but permanent corpus of pedagogical thought. The purpose of
this chapter is merely to name some of those men who were concerned
about education and to indicate the reasons for and the nature of that
concern. It should be borne in mind that the seventeenth century was
one of competition for souls between advocates of various types of
Christianity and other religions, so that a particularly significant
catalyst for thinking about schools was the defense of religious belief.
That kind of motivation, which was eminently practical, helped shape *ok,*
secular attitudes towards the purpose of instruction as well, and it gave *maybe*
to early school institutions and plans a utilitarian character.

One of the first written schemes in Russia which was related primarily to the instruction of youth was the sixteenth-century *Domostroi,* or
household guide. A collection of rules to direct parents in the rearing of
children at home, it urged that Muscovy's youth be taught to fear God,
to live decently, and to be obedient.[1] These, of course, were the standard criteria for proper upbringing everywhere. Although not an official government document, the *Domostroi* exemplified a principle
that was to be reformulated under Peter the Great and Catherine II
two hundred years later, and once again under the name "Official
Nationality" in the subsequent century. In essence, it assumed the

family unit to be an institution of the state and recognized the father as an autocrat at home, with the obligation to manage his estate within his means and to raise his children in the best interests of crown and Orthodoxy. Elementary education, that is, basic reading, writing, and religion, remained the responsibility of parents well into the eighteenth century even though alternatives were actively sought out. The *Domostroi* was designed specifically for those families who could not afford to hire domestic teachers.

The state, the family, and the Church were depicted in the *Domostroi* as the three closely related parts of Russian life. The state was the political force which assured that God's law would be the guiding light for the community, the family served as the social unit which kept individual parts of the state believing in a political ideal, and the Church was the cohesive force which maintained the connection between family and state. Religious tenets were carefully spelled out in the first six of sixty-four rules, and the seventh ordered that subjects "hold the Tsar in awe and serve him faithfully." There followed more religious commandments, instructions on the role of each member of the household, including servants, and suggestions on how they were to treat with each other. A number of the regulations embodied specific lessons for the rearing of children. Save and educate them through fear, the *Domostroi* suggested; punish them frequently so that their souls will be saved.[2]

Women were given guidance in household economy even to the proper arrangement of furniture. The master of the house was instructed on purchasing practices, estate management, and on how to keep his wife in a subordinate and humble frame of mind. The book ended with a long semi-sermon on life from a father to his son, which foreshadowed similar testaments from the eighteenth-century thinkers, Tatishchev and Pososhkov. It was the first in a series of state-sponsored catechisms on life and living which culminated with Catherine II's, *On the Duties of Man and Citizen*.

Similar but more sophisticated educative rules were laid down in 1624 for the School of the Lutsk Brotherhood in Kiev, which at that time was in Poland but was soon to be integrated into Muscovy. Although these rules were designed to guide teachers and had little general circulation, they mirrored an overall notion about the purpose of education which was eventually absorbed by northern educators. Above all, the teachers' job was to instill the fear of God into their students. "If it is written down," said article five, "it has been written down for our instruction." This was an easy enough assertion to make at that time, for there were relatively few books published in seventeenth-century Russia. Their content was screened by Church and state authorities, whose monopoly on the published word was to remain a characteristic of Russian cultural life. More concerned with behaviour than with actual learning, this series of twenty regulations set a pattern for proponents of education in the seventeenth century and the subsequent century as well. Similar rules existed at other brotherhood schools.[3]

In a recent study, Max J. Okenfuss has shown that the Orthodox brotherhood schools provided 'a more extensive education for their pupils than has usually been assumed, and that Latin rather than Church Slavonic was their main language of instruction.[4] Thus, intellectual contact with the West was possible for young Russians, especially when Peter Mogila dominated Orthodox Slavdom between 1633 and 1647. But the Church's tendency to make learning and heresy synonymous assured that the few existing educating institutions paid little attention to broad knowledge. Since they owed their very existence to Orthodoxy's need to take the offensive against Lutheran and Roman Catholic inroads among Muscovy's faithful, instruction or propaganda was their chief concern. As a matter of fact, school authorities forbade their teachers any free access to foreign books to the extent that alleged breaches in conduct could lead to exile in Siberia, or even to burning at the stake.[5] By the middle third of the century, many Orthodox Church Fathers at least had recognized a need for an organized programme of instruction, and it was the argument between proponents of either a Latin or Greek predominance in religious education which prompted competition for students. Silvester Medvedev was one of the leading advocates of the Latin language and culture and, as head of the Zaikonospassky Monastery, he tried to develop a latinizing school and academy in Moscow during the 1670s and 1680s. The Greek faction, led in the mid-eighties by the Likhud brothers, resisted Medvedev's efforts so effectively that the leader of the Latin group was burned for heresy in 1691. But in the long run, the Grecophiles could not withstand pressure from the Western-looking latinizing theologians. The Likhuds were expelled from the Moscow school themselves in 1694, and by the end of the century Latin had become the intellectual language of Russia. Since that tendency of thought had a relatively more tolerant attitude towards secular thinking, the trend was important to the future of learning in Russia.

The Kiev-Mogila school (founded 1632) remained the closest thing to a Western style arts institution long after Kiev was incorporated into Muscovy. The Slavonic-Latin-Greek academy at the Zaikonospassky monastery in Moscow (opened in 1687) was the only other significant educational operation in Russia at the turn of the eighteenth century. The Likhuds brought Aristotelian physics to the academy, which gave it a broader curriculum than that at Kiev. In its first year it attracted more than seventy students. Members of the school's faculty functioned as censors of imported books and were asked to keep an eye on the non-Orthodox teachers in Russian schools. Nevertheless, from its classes came M. V. Lomonosov and L. F. Magnitsky, both very important cultural leaders in eighteenth-century Russia. The learning process was a strict one and its purpose was to inculcate in Muscovites a monastic-type sense of virtue, which involved absolute obedience to church and state, and the relegation of one's own free-will to a position where it could not contradict those institutions. Some Russians kept aware of Western education developments, and the ideas of Comenius (1592-1670), which were so influential in Europe, were known in Kiev and Moscow already in the seventeenth century.[6] It is true that the relationship of secular to church authority was to change, and the acquiring of knowledge was to take on different characteristics; but the basic concept of the complete subservience of individual to institutional needs was to remain a starting point for Russia's education systems.

In the long run, it was the political interests of various factions in the state of Muscovy which determined the direction of educative practices. The bitter feelings which had arisen from arguments over Patriarch Nikon's liturgical reforms of the 1650s coloured Orthodoxy's attitude towards learning and literacy. Control of the publishing press had proven an important advantage to Nikon, and the lesson was not lost on his opponents or on Tsar Alexei (1646-1776), who benefited from the dispute in the sense that among its consequences was the subjection of the Russian church to the state. Nikon was deposed from his office as Patriarch in 1667 when a panel of Eastern Patriarchs determined that he had overstepped the bounds of his office in the face of tsarist supremacy. His downfall meant the affirmation of ancient eastern church-state relations and also implied the acceptance within Orthodoxy of the more modern Hobbesian-like principle that the Church should be controlled completely by the state.[7] With Nikon reduced to the rank of monk, advocates of absolutism in Muscovy were free to strengthen their position by sermons from the pulpit, control of schools, and use of the printing press.

A valuable by-product of the Nikon episode was an increase in

scholarly and pedagogical activity in Muscovy. Nikon's emphasis on
the proper translation of the Bible into Slavonic made Moscow a
vortex into which educated men were drawn for this work. At mid-
century about thirty of them moved to Moscow from Kiev. One of
them, Epiphany Slavinetsky was made head of a school at the Chudovsky monastery, which tended to train young aristocrats to take
their place in society as Muscovy's leaders. Foreshadowing the proposals made for seminaries in Peter the Great's *Spiritual Regulations*
(1722), students at the Chudovsky school were isolated from their
families until they reached the age of sixteen. In that way, they could
learn without being subjected to the baneful influence of the semi-
barbaric and illiterate communities into which they were born. Slavinetsky prepared for his charges a textbook, *Citizenship Rules for*
Children (Grazhdanskoi obychaev detskikh), which had fairly wide
circulation and which followed the natural law philosophy of Western
Europe. Its questions and answers were designed to create well-
rounded gentlemen capable of functioning effectively as adults. According to one Soviet scholar, the model for the textbook was a
sixteenth-century book by Erasmus. Others see in it the hand of
Comenius.[8] Whatever the case may be, the text provides an interesting
precedent to subsequent efforts by Peter the Great, Prokopovich, and
Catherine II. Slavinetsky also translated scholarly and scientific
Western books and prepared a new Church-Slavonic version of the
New Testament.

Other monks helped bring the first lobby on behalf of education to
Russia, Simeon Polotsky and Yuri Krizhanich being the most outstanding. Both were advocates of knowledge for its own sake and recognized the need for state initiative in matters of education. Their
interests, however, were above all in the field of religion, although
Krizhanich was less concerned with theology than were the others. The
fact that together they attempted to make priests and monks more
learned in their defence and espousal of theology helped undermine the
traditional Orthodox Christian aversion to study. Polotsky was a tutor
to Tsar Alexis's children, a leading sponsor of the Slavonic-Latin-
Greek Academy, and represented the latinizing trend among Muscovy's small coterie of intellectuals. Dogmatic in his adherence to Orthodoxy, he still criticized superstition and acknowledged the merits of
western scholarship.

Polotsky was particularly interested in the education of children at
home, and he expressed the growing conviction among educators that
one's adult habits are formed from the earliest years spent at home.

Therefore, he insisted that parents must set the best possible examples for their children and guide them carefully through their formative years, for it is the actions of parents that youngsters are most likely to emulate. But Polotsky did not concur with the harsh disciplinary measures recommended in the *Domostroi.* His pedagogy resembled that of Comenius, whom he followed, and of Locke, whom he preceded. In fact, he was among the first in Russia to carefully outline the basic periods of life which determined the content of a child's education: (1) from birth to the age of seven were the years in which a child's moral values were decided; (2) from age seven to fourteen, he or she was ready for practical learning, and (3) until the age of twenty-one the young adult was ready for serious knowledge and the implications of citizenship.[9]

Krizhanich brought a more secular current into Muscovy and added it to the religious rationalization of political power which had been the single dimension of political philosophy until the end of the seventeenth century. A Croatian Catholic who advocated Slavic unity under Russian leadership, he was an indefatigable writer who constantly cited from the classic works of Homer, Plato, Plutarch, Livy, and others. Moreover, he insisted that wisdom and learning were the keys to Russian greatness and, in the manner of Prokopovich and the eighteenth-century "Learned Guard," heaped scorn on those of his fellow clergymen who were fearful of education. In contrast to the generally-held assumption that learned men are the bearers of heresy, he stated without equivocation that "man is in need of wisdom."[10] Krizhanich saw autocracy as a divine institution and religion as the most important bulwark of the state. Although an alien to Muscovy himself, he warned constantly against foreign influences, above all from Turkey and Germany.

After arriving in Moscow in 1659, Krizhanich had the misfortune to offend the tsar, so spent some fifteen of his eighteen years in Muscovy in Siberian exile. While in Siberia, he wrote his famous *Discourses on Power* (*Razgovory ob vladetelstvu*), a Slavic grammar, theological tracts, and an historical geography of Siberia. In the *Discourses* he quoted at length from Machiavelli in support of powerful monarchy and, quite ironically in the light of later development, said that Russia was better suited than other countries for absolutism because its nobility was weak and women had no power at court. These works and the fact that he had many friends and acquaintances from a broad sector of Siberian and Muscovite society assured that his ideas gained a reasonably wide circulation. Krizhanich was one of those who helped spread the assumption that education was important, and who, at the same time, helped expand the framework of secular political thinking in Russia. In short, he foresaw the replacement of a medieval theology based on myths and on Greek religious doctrine with a modern, uniquely Russian political philosophy. Schools could be a means to that end.

There were other individuals who worked on behalf of education in Muscovy and early petrine Russia. Dimitrii Rostovsky (1651–1709) was one of those who played an extremely important role in maintaining some semblance of educational activity in Russia during those politically turbulent times. Educated at the Kiev Academy during the 1660s, and then learning in the company of Innocent Gizel at the Kievo-Pechersky monastery, he was the one most responsible for organizing the writing of the lives of the Saints, undertaken there in the 1680s. Rostovsky, as well, wrote catechisms and treatises against the Old Believers, and for this work he was appointed Metropolitan of Rostov in 1702.

At the same time that Peter began opening up technical schools, Rostovsky created a school of his own which trained some two-hundred youngsters in Russian grammar, Greek, and Latin. He administered the institution in Rostov himself, opened its doors to children of all classes and produced theatrical pieces for and with the pupils. He made no attempt whatsoever to direct students along the religious/political lines supported by either Prokopovich or Stefan Iavorsky, who argued about the relationship between state and church during Peter's reign. Instead, he based his entire programme of instruction on the Christian principles as they were expressed in the Bible. Most of his students were expected to become priests, but not all of them, and he emphasized to his charges their obligation to practice Christianity and to ignore the political side of life. Thus, his views were quite different from those of Krizhanich. In his school, grammar was taught seriously, so that graduates were well-versed in the learning tools of Western civilization.[11]

Aside from these individuals, there was one particular event of the seventeenth century that had important repercussions for the evolution of pedagogy in eighteenth-century Russia. That incident was the placing of the city of Kiev and its autonomous metropolitanate under the jurisdiction of Muscovy in 1686. With that incorporation, the Mogila school at Kiev, often referred to as the Kievan Academy, brought Latin-scholastic methods to Russians. Faced with the possibility of closure due to pressure from antagonistic forces among

Russian Orthodox hierarchy, the Academy widened its curriculum to include comprehensive courses in philosophy and theology. Blessed by highly-qualified instructors, including the subsequently controversial Iavorsky, the Academy was able to prove its worth enough to earn a charter from the tsar in 1694. It gave the school formal recognition, allowed it to enroll students from areas still dominated by Poland, and allotted to it funds from the Muscovite treasury. More important, the charter granted to the Academy a certain autonomy from the civil authorities of Moscow and Kiev.

In spite of difficulties incurred by the Academy after 1694, especially during the Mazepa insurrection which ended in 1709, the school continued to provide educators, writers, artists, and theologians of high standard to Petrine Russia.[12] It was from there that Feofan Prokopovich came to serve as Peter's most valuable panegyrist in the early eighteenth century.

The efforts of Polotsky, Krizhanich, Slavinetsky, Rostovsky, and their colleagues, and the overall contribution of the two main academies, were not orchestrated and sometimes represented conflicting aims. They did not go very far towards bringing learning to Russia, but they broke the monopoly on ideas held by isolationist and obscurantist officials of the church. A seventeenth-century foreign visitor to Muscovy, Adam Olearius, remarked on the existence of schools, although not in a very favourable light. He expressed some astonishment, however, at the fact that some Greek and Latin was being taught, even in a school for youngsters which had been opened close to the Patriarch's home.

Other schools came into existence, usually on the initiative of individual churchmen or nobility. Kievan monks staffed a school instituted at the Andreevsky Monastery in 1649, sponsored by a boyar, Fedor Rtishchev. Latin, Greek, rhetoric, and philosophy made up its curriculum; so it furthered the trend started by Slavinetsky and Polotsky to educate Muscovite children in the manner of the Kievan Academy. Yet the old hostility towards curiosity and the fear of scepticism remained a fixture of Orthodoxy for some time hence. All teachers had to be Russian and Orthodox, and they were very carefully chosen. Only with the appearance of Peter the Great did the Russian state have an emperor determined enough to set in motion plans for institutionalizing and secularizing education, in the main against the wishes of his own national church.

II

Peter I:
Ideas and Their First Practitioners

Peter I's desire to make Russia a major European power was the incentive behind the numerous and eclectic 'reforms' which so characterized his reign. He recognized that Russia would have to match the technical skills and knowledge of the western nations and that his government machinery would have to be made efficient if his ambitions in foreign policy were to be achieved. Peter's domestic dictates were born of military needs, were ruthlessly adopted and barely survived him, but they created precedence for all institutional developments in Russia during the remainder of the century.

The "Tsar Reformer's" first aim for education was to create a class of educated bureaucrats, for he was aware that only through an increase of knowledge could Russia obtain political power and material prosperity. Education, Peter assumed, was simply a matter of preparation for state service. His own education was limited, but Peter's first teacher, N. M. Zotov, instructed him in religion and gave him a general knowledge of Russian history, the glories of earlier princes, reigns, and wars of the past. The lengths to which Peter was willing to go to achieve his ends were shown by the institution of the Table of Ranks in 1722. By classifying all civil, military, and other positions into fourteen ranks and making them open to everyone, including foreigners, he established the principle that ability was more important than birth for advancement in service. Education was obviously to become increasingly important even though the merit principle was often ignored.[1] Even more obviously, foreigners would have an initial advantage over Russians in the state service, for at this time they were more likely to have an education, or at least have pretensions to one.

The pressing requirements of a nation at war prompted Peter's first educational legislation. Special schools for artillery men were opened in 1699, soon after he returned from his trip through Europe. The Slavonic-Greek Academy in Moscow was latinized in 1701 and told to broaden its curriculum, and in January of that year the Mathematics

and Navigational school, one of the first non-classical schools in
Europe, was opened in Moscow. Its first director was a Scotsman,
Henry Farquharson, and the teachers of navigation were two English
teenagers, Stephen Gwyn and Richard Grice. L. F. Magnitsky
(1669–1739) was the most important Russian in the school. Well-
educated in contemporary pedagogy, he wrote a textbook on mathematics which had widespread use throughout the century.[3] The language of instruction was English until Farquharson and his colleagues
learned Russian and while textbooks were being translated. The programme was completely secular and discipline was strict, for time spent
there was regarded by Peter as part of the student's state service. The
school had produced some 1,200 graduates by 1716, which meant that
more and more Russians served as officers and that foreigners became
less indispensable in military matters.

The upper class of the school, plus Farquharson, Gwyn and eight
other navigators were moved to St. Petersburg in 1715. Ten years later
that section of the Moscow institution was designated as a Naval
Academy. Its first director was a French baron, but he was replaced
within two years by a Russian, A. A. Matveev. Magnitsky joined the
new Academy in 1725 and took over its directorship from Matveev's
successor. According to its charter, the Naval Academy was made up
of six fifty-pupil brigades, each of which were assigned officers who
were in charge of discipline and military matters. The course of study
was limited at first to arithmetic, geometry, navigation, artillery, fortification, and geography. Okenfuss has shown that the variety of dates
which appear for the establishment of this institution and others
demonstrate their stop and start nature. But they were a beginning and
the programmes took on a more permanent character with the close of
the Great Northern War in 1721. The academies were not elementary
schools; rather they gave technical training to students who had already developed basic skills.[4]

In 1714 Peter legislated for elementary, Cypher (Mathematics)
schools throughout the empire and demanded that attendance in them
be compulsory for sons of the *dvorianstvo*.[5] But only two years later
the children of the nobility were freed from obligatory participation in
the Cypher schools and were allowed to acquire an education at home,
dubious as that privilege might have been academically. Thus, in 1726,
a year for which we have statistics, children of the nobility made up less
than three percent of the 2,000 students who were spread over twelve
such schools. Almost half were sons of clergymen, and the remainder
were offspring of officials and soldiers. The fact that admittance to the

Cypher schools was also limited to those who already had a command of basic grammar and writing skills helped reduce their effectiveness. But the Russian nobleman was still expected to educate himself, whether at home or in school. The Heraldry Office, which Peter established as a means to administer the service dimension of their lives, regularly inspected the level of a young noble's education, and, on the basis of that, determined the times at which he could marry, inherit property, or be made an officer.[7] With the opening of the Naval Academy, the Navigational school in Moscow lost much of its significance; and the Academy assured the evolution of a schooling system which in practice if not yet in theory was to be a preserve of the nobility. Order and discipline were stressed in those schools to the extent that the *ustav* which called for their establishment made it quite clear that everyone was equal when it came to punishment for disobedience. In fact, each class was assigned an attendant with "a whip in his hand" to maintain order.[8]

Peter also pressured the Church to educate its priests, and in 1705 orders were directed to Dimitrii, by then Metropolitan of Rostov, to ordain only candidates who were fully literate. Several later decrees insisted that sons of clergymen should study Greek and Latin. New schools were opened by bishops in Novgorod, Tobol'sk, and Rostov, and the Moscow Academy was expanded so that it held more than two hundred students and offered a full syllabus of study, which was predominantly secular. The school in the Rostov area also had two hundred students, but in the way of many petrine initiatives, the school failed soon after Dimitrii's death in 1709.[9]

Peter made a crusade against ignorance and superstition one of the characteristics of his reign, if a somewhat Quixotic one. Experts in the military sciences, mathematics, fortification, artillery, geography, military and civil law were needed desperately in his beleaguered state. Therefore, new institutions abounded. An engineering school opened in Moscow in 1703, and another in St. Petersburg in 1719. The new capital was granted an artillery school in 1721. A training centre for physicians was attached to the Moscow military hospital in 1707, and a medical school opened in St. Petersburg nine years later. Institutes for foreign-language instruction also appeared. Furthermore, Peter's desire to propagandize his cause to Russians and foreigners alike stimulated the publication of journals, the opening of printing houses, libraries, and museums. He issued Russia's first newspaper in 1703 with the expressed intention of bringing current news to his public. The *Vedomosti o voennykh znaniiakh i inykh delakh dostoinykh znaniia i pamiati* appeared on a regular basis until Peter's death in 1725.[10] Unlike his predecessors, Peter welcomed foreign books in translation. Books were printed in the Russian language and in inexpensive editions. To this end, Jan Tessing (Thessing) and Il'ya Kopievsky, both from Amsterdam, were the main figures in Peter's printing and propaganda exercizes; and Baron von Huyssen acted on his behalf in Berlin. In fact, von Huyssen was Russia's main link with the Berlin Academy of Sciences. He was responsible for the election to that institution of Dmitry Kantemir and the Englishman, Thomas Consett, Chaplain to the British Factory (Russian Company) in St. Petersburg and the first translator into English of Peter's *Spiritual Regulations*.[11]

P. P. Shafirov (1669–1739), one of Peter's leading diplomats, contributed in the same way. The publication in Paris of the short book, *Abrégé de l'histoire de Czar Peter Alexceevitz* (1714), was his work and he collaborated with Feofan Prokopovich and others on similar Russian-language studies. Shafirov also wrote a defence of the Russian side in the war against Sweden. Printed in 1717 on the orders of Peter, to whom such a justification had been suggested a few years earlier by F. S. Saltykov, then his diplomatic representative in London, the *Discourse Concerning the Just Cause of the War Between Russia and Sweden* (*Razsuzhdenie kakie zakonnye prichiny Ego Tsarskoe Petr Velikii . . .*) represents the first serious Russian essay in international law. The *Discourse* opened with an historical rationale of Peter's actions in which the writer saw the affair as a simple attempt by Russians to regain lands rightfully theirs, but taken away from them by Sweden during the Time of Troubles. Sweden's ties with the Porte persuaded Shafirov to portray Peter's cause as a Christian one against Islam. But the essence of the paper was a detailed look at the rights and recourses of the combatants, specifically those of the Russians, so that it reflected the care that Peter took to place his activities in a legalistic and messianic light. In this area, the influence upon Shafirov of Pufendorf, whose *Introduction to History* was cited twice, is clearly visible.[12]

Peter attempted to have the *Discourse* read all over the Russian Empire and had the incredible number of 20,000 copies printed in 1722, the third edition according to William E. Butler. It was translated into German and English. At the same time that Peter was organizing his own propaganda, he decreed, in a typically Muscovite fashion, that his subjects must "not believe or keep in their possession" any anti-government (mainly Swedish) pamphlets.[13]

The contract given to Tessing in 1700 stated specifically that the books were to be for the "greater glory of the great sovereign . . .

[and for] general national benefit." Nothing could be printed that might detract from that aim.[14] Among the twenty or so titles which were produced for Russians in Amsterdam were grammars of the Russian language, morality books, and books instructing youth on how to behave in society and at home. Peter's own library of some 1,600 books was dominated by titles in religion, naval, and military affairs. History and geography ranked next, with one hundred and fifty books.

Peter Polikarpov was put in charge of the Moscow publishing house in 1701, and he used it to print secular items even though it had previously produced only religious materials. Four years later a press was created by a private citizen, V. O. Kiprianov, who limited his efforts to secular books. He was asked to print textbooks for schools, mainly in the "scientific" fields. The press was managed in its first four years by Jacob Bruce, who made it into Russia's leading typography for maps and other geographical documents. Eventually the press was expanded into a library (*Publichnaia vsenarodnaia biblioteka,* 1724) and a book shop managed by its founder's son, V. V. Kiprianov. By the end of Peter's reign, there were eleven official printing houses and several private ones. Slightly less than two thousand books had been printed, a third of which were government decrees.[15]

On the face of it, the amount of literature available in the Russian Empire in the 1720s and the number of people able to take advantage of it were slight enough. But there was progress towards a reading public of sorts, and for the Orthodox Church a reading public still meant a potentially heretical one. The extent of Orthodoxy's intransigence against the introduction of education, especially a secular one, may be illustrated from comments made by foreign observers of Russian society. The first of these, Giles Fletcher, who was sent to Moscow as England's ambassador in 1588, had this to say in his book, *Of the Russe Commonwealth* (London, 1591):

> As themselves [clergy] are voyde of al maner of learning, so are they warie to keepe out all meanes that might bring any in: as fearing to have their ignorance and ungodliness discovered. To that purpose they have perswaded the Emperours, that it would breed innovation, and so danger to their state, to have anie noveltie of learning come within the Realme [sic].

Father Antonio Possevino, who was sent to Muscovy in the 1580s by Pope Gregory XIII, reported almost exactly the same thing.[16]

A half-century later, Adam Olearius noted that Russians saw "witchcraft" in astronomy and astrology. And, as a sign that little change seemed to have taken place, one could turn to the observations made by Johann-Georg Korb, secretary for the Austrian Legation to Russia, who wrote the following in 1700:

> [to prevent schism over the Nikonian reforms] it would have been far more useful and far more wholesome labour to organize schools, to appoint masters for the instruction of youth, to teach the ignorant, to lead back the erring to the right road to salvation. But as they are, to the last degree, unskilled in divinity, and haughtily despise all learning from abroad, they envy that enlightenment to those that are to come after them, and they themselves are ashamed to emerge out of their benightedness . . . In their schools positively the only labour of the schoolmasters is to teach the children how to write and shape their letters. The height of learning consists in committing to memory some articles of their creed. They despise liberal arts as useless torments of youth, they prohibit philosophy, and they have often publicly outraged astronomy with the approbrious name of magic.[17]

Korb's picture of Russian education just before Peter the Great began to re-organize it was confirmed by a book published in Cologne in 1698. In that book it was said that the Russian clergy frowned upon preaching because the passions of the speakers may "raise questions and disputes, which make the common people fall into error." The book was cited in an overview of Russian religion which was printed in England in 1723, whose author also remarked upon the fact that the Russian clergy was "utterly unlearned both in the Scriptures, and all other sorts of knowledge . . . [and that] . . . the people live in gross ignorance."

Another visitor, Captain John Perry, who returned to Russia with Peter from England in 1698, noted the abysmal ignorance on the part of Orthodox clergy and commended the Tsar's efforts on behalf of education. Writing in 1716, Perry said that Peter built schools and had books on morality and divinity translated into Russian in order that they "instill principles of virtue into the minds of the people."[18] Obviously, assuming that the observations made by these foreigners on Russia's soil were even partly accurate, the attitude of Muscovy and Imperial Russia's most persuasive body had changed very little in the century which followed Fletcher's time in Moscow. No decree from Peter was going to ease the dread which most of his nation's church leaders and parish priests had of learning. Ironically, financial demands of constant warfare assured that the Church would retain a powerful hold on the education of Russia's youth. Without the resources to spare for a completely secular system, Peter insisted that the

Church had to administer and pay for one, and that institution's lack
of enthusiasm for secular subjects was mirrored in the careless circumstances of most of its schools.

The *Spiritual Regulations* of 1721 illustrate the extent of Peter's
conviction that education was the panacea for Russia's weaknesses. A
body of rules to govern and organize the ecclesiastical administration
of Russia's church and to fix its relationship to the state, the *Spiritual
Regulations* also incorporated Peter's thinking on education, and the
role of the Church and State in it. Few schools were actually opened as
a direct result of the *Spiritual Regulations,* but they appear as the first
set of principles for lower and middle schools in Russia.

One function of the Spiritual College (Synod) was to organize an
Academy and seminaries, for "foolishly do many say that education is
responsible for heresy . . . learning is beneficial and basic for every
good, as of the Fatherland, so also of the Church."[19] The *Spiritual
Regulations,* written in the main by Feofan Prokopovich (1681-1736),
and echoing Polotsky and Krizhanich, pointed out that "learning"
(*uchenie*) had to be carefully watched so that it would be "good and
sound." Particularly interesting and challenging was the importance
which was given to the constant acquisition of knowledge: "a person
enlightened with genuine learning never reaches satiation in his knowledge, rather he never ceases to learn even though he should live as long
as Methusalah." Prokopovich went on to stress the necessity of good
teachers, and special rules were set down for their training. The funding of libraries, without which "an academy is as without a soul," was
also recommended. Poorly trained teachers and people who think that
they know everything, "are extremely harmful to their colleagues, to
the fatherland, and to the church." They become heretical through
ignorance and obstinacy and, in contrast to wise people who have "the
ability to change their opinions," are inclined towards rebellion.

Between 1721 and 1724, the Holy Synod slowly carried out the instructions from *Spiritual Regulations,* which called for compulsory
diocesan clerical schools. Forty-five of them were opened in those few
years. Since a major seminary already existed in St. Petersburg, another was established in Moscow. The Church Slavonic elementary
schools which were then organized were administered at the expense
of monasteries, where most were located, or through diocesan offices.
As the schools took on more advanced classes, Latin became their
language of instruction. Their organization tended to be eclectic; in
fact, the most effective one had its roots in Novgorod as early as 1706,
where the Likhud brothers were requested by the Metropolitan to con-

struct a programme in which Latin, Greek, and Slavonic were taught. An entire system of elementary schools evolved from it in the Novgorod district, encompassing, according to Vladimirsky-Budanov, about one thousand students. Eventually, these and other such schools progressed so that by the 1740s they were training centres for clergy, and that entailed the building of further elementary institutions from which to feed the diocesan schools. Such a programme was finally established in the Novgorod area by 1737. Throughout the empire the clergy were ordered to educate their own children in reading and writing, so that by the age of twelve they were supposed to be ready for professional training with the diocese.[20] But in spite of the eloquent words in the *Spiritual Regulations,* the usual lack of funds and the failure of the clergy at all ranks to make a serious commitment to its principles assured that the level of learning among the clergy did not improve very much.

Included in the *Spiritual Regulations* were a curriculum and a set of rules for the seminaries. These schools were intended for students from ten to fifteen years of age who were "not to be let out anywhere" for three years after their arrival at the institution. In this way, they might realize "the obvious advantages of such an education."[21] Many years later, just such an idea was taken up by Ivan Betskoi, who prepared schooling projects for Catherine II which assumed that children should be isolated from their normal family environment so that they might be made into better citizens of the state. Elsewhere, Prokopovich voiced the opinion that the peasantry also should be assisted towards literacy, for they became Russia's soldiers, servants of the state, its clergy, and its monks.[22] His own school for orphans and poor children in Novgorod was open to youngsters from all walks of life. Another which he instituted in St. Petersburg in 1721 for the same purpose offered such courses as languages (Slavonic, Russian, Latin, and Greek), rhetoric, logic, Roman history, geography, drawing, and music. On Prokopovich's death, this school was taken over and maintained by the central government. Prokopovich's conviction that universal education was in his nation's best interest was a notion that was to have a sad history during the subsequent life of Imperial Russia.

Education for all classes in society was an idea which developed naturally from the petrine demands for total mobilization of the empire's resources, including its manpower. Others sponsored the notion as well. Fedor Saltykov (d. 1715), whom Peter sent to England and Holland in 1697 to learn navigation and who then represented Russia in England, 1712–1715, sent from there a *Propositions* (1712) on behalf of universal school instruction. He recommended that nine academies, which altogether would accommodate eighteen thousand students, be opened under the auspices of the monasteries. Pupils from all social ranks would be invited to attend. Languages (Latin, Greek, English, German, and French), rhetoric, poetry, philosophy, religion, the natural and mathematical sciences, history, geography, architecture, drawing, navigation, fortification, artillery, swordplay, and horsemanship would be their intended objects of study. If fathers refused to send their offspring to the schools, then fines should be applied to stimulate participation. In order to get through such an all-encompassing curriculum, youngsters were expected to enroll at the age of six and continue their instruction until they reached the age of twenty-three. Little of note came from Saltykov's proposals, but Peter did issue instructions to his magistrates in December, 1724, in which he admitted that an efficient society was possible only after all his subjects could read, write, and count.[23]

Implicit in the *Spiritual Regulations* was the notion that pedagogy was a means for generating a new type of Russian citizen. The same document spelled out clearly for Imperial Russia the idea that absolute obedience to the autocratic emperor in all things was the wish of God. Many individual Church leaders, like Iavorsky, were more reserved about the emperor's secularization of church institutions than was Prokopovich,[24] but Prokopovich was in a far stronger position than the others to have his view prevail. He insisted, however, that the enormity of the power taken on by the ruler made it necessary that it be used for the common good. Thus, the monarch must be enlightened and spread education in order to eliminate the social vices which arise from ignorance. In this, if not much else, Prokopovich preceded M. V. Lomonosov and the enlighteners of the Catherinian era.

Textbooks written for Russia's youth carried Prokopovich's political message and demonstrated the extent to which schools might be employed. In a primer widely used by the church, Prokopovich wrote:

> . . . kings and magistrates, who rule over us in the Lord, are to us in the place of fathers . . . Inferiors must love and respect their superiors, pray for them and cheerfully obey all their just commands.[25]

Peter also called for the translation in 1724 of parts of Pufendorf's *De Officio hominis et civis Juxta legem naturalem libri duo* (1673), an abbreviation of which finally appeared as *On the Duty of Man and the Citizen According to Natural Law* (*O dolzhnosti cheloveka i grazhdanina*) in 1726.[26] This book, which Prokopovich adopted for use in his own school, and recommended in *Spiritual Regulations* was the predecessor to subsequent citizenship books. One, in particular, which appeared with nearly the same title in 1783, was prepared as compulsory reading for Catherinian schools.

There were a number of educational projects offered to Peter during his reign. Saltykov, von Huyssen, Pososhkov, Tatishchev, Leibniz, Baron Christian von Wolff, and others all contributed their ideas to him.[27] Both Saltykov and Werner Pause (1670–1735), who was a tutor to the Tsarevich Alexei and director of a gymnasium in Moscow, 1705–1706,[28] put together treatises on education which included recommendations for the instruction of young women. Although they held some ideas in common with the *Domostroi,* Saltykov's views were the more sophisticated of the two, for he applied to female education the fundamentally utilitarian precepts of the petrine era which demanded full mobilization of Russia's human resources. Saltykov wanted women to be instructed to be good wives, and he recognized that mothers were the ones to leave the most lasting impressions upon young boys who were to become servants of the state. Therefore, girls had themselves to have basic knowledge. His *Propositions* carried a detailed programme for their instruction, which resembled his recommendations for boys.

As a beginning step, Saltykov suggested that schools for girls be opened in every province, that they be run by the monasteries, and that schooling be compulsory for selected girls who would begin a course of study at the age of six and complete it at the age of fifteen. Fines would also be levied against fathers who failed to send their daughters to the schools, which could have an enrollment of 500 pupils each. In Saltykov's opinion, the academic side of the schools should be limited to reading, writing, and numbers. The remainder of the curriculum would be filled with matters of refinement, learning the German and French languages, and "for their own amusement and gay manners in company," drawing, dancing, vocal and instrumental music. All this in the hope that "the clever girls will be wiser and more pleasant than those who live with their fathers at home until they are married, not knowing the manners and conversations of civilized people."[29]

Coinciding as it did with Peter's decree of 1718 on "Assemblies," that is, his demand that upper class Russians entertain weekly in their homes with wives and children in attendance,[30] Saltykov's *Propositions* was part of a general movement to bring Russia's noble women, however reluctantly on the parts of their husbands, out of the *terem.* Saltykov's advice about girls was ignored in the same way that his suggestions for boys were, but the type of education which he proposed later became fashionable and was turned over to often incompetent foreign tutors. The one element of consistency between all the submissions which came to Peter was the feeling that Russia's backwardness could be cured only by greatly expanded educational facilities. Among the foreigners who advised Peter, Leibniz was the leading advocate of an education in which the fear of God was combined with love of virtue and science. And it was while he was in Germany in 1711 that Peter first discussed with Leibniz, then the director of the Royal Society of Scientists in Prussia, a plan for the future Russian Academy of Sciences. In the next year Peter accepted Leibniz into the Russian service by decree (1 November, 1712), saying that "we know that he can be of great help in the development of mathematics and of other arts, in historical research, and in the growth of learning in general. ..." Leibniz did not travel to Russia and it is difficult to tell whether or not his long time correspondence with Peter, which began in 1697, had much lasting influence upon the development of education there. But the German rationalist undoubtedly swayed Peter. He told the emperor that Russia needed foreign expertise, libraries, educational material, and schools right away. The schools, he said, should emphasize mathematics, languages, and history, and his letters carried the German emphasis on the practical and cameralist view of education. In 1716, Leibniz sent a specific recommendation for public schools, academies and universities, which included, among other things, the idea that education must be a monopoly of the state, and that history and philosophy were as important as practical sciences. There was very little in the way of material results from Leibniz's letters to Peter, but his famous protegé, Wolff, was Peter's main adviser when it came to finally working out plans for the Academy of Sciences at St. Petersburg and for a university.[31]

Ivan Tikhonovich Pososhkov (1652–1726), who was of humble birth, spoke in favour of an education in which children would be taught to fear God and tsar, to respect autocracy, and to be cautious about foreigners. In his *A Father's Testament to his Son* (*Zaveshchanie otecheskoe k synu svoemu*), written in 1719 but not printed until 1783, Pososhkov also stressed patriotism, strict instruction in good habits at home, rigorous reading, and concentration on practical subjects like Slavic languages, Greek, Latin, German, French, mathematics, geometry, architecture, and fortification. He offered a word of warning, however, about the overuse of Latin, because it was the language of Orthodoxy's opponents, and for the same reason he insisted that no

Polish be offered to Russian youngsters. His devoutness was such that Pososhkov actually suggested that Lutherans be commissioned to help raise the educational standards of Orthodoxy's all too ignorant clergy.[32] The Lutheran flock had a seminary of its own in Russia from 1703.

Although his views on methods in education were more along the lines of progressive seventeenth-century thinkers, Pososhkov was enough a part of eighteenth-century trends to recognize the necessity of schooling. Like Prokopovich and later educators, he gave pride of place to moral training, saying that children must be directed firmly towards good habits very early in their lives. In that belief he was well in tune with Western pedagogues who emphasized both practical training and character-building in education. However, Pososhkov maintained the Muscovite notion that coercion and severe punishments were the best means to make a child learn and to be obedient.[33] He was convinced also that education should be extended to the peasantry, and that a peasant's relationship with his landlord be regularized. He was ahead of his time in that regard. Pososhkov went so far as to suggest that instruction be compulsory for children of peasants under ten years of age, and that harsh treatment be meted out to parents who refused to have their children trained at least in reading and writing. "Having learned to read and write, they will not only conduct more intelligently the business of their lords, but they will also be useful to the government," he wrote in his best-known publication, *Book on Scarcity and Wealth (Kniga o skudosti i bogatstve*, 1724). A pragmatic, nationalistic man of Peter's era, he saw education as a means whereby Russia could gain more efficient producers for its economy.

Pososhkov was a firm exponent of a well-ordered state in which the nobility could devote their time to state service; the merchants, and they alone, should manage state finances, while the peasants provided the nation with labour and taxes. *Book on Scarcity and Wealth* was a striking example of the petrine trend towards a secular rationalization of Russian society. Not printed until the next century, it was read in manuscript form by Tatishchev and later by Lomonosov. It had its predecessor too, insofar as L. M. Mordukhovich suggests that Pososhkov and Krizhanich had very similar economic and political viewpoints.[34]

Pososhkov formulated educational ideas as a by-product of his feeling that economic prosperity was only possible in a community with a dynamic merchant class and a policy which would encourage that class to work hard for themselves and for the general welfare. Wide-spread learning, advanced technology, and a benevolent government were the basic ingredients for his plans for Russia's transition into the modern age. Although Pososhkov's concern for the peasantry was a consequence not of humanitarian inclinations, but of his desire to make them productive, it and other non-conforming ideas earned him a cell in the Peter and Paul fortress where he died in 1726. He was by no means the last Russian intellectual to suffer for being ahead of his time or, indeed, for his patriotism.

Interesting though the 'think-tank' procedures of Peter's reign were, since they marked the origins of serious educational thought in Russia, the value of the proposals lay more in the enunciation of a principle than in concrete results in the form of schools. In practice, Peter's educational endeavours had only a fleeting impact on the expanse of the Russian Empire, for the greatest and ultimately insurmountable roadblock to education in the eighteenth century in Russia was the almost universal apathy, even hostility, with which such proposals were greeted by Russians. Peter was aware of this situation and explained his own forceful methods in a preamble to a decree of 1723. "Our people are like children," he said, "who would never undertake to study the alphabet if they were not forced to do so by the teacher."[35] The nobility resented compulsory education and by the 1720s it was the Church that carried on the real business of educating Russia's youth once again. With the promulgation of the Table of Ranks, new efforts by Peter to systematize Russian society had some effect, and teachers were given the right to the tenth rank. Unfortunately, most of these efforts came to naught after the great monarch's death. According to most accounts, the number of students in Peter's secular schools in the late 1720s was approximately 2,000, of a population of some thirteen million. Diocesan schools, which had been ordered opened in 1721 accounted for about 2,500 more pupils by the end of Peter's reign.[36] Nonetheless, the door to a purely secular enlightenment was now at least ajar.

Although literacy had been made compulsory for the clergy and children of the nobility, even that ruling was not rigidly adhered to. By mid-century, the university section of the Academy of Sciences (founded by decree, 1724, opened 1727) was closed for lack of students. The sons of the nobility flocked to the military academies, which became their preserve and in which they learned West European languages and subjects attuned to the "polite" society of St. Petersburg, rather than solely military sciences. In fact, the founding of the Land

Cadet Corps in 1731 represented in part an attempt to give a special place on the Table of Ranks to the sons of nobility.

In his classic study on books and the book trade under Peter, P. P. Pekarsky showed that even though there was an increase in typographies and in the number of books published, a great many printings were not sold out. He suggested, therefore, that Peter's efforts to spread learning through the distribution of books was largely a failure, although progress of sorts was made. However, a Soviet study of 1973 has demonstrated that there was a considerable, if relative, expansion in the use of books and that many of the unsold items were actually government decrees, informational documents, or issues of journals. Secular books, especially the histories and geographies, sold very well.[37] Books were certainly more readily available than they had been in Muscovy. The important thing was that books in general and secular ones in particular were now part of Russia's cultural life.

The writings of Pufendorf, Leibniz, Wolff, and other representatives of the German *Aufklärung* were especially well suited to Russia's intellectual and social needs for at least two-thirds of the eighteenth century. The Germanic conception of natural law stressed man's duties and obligations to society. Thus, the Russian tradition of autocracy and service found a ready-made philosophy with which its thinkers could feel comfortable. With the Hobbesian notion that mutual obligation meant absolute power in the hands of a ruler expressed so well for Russians by Prokopovich, who examined the works of Grotius, Hobbes, and Pufendorf, political and social theorists in the empire had a firm commitment to an ordered society. In a recent article, Sumner Benson points out that these men may well have advocated individual rights and the idea of contract between ruler and his subjects, but "all agreed that civil authority was established by God and that order could only be preserved in society if each subject believed that obedience was a religious obligation." Even Peter had cited the case of Louis XIV's France, where absolutism was so carefully awarded divine status by Bossuet, when he accused his own son of being ill-suited for his position as heir to the throne. It was partly his sense of obligation for the well-being of his realm that prompted Peter to alter the law so that he could select his own successor. It was Prokopovich who used the assumptions of *Aufklärung* to give Russian autocracy a systematic justification. These were the ideas which were to be built into the curricula of Russian school systems. The *philosophes* whom Catherine II cultivated during the decades before the French Revolution were not likely to find an enthusiastic audience in academic circles so fully grounded in the Germanic *Weltan-schauung*.[38]

Prokopovich's best known theoretical statement about the auto-cratic powers of Russia's monarch appeared in his "Justice Is The Monarch's Will" ("Pravda voli monarshei," 1722). But he had expressed it often before that, above all in a sermon delivered on Palm Sunday in St. Petersburg, 1718, in which he sponsored blind obedience, saying that "the highest power is established and armed with a sword by God and that to oppose it is a sin against God himself, a sin to be punished by death, not temporary but eternal." He cited at length from the Scriptures to corroborate his opinion and at the same time drew support from the doctrine of natural law as it was expressed by contemporary Western writers: "And behold, might there not be in the number of natural laws this one too, that there are to be authorities holding power among nations? There is indeed! And this is the very chief of all laws. . . . For we hold it certain that supreme authority receives its beginning and cause from Nature itself. . . . From this, then, it is likewise evident that Nature teaches us too of the obedience due to authorities. . . . Therefore to resist the powers is to resist God himself."[39] Such an argument was simplified even further for a text-book of moral, religious, and political instruction which Prokopovich prepared in 1720 for use in Russian schools (see above, ch. 3), and was to be the essence of Catherine II's *On the Duties of Man and Citizen* of 1783.

The man who was to become the first modern historian of Russia, V. N. Tatishchev (1686-1750),[40] took up the cry for increased educa-tional services and for a popular history of Russia to serve as an educational tool. One of the men whom Peter sent to Europe to study in 1716, he spent most of his life in the service of the state. A strong patriot and supporter of Peter's attempt to create an efficient, secular state system, Tatishchev was convinced that history could play a role in creating the new age for Russians.

Tatishchev preferred absolute monarchy to any other political system and, besides his natural patriotism, it was the potential for order and efficiency which impressed him most about Peter's practices. His well-documented opposition to those who tried to impose constitutional restrictions on the new Empress, Anna, in 1730 is evidence enough of that.[41] Combined with his research in history, the events of 1730 helped persuade him that schools should be employed to prevent any such challenge to central authority in the future. Consequently, his writings all had a clearly didactic tone and his historical work carried specific socio-political lessons. A treatise written by him in 1733, *Conversations between Two Friends on the Usefulness of the Sciences and Education* (*Razgovor dvukh priiatelei o pol'ze nauk i uchilishch*) contained 120 questions and answers about the value of enlightenment and the role of teachers. This essay and a *Testament* (*Dukhovnaia*), which Tatishchev prepared for his son in 1740, continued the tradition of the *Domostroi* and of Pososhkov's *A Father's Testament to His Son*.

In each of the essays, Tatishchev stressed the value of knowing the scriptures and of training Russians to teach. He told his son that Russia's nobility had to be well educated in order to serve the state properly, saying that they must learn to write correctly, and then "turn to mathematics, geometry, artillery and fortifications..., and Russian history... which you will find in my papers... and Russian geography which all noble Russians need to know."[42] He also insisted that Russians should learn the civil and military laws of their own land. Echoing the words of Prokopovich and Pososhkov, Tatishchev stated in the *Testament* that each man had to know the laws of citizenship, be "faithful and diligent in his service to the state, no matter his position," and be prepared to defend "the power and honour of the monarchy" to his last drop of blood.[43] Tatishchev followed them too in his conviction that societal progress was determined by the growth of human wisdom. But there were limitations: "Another qualification of the nobility," he continued, "is citizenship," for no foreigner will be properly committed to the interests of the Russian Empire.

Taking exception to the principles espoused in *Domostroi* about the role of a wife in a family, Tatishchev admonished his son, Evgraf, to earn the respect of his wife, children, and servants by treating them and his own parents honourably.[44] His sentiments in this regard were exactly those expressed in Prokopovich's *Primer for the Instruction of Youth* (*Pervoe uchenie otrokom*) and again fifty years later in Catherine's *On the Duties of Man and Citizen*. They represented the paternal but essentially co-operative type of family envisioned by many Russian intellectuals. He followed Saltykov in advocating that women be allowed access to education because they must have knowledge in order to be useful to society. "For success in marriage," Tatishchev advised his son, "look more for virtue and a good education [in a woman] than for wealth."[45] Here, too, Tatishchev foreshadowed ideas implicit in the planning and curriculum of Catherine's Imperial Education Society for Noble Girls, established in the 1760s.

The *Conversations* was more specifically an essay on education, and he emphasized in it that science and knowledge must be freed from religious restrictions. Only then could man reason properly and effectively. He supported this claim by showing that such a policy would be to the advantage of the state by creating a citizenry that would understand the merits of the status quo. "It is never the intelligent people who start revolts," he wrote in a tone like that which permeated the *Spiritual Regulations.*[46] It was not to be the last time during the century that this argument was to be used, often vainly, in defence of enlightenment. In fact, Tatishchev saw in education the means to make the nobility capable of administering the Russian Empire.

Convinced of the need in Russia for centralization and service, he assumed that intellectual disciplines were no exception to the rule. In serving the specific ideological and practical needs of the state, schooling therefore worked to the advantage of everyone. Only under absolute monarchy, Tatishchev continued in the *Conversations,* could Russians find true security. The national history constantly proved this to be the case.[47] He was sure that the role of science was to enable man to "know himself," so that he would be better able to choose the proper way in which to serve his community.

Tatishchev tried to categorize the sciences in order of their usefulness to the state and to man. The "necessary sciences," he said, were those that satisfied man's practical needs: basic grammar, home economics, law, medicine, logic, and religion. The "useful sciences" included advanced language study, rhetoric, foreign languages, mathemathics, physics, history, and geography. Others he listed as "foppish" (music and poetry), "futile" (astrology and alchemy), or even "harmful" (divination, sorcery). He even suggested that there be corporal punishment for those who waste their time in "useless occupations."[48]

The entire second half of the *Conversations* which was supposed to have been based on discussions between the "Learned Guard" and the Academy, 1731–1732, had to do with Russia's contemporary problems, above all the lack of a proper system of education. Tatishchev predicted that the Academy, valuable institution though it was, would accomplish nothing for Russia until a productive lower school organization was established. A mill without water to turn it, was his apt description of the situation. From education came respect for law, for government, and for nationhood. It would bring moderation and popular acceptance of life as it was, he wrote, adding that the gentry in particular must be educated well for their role as backbone of the Russian Empire. He also suggested that school curricula and text-books should be centralized and overseen, to provide uniformity and the "right" ideas everywhere.[49]

The qualification of teachers was one of the matters which Tatishchev undertook to clarify in the *Conversations*. He did not insist upon purely academic training as the basis for selecting instructors, saying that both knowledge and social status should be considered, along with the candidate's degree of learning in theology and his morality. He suggested that monks over the age of fifty were the best potential teachers, but that "secular persons with wives" could also be suitable. In military schools, officers should be the main instructors, and they must be neither arrogant nor too strict. Tatishchev recog-nized that foreigners would have to carry much of the pedagogical burden in Russia at first, but said that Russians should be trained to replace them as soon as possible. The *Conversations* also carried the first proposal that the government open up a special administrative office or College to handle all educational matters. That this was not done until the subsequent century was explained by Vladimirsky-Budanov as a result of the fact that the entire purpose of education was to train skilled bureaucrats for the various agencies of government. For that reason, he said, there was no consensus as yet about education as a phenomenon in its own right.[50]

Not satisfied with merely writing about education, Tatishchev acted on his own to remedy the lack of educational planning in Russia. As an administrator in the Ural region, he came to recognize the practical need for schools, so he issued instructions for the founding of mining and metallurgical schools in his province. These were not the first such schools, for George-Wilhelm de Gennine (1676–1750) had organized some training centres to prepare skilled workers in the Olonetsk province (Karelia), where he was commandant in 1716. The Admiralty College had provided him with teachers and with some twenty students from poor gentry families. But Tatishchev's plans were particularly important to the history of education in Russia. Prepared in 1736, at a time when the clergy once again controlled all elementary education in Russia, his schools were secular, directed by the government, and called for compulsory attendance. Designed for sons of craftsmen, administrative and skilled workers, Tatishchev's programme was Russia's first attempt at mass education. Besides reading, writing, and other basic lessons, students were to be taught technical matters which would suit them for work and management in a factory system. Their

course of study was loosely organized on a fifteen year basis. The
psalters were required for first year pupils only, but the religio-political
Primer for the Instruction of Youth prepared by Prokopovich in 1720
was also part of the syllabus, along with a commonly-used morality
book which had been printed in St. Petersburg in 1717. Tatishchev
founded twelve elementary schools in the Ural area. By 1737, they
contained over six hundred students; the emphasis in each of them was
secular knowledge, though religious learning was encouraged as well.
His own large library was opened up for use by advanced students,
who were sent to school in Ekaterinburg for further study. Another
four hundred future mining experts were learning in that city by
1738.[51]

Several of Tatishchev's essays were classics on the training of skilled
workers and on public education.[52] Among the practices he insisted
upon was the total responsibility of teachers. They had to instruct
youngsters in specific sciences and skills and also in the general
conduct of their lives. Teachers were to set personal examples for the
children in their care and were told to treat them as the valuable and
respected citizens they were intended to become. A typically utilitarian
disciple of Peter I, Tatishchev was one with Pososhkov in advocating
that all Russian citizens be educated.[53] This principle, which was
eventually adopted in most West European nations, was to be greeted
with increasing distaste in autocratic Russia. However, that does not
mean that Tatishchev or Pososhkov's counsel in support of universal
education was based on an egalitarian outlook, for even proponents of
such a policy in the West were only rarely that democratic. Their
concern was that their fellow countrymen become more proficient in
the vocations usually associated with their prescribed stations in life.
Tatishchev also recommended that Russians be sent abroad to learn,
so that Western technology and other skills could be harnessed to the
service of the Russian state.

Tatishchev worked for a decade after 1729 on a manuscript for
Russian history, the first draft of which was sent to the Academy in
1739. His historical work was closely connected to his interest in
education, for he saw history as a discipline through which one could
be "warned about evil." In that, of course, he typified the eighteenth-
century pragmatic conception of history as a guide for actions in the
present. In keeping with this educational rationale, he insisted that
government could not embark on new politics without basing them on
examples set in the past, nor could members of the clergy, jurists, and
other professional people function without a knowledge of history:

". . . no man, no condition of life, no profession, no science, no government, much less a single individual, can be perfect, wise and useful without a knowledge of [history] . . . ."[54] Thus, for reasons of edification, Tatishchev claimed that one of the foremost responsibilities of the literate classes was to make themselves aware of the national history and geography. To serve that end there had to be schools.

The paternalistic view disseminated by Prokopovich in religious terms was repeated by Tatishchev in his history in secular, political terms. He saw more logic in citizens having obligations than in their having rights, and cited Pufendorf, Machiavelli, Hobbes, and Locke (in this instance, *Two Treatises of Government,* 1690), to make his case. The state, Tatishchev wrote, could be compared to a family in which the father had an obligation to care for the interests of his wife and children; in their turn, they owed to the father respect and obedience. To prove his position, Tatishchev turned to parts of the Old and New Testament which, though he did not cite them in full, read as follows:

> Servants, be obedient to them that are your masters, according to the flesh, with fear and trembling, in singleness of your heart, as unto Christ (Ephesians, 6.5)

and:

> Masters, give unto your servants that which is just and equal; knowing that ye also have a master in Heaven (Colossians, 4.1)[55]

In common with other eighteenth-century political thinkers, and Aristotle long before them, he saw only three possible forms of government, Monarchy, Aristocracy, and Democracy: "In all three circumstances it is not possible to say which government would be the best and most useful to any society, but it is necessary to draw on the conditions and circumstances of each society." He argued that Democracies might exist in small towns and Aristocracies in larger but geographically protected states. But only Monarchies were valid in large, geographically vulnerable states.[56] This was exactly the argument used by Prokopovich in "Justice Is the Monarch's Will," and was the message to be conveyed in Russia's school programmes.

From Peter I to Catherine II, those who tried to formulate an educational policy for Russia accepted to a man the dictum of Plato; that is, that education "is the constraining and directing of youth towards that right reason which the law affirms."[57] In his *Republic,* educational institutions were planned by the state with the expressed purpose of creating good citizens. Furthermore, members of the ruling oligarchy were fully trained for service to the state. It is unlikely that Peter took his ambitions for education from Plato purposely, but his goal was the same. Subsequent educators accepted state supremacy in matters of learning and, though Tatishchev and others spoke of the need for freedom of thought, they granted to the state the right to channel the thinking of its youth in an approved direction as the first step towards the achievement of that end.

Under the leadership of Prokopovich, Tatishchev and Prince A. D. Kantemir, who will be discussed in another context, Peter's bureau-cratic programme and faltering steps towards enlightenment were kept alive after that great monarch's death. Together, these men laboured to foster enlightened thinking and practices in the face of an indifferent court and apathetic nobility. They actively endorsed the idea expressed in *Spiritual Regulations* to the effect that ignorance, and not knowledge, was the source of heresy. It was Prokopovich who prepared the most clearly reasoned rationale for absolute obedience to the ruler and who was the leader of the "Learned Guard," which the group tended to call itself.[58] Tatishchev and Kantemir employed persuasive pens in a desperate but seemingly vain attempt to have "reason" accepted as the ideal means through which Russian society and political life could be transformed for the better. The "Learned Guard" advocated state-directed education for all of the Russian people, and they assumed that in order for it to be successful, all educational policies must remain in the hands of the Emperor. In many ways, the Marxist George Plekhanov was correct in saying years later that they were the first real ideologists of absolute monarchy in Russia.[59]

Pragmatic and empirical as these apostles of learning doubtless were, they were aware that they were almost alone in a vast sea of ignorance and superstition and were thwarted by a conscious effort on the part of government to keep the bounds of knowledge within limits. Their ideas had little, if any, effect on the society of their own day, but they kept the thirst for information alive and served as models for the likes of Lomonosov and others who came after them.

III

The Interim Years: 1726–1762

The governments of Anna (1730–1740) and Elizabeth (1741–1762) made no serious attempts to strengthen or even to maintain the educational projects undertaken by Peter the Great. The entire subject of systematic education slipped into the background as far as the central agencies were concerned at least until the 1750s, but there were events worthy of note for the history of Russian pedagogy. New institutions for instruction were established during the nearly forty years which separated the reigns of Peter and Catherine II. Books of general interest and school textbooks were printed and reprinted, libraries and typographies were opened, and an important nucleus of lay teachers was slowly formed. This growth tended to be of an ad hoc nature and the adoption of specific educational policies was usually subject to their sponsors' current position in the lobbying and intrigue which prevailed at court. But together the quite disparate trends in pedagogical matters combined to keep the habit of education alive.

Russia's first durable gymnasium was opened in 1726, with 112 pupils, as an adjunct to the Academy, and its students tended to be those who were being groomed for academic service; that is, they were to be recruits for the small university which was also attached to the Academy. But actual enrollment in the gymnasium dropped rapidly in the first decade of its existence and by 1744 it had only six students, four of whom were German.[1] Furthermore, the state was still primarily interested in practical subjects, and the curriculum included mathematics, machinery study, drawing, and the natural sciences. History, linguistics, philosophy, and similar courses of study were generally ignored.[2] This dismal state of affairs prompted an attempt at reform in 1737, but with little effect. Five years later, A. K. Nartov (1694–1756) suggested that the institution become a Russian one and that its predominantly German teaching staff either be discharged or that a syllabus suitable for a Russian student body be organized. In 1750, S. P. Krasheninnikov (1713–1755) was made its director and K. F.

Moderach (1720–1772) was named its inspector. Although foreign teachers were still important at the gymnasium, Russian students from the Academy university lectured on arithmetic, geography, and Latin. German was once again taught. But until 1760, no graduates were prepared well enough to be accepted at the University of Moscow, after its founding in 1755, mainly because of the Latin requirement. In 1758, Russian was made a course of study at the gymnasium, probably on the urging of M. V. Lomonosov, and, although G. N. Teplov had suggested as early as 1750 that noble and bourgeois students be taught separately in the school, the two classes were still instructed together. An inevitable result of that situation was the fact that by the mid-1750s, the gymnasium had in it a majority of students from the middle echelons of society. In 1753 their number had risen to 150, almost all of whom were Russian and bourgeois.

During Anna's reign a second system of primary schooling was given a formal existence. Schools for the education of children of soldiers had been established in the early years of Peter's regime, and in 1721 plans were drawn up for the instruction of children under the auspices of each regiment. The following year an "Admiralty Regulation" called for Russian language elementary schools at the main naval centres. The regulations recognized the admiralty schools already opened in St. Petersburg, Kronstadt, and Revel (all in 1719), and in Tavrov (1720). They were sometimes called "Russian" schools to differentiate them from those in which the teaching language was Latin or German. In 1732, however, a more widespread organization of Garrison schools (*garnizonnye shkoly*) was founded by decree. They were designed to give basic instruction to sons of active-duty soldiers and of junior officers who were not of the nobility. Pupils were sent from such schools directly into the army at the age of fifteen, so their purpose was also partly for recruitment. The new institutions were quite widely dispersed, appearing in St. Petersburg, Moscow, Kronstadt, Riga, Revel, Narva, Vyborg, Kazan, Smolensk, Siberia, Astrakhan, Voronezh, and Belgorod.

By the 1740s, the old Cypher schools had outlived their usefulness. Nobility did not attend them; nor did sons of city-dwellers, most of whom could learn at home if their parents could afford it, nor those of the clergy, who had access to seminaries. In 1744 there were only 222 students in Cypher schools, and the Admiralty College, which provided teachers for them, actually had more teachers than it could find places for. Therefore, in that year the Cypher schools were absorbed by the Garrison schools, which remained an important agency for educating young Russians outside the gentry until the end of the century.[3] Although they received little attention from the state, Garrison schools flourished, having some 4,000 pupils in the 1730s, 9,000 in the early years of Catherine's reign, and 12,000 in 1797. Youngsters were taught to read and to write, and special attention was given to mathematics. At the upper levels they studied geometry, the basics of fortification, artillery, and military engineering. Some of the schools took in sons of merchants, especially in the peripheral parts of the empire, and in those schools courses were often offered in navigation, geography, and languages, at extra cost. Cossack regiments in the Ukraine also had schools for their children, to the extent that in the Nezhinsky district there were about 200 small elementary schools administered by Cossack personnel.[4]

As a matter of fact, it was in the Ukraine that educational activity continued with reasonable consistency throughout the first half of the eighteenth century. The Kievan Academy broadened its curriculum (geometry was added by Prokopovich in 1707; Greek, German, and Hebrew in the 1730s), and a number of seminaries modelled after it produced educated young men for Imperial Russia. The Kharkov Collegium, in particular, conducted a programme which included French and German, architecture, geography, and mathematics. But the Ukraine did not acquire the higher secular facilities which Catherine II brought to Moscow. After the introduction of a university in Moscow in 1755, a campaign was launched for a similar institution at Baturin. A detailed proposal was submitted to Elizabeth in 1760 by Count K. G. Razumovsky, Hetman and President of the Academy of Sciences. His suggestion was ignored, apparently because Teplov (1711–1779), an influential official in the secretariat of the Academy and in Nikita Panin's office, did not bother to act upon it. P. H. Dilthey was to make the same suggestion a few years later, but to no avail. Similar appeals for more advanced educational facilities in the Ukraine were to be presented to Catherine's Legislative Commission by Ukrainian gentry in the late 1760s.

There was another form of schooling extant by the 1740s, and that stemmed from a desire on the part of wealthy landowners to train serf children to assist in the administration of their large and scattered estates. Privately sponsored study programmes also produced home-grown musicians and artists who could provide rural gentry with cultural amenities usually found only in cities. The most extensive example of such serf schools can be found within the widespread Kurakin family holdings, which extended throughout the Ukraine and areas south of Moscow. Family archives carry reports of schools in the 1740s and continue to mention them until the late 1780s. A note from A. B. Kurakin, one of four brothers, to an overseer on one of his estates indicates clearly the purpose of the family's training centres: "I am sending twelve young sons of my serfs to learn their letters so that they can be made suitable for my service."[5] Enrollment in the six Kurakin serf schools varied considerably according to time and place, but it ranged between ten and forty-seven pupils, from ages seven to nineteen.

Education for the peasantry remained a matter for the inclination of church and landowners, but for the nobility an especially important event was the opening in St. Petersburg in 1732 of the Russian Cadet Corps College. Planned and directed by Anna's leading military adviser, Count B. C. Münnich, the college was designed specifically for sons of the nobility. In it, a student could gain a broader education than that given in Peter's military training schools. The decree which called for the institution named arithmetic, geometry, drawing, fortification, artillery, fencing, horsemanship, and swordsmanship as preliminary subjects. It went on to say, however, that "since the state needs political and civil education no less, let this school also have teachers of foreign languages, history, geography and law."[6] Except for its references to social rank as a criterion for admission, the Cadet Corps syllabus was quite like that proposed by Saltykov many years before.

Its founders recognized that the school's graduates would have to perform other than military services for the state, so they tried to include in its curriculum every potentially useful subject. The Russian language was supposed to be taught in all classes, along with German, French, Italian, and Polish. Latin was given only cursory attention, and other Classical interests were by and large ignored, for the school was to train its charges for careers in the Imperial service. No suggestion was made that this be merely a prototype of many such schools, and enrollment was limited at any one time to 150 Russians and fifty Livonians and Estonians. Between 1732 and 1762 slightly over two thousand students entered the school and 1557 graduated. Already in 1731 the charter of the Russian Cadet Corps insisted that there be no harsh coercion of pupils, thereby marking a break with petrine traditions and setting a pattern later adopted by Ivan Betskoi in all of his school programmes.

Among the initial class enrolled in the Cadet Corps was A. P. Sumarokov (1717–1777), who wrote his first songs there and founded a literary circle called the Society of Lovers of Russian Literature.

Throughout the next twenty years the society grew and its cultural and patriotic tone became an integrant of the school. Through it, Sumarokov left his mark on other famous men-of-letters who passed through the Cadet Corps, including M. M. Kheraskov, I. I. Melissino, Peter Panin, and I. P. Elagin. The school also pioneered the institutionalizing of the ballet and of the Russian theatre, which Sumarokov began by organizing a group to perform a play by Racine.

Separate artillery schools were opened in the 1730s as well. The first was established by Münnich in 1730, with some sixty students in attendance. Five years later an academy for military engineering was inaugurated by the Prince of Hessen-Homburg. The two institutions were merged in 1758. Modelled after the technical training schools devised for Peter I, their curricula were limited mainly to mathematics and military skills. We have the testimony of M. V. Danilov (1722–1790) as to the calibre of instruction given to students in at least some of the institutions for learning which existed in the thirties. He attests to the drunkenness, viciousness, and incompetence of the teachers with whom he had contact.[7]

In the same year that the Russian Cadet Corps was founded, enrollment at the old Moscow Mathematics and Navigational School was fixed at 100. Its naval branch in St. Petersburg had been officially termed a Naval Academy in 1725, when Magnitsky became its director. Nonetheless, by 1731 enrollment in the capital city institution had dropped considerably, to about 150, and the decline continued for the next dozen years. The Senate tried to solve the problem of declining enrollment by creating a Naval Cadet Corps in 1743 and another corps for artillery cadets. It was hoped that elitist units of this type might attract more sons of nobility, for only about one-half of the combined recruitment in the Naval Academy and the Moscow Mathematics and Navigational school were from that class. It was also in 1743 that the Russian Cadet Corps was renamed the Land (or Infantry) Cadet Corps. The three were analgamated briefly by Peter III in 1762, but then they were separated once again by Catherine II. In 1752 a second Naval Cadet Corps was opened in St. Petersburg, also as a preserve for the nobility, and Peter's old school, from which the new institution drew most of its students, was abolished. At first the naval cadets studied subjects attuned to the seaman's craft, but their curriculum was broadened in the early 1760s to include the teaching of Russian and foreign languages, geography, and history. Its first inspector, G. A. Poletika (1723–1784), was appointed in 1764. A new medical college was ordered into existence in 1733, with twenty students; so even in the face of monarchical indifference, educational activity was sustained and actually increased in the decades following Peter's death.

Elizabeth was conscious of the fact that her subjects were badly instructed, and was particularly concerned about religion. She issued an ukaz in 1743 which called for a fine of ten roubles from all nobility and free people who failed "to instruct their children from learned Russian books . . . the Christian duties and the dogma of the Orthodox faith so as to preserve them from foreign profligates."[8] Her concern was for spiritual adherence rather than for their minds, and the fact that there were too few teachers available to parents who wished to follow her instructions made the impact of the ukaz slight. But she at least helped maintain some of those things for which Prokopovich had struggled so long. By far the most important pedagogical event of Elizabeth's regime was the institution of the University of Moscow in 1755 and the two gymnasiums which were associated with it. M. V. Lomonosov (1711–1765), who had written the year before that a university without a gymnasium "is like a field without seeds," prepared regulations for the lower schools. He emphasized that schools had an obligation to train Russians for service to the state.[9]

It was Lomonosov who sustained the initiative which turned the Moscow gymnasiums into Russian institutions, for he insisted that in them Russian be both the language of instruction and an object of study.[10] But it was only by 1768 that all subjects except philosophy, which was taught in Latin, were conducted in Russian. Lomonosov made a personal contribution by translating books into Russian for use in the schools, among them a treatise on Wolff's philosophy. The most difficult task was finding Russian speaking teachers to carry out the programme, but that too was accomplished even though the major Russian appointments did not come until after S. K. Kotel'nikov (1723–1806) was assigned a senior post at the school in 1761. Throughout the early 1760s, the most capable upper class students of the gymnasiums were also used as instructors. Lomonosov laboured to persuade the Academy to expand enrollment and to provide stipends for good students, but he was often opposed by German members of the Academy who continued to assume that Russian was not a suitable language for scholarship.

At the same time, Lomonosov bemoaned the fact that Russia had far too few native doctors, chemists, mechanics, jurists, engineers, and other professional people, and he used that as a plea to get funds for the gymnasiums. His efforts proved successful in that between 1760 and 1765 twenty-four gymnasium graduates, after being examined by professors, were accepted into the university. Thus, the fledgling university slowly gained a supply of Russian students with basic prerequisite knowledge.

The matter of language was one of vital concern to Lomonosov, and he harped on it more than any other Russian intellectual at mid-century. He spoke of Russian as having "the grandeur of Spanish, the vitality of French, the power of German, the tenderness of Italian, and above all the wealth of expression of Greek and Latin."[11] The author of two glowing histories of ancient Russia, one of them a popular text book, he worked diligently to create schools designed to shape a Russian national consciousness. His own book on Russian grammar was used by several generations of Russian students and served as a model for later texts.

Teaching methods were also subject to Lomonosov's analysis. He insisted that students proceed from one class to another only after they had learned fully the material taught in the lower class. Students should be treated as individuals, he said, and instructors should learn the capacity of each pupil who then might be directed towards making use of his own special talents.[12] Moreover, Lomonosov was one of the first Russian educators to stress the need for careful progression from class to class in schools. He called for the use of homework, writing that teachers should lecture, explain, and then examine, until pupils understood prescribed material. As a matter of fact, his recommendations were much like those adopted formally in Catherine's schools more than twenty years after Lomonosov's death.

Just as his predecessors and later educators in Russia were to do, Lomonosov advocated the inculcation into students of certain basic civil and moral rules of conduct, and he suggested that each youngster be given a list of such rules to memorize. To the teachers he assigned the most important task. They had always to act as good models for youth, and so needed to be pure in their speech and actions, and at the same time be capable of instructing in the Russian language. His ideas differed from many subsequent proposals, however, in that Lomonosov believed that much of the pedagogical work in the Russian Empire should be conducted in Church seminaries.

Count I. I. Shuvalov (1727–1797), initial curator of the university in Moscow (in association first with L. Blumentrost, and then with F. P. Veselovsky), also worked hard at maintaining the gymnasiums and actually proposed that such institutions be opened all over the empire for children of the gentry. Shuvalov was a well-read intellectual who had some influence at court, and it was he who appealed to the empress for a university. He acted as a sponsor to Lomonosov and helped him in his several confrontations with members of the foreigner-dominated Academy. Shuvalov was a favourite of Elizabeth's and so wielded some clout when it came to having projects considered. It was also Shuvalov who persuaded Voltaire to undertake the writing of a history of Russia during the reign of Peter the Great, and who was the main mover behind the founding of the Academy of Arts in 1757. He was its president until 1763, when he was replaced by Ivan Betskoi. But, as Shuvalov's position of favour deteriorated during Elizabeth's last years, so did the likelihood of the Senate acting on his proposals; nothing further was done about gymnasiums after the granting of one to the city of Kazan in 1758.[13] Shuvalov's role in maintaining at least some semblance of academic decorum and in continuing the practice of sending young Russians abroad to study in disciplines which were still undeveloped in Russia, especially medicine, has probably not yet received the full attention it deserves, in the main because Lomonosov so dominates the literature about the period.[14]

The school in Kazan was the lone and paltry result of a recommendation which Shuvalov sent to the Senate calling for gymnasiums in each of the empire's large towns. The Senate went so far as to ask the Academy of Sciences for a list of appropriate towns and a suitable curriculum, but that was the extent of their efforts. G. R. Derzhavin (1743–1816), whose accounts of his early education in the 1750s were as hair-raising as those of Danilov some twenty years earlier, was a member of the first class enrolled at Kazan and reported much later in his memoir that the gymnasium was provided with only one instructor, M. I. Verevkin (1732–1795).[15] Yet the school grew so rapidly that its small original enrollment of fourteen pupils had grown to 116 within a year. Like its Moscow counterparts, the Kazan gymnasium was organized so that nobility and middle class students were kept apart. A course of study in the Tatar language was instituted in its second year, and special textbooks were created for it. By 1761, the gymnasium had its own director in the person of D. V. Savich.

In her ukaz announcing the university, Elizabeth linked patriotism and the national well-being to education and, as she did with almost all her pronouncements, implied that her policies were a continuation of those of her father. She directed the new institutions to teach "all useful knowledge" and pointed out that home educational methods were not producing people capable of performing efficient services for the state. She recognized that most of the tutors of landlords "are incapable of teaching anything, never having mastered the rudiments of knowledge themselves; thus, they only waste the young years of their charges — the best time to receive instruction. . . ." Elizabeth also bespoke the connection between education and morality which was the guiding principle of schooling in eighteenth-century Russia after the petrine era. "All that is good proceeds from an enlightened mind, which also serves to eradicate evil," the empress wrote in a tone reminiscent of sentiments expressed earlier by Kantemir and Prokopovich.[16] This was all quite normal verbiage, however, and did not signal a flurry of activity in pedagogical matters.

Elizabeth did not pursue the problems of education any further, although in 1757 she made all persons who wished to open a *pension,* or private school, apply for permission and submit their teachers to an investigation of their competency. This ruling applied also to foreigners teaching in the homes of nobility or merchants and was intended to be acted upon retroactively. In theory, the nobleman who kept in his house a tutor without accreditation could be fined heavily. Unqualified persons in the schools could be sent out of the country, but there is little evidence to suggest that this law was ever enforced.[17] In the same month, the Land Cadet Corps college was given its own typography in order to print school textbooks in arithmetic, geometry, geography, and general history; so that some educational activity and concern was demonstrated by the government.[18]

The gymnasium at the University of Moscow and in Kazan had French and Latin as their initial language of instruction. From the beginning their formal, if not always real, division according to class, one school for the nobility and another for those of lesser rank, had not gone unopposed. Shuvalov saw gymnasiums strictly as town schools which would provide students for the Cadet Corps and universities. But when the Academy of Sciences was asked to prepare a detailed prospectus for the schools, there were several outlines put forward. The German professor of history, J.-E. Fischer (1732–1771) suggested a rigid separation according to caste, children of merchants and peasants in one school, those of gentry in another. Lomonosov and a few others recommended that the classes be mixed. A. P. Protasov (1724–1796), a Russian professor of anatomy, supported the idea of a single school, but called for special courses designed to train only the sons of nobility for state service. S. K. Kotel'nikov went further and insisted that all children be given the same syllabus in the gymnasiums and that a study of the Russian language be a compulsory component of it. The final decision could hardly be called a compromise. Although some provision was made for instruction in Russian, it was Fischer's

Yet earlier he seemed to suggest that only the Ch. not the state regarded ed. as dangerous. Also he doesn't deal w/ possibility that relations of nobles to send children to mix...

recommendation that was adopted by Shuvalov. The caste basis of education limited the chances for rigorous and competitive learning. In fact, the Academy gymnasium in St. Petersburg was divided by social rank already in 1735, although it and the practically nonexistent university there were theoretically open to all classes until 1747, when the Academy was granted its first official charter. It was in the 1750s that schooling took on a permanent class alignment, and those who advocated a system based on the principle of advancement by merit alone no longer found a receptive ear at court.[19] The old church-state premonition that learning was a potentially subversive force once more won the day.

Although a number of institutions with considerable potential were created between the reigns of Peter I and Catherine II, the matter of learning for its own sake was left mainly to individual inclination. As Danilov and Derzhavin's testimonies show, harsh brutality, ignorance, and laziness were commonplace traits among the tutors of the sons of Russia's gentry. Not surprisingly, many grew up with a distaste for education, but a fortunate few have left accounts of experience with enlightened, earnest instructors.[20] There were also a small number of thinkers who struggled against the tide of obscurantism in the church and government lethargy about education after Peter's death. Among the earliest laymen who fall into this category was the poet-diplomat, A. D. Kantemir (1709–1744), who had been one of the first students at the Academy university, where he studied the translation of Pufendorf when it was adopted there in 1726.

Kantemir was closely associated with Prokopovich and the "Learned Guard" and like them was an advocate of the principles basic to Peter's bureaucratic absolutism. When only twenty years old, he wrote a revealing satire on learning in Russia and its detractors. Circulated in anonymous manuscripts, his, "To My Mind: The Enemies of Learning," assailed church leaders and others who threw obstacles in the way of enlightenment for Russians. He especially liked to attack the religious hypocrites who saw in learning the seeds of heresy and atheism, and the gentry who felt that schooling was useless. A decade later, Kantemir dedicated another satire to education, insisting that a poor one, or the absence of one altogether was far more likely to lead to bad habits in children than would a progressive school system.[21] Kantemir, who spent most of the 1730s in Paris, translated Molière and played an important part in bringing French culture to Russia.

After Kantemir and Lomonosov, the advocacy of modern, national and secular learning was taken up by N. I. Popovsky (1728–1760) and

A. A. Barsov (1730–1791), both of whom taught at the new university of Moscow. They too continued to speak for an expanded and open education for Russians. A student of Lomonosov's, Popovsky attacked the predominance of religion in Russian education and demanded in vain that schools begin to concentrate on knowledge from the secular world. These ideas were contained in a long poem written in 1756, "About the Uses of Science and About the Education of our Youth" ("O pol'ze nauk i o vospitanii vo onykh iunoshestva").[22] Over the protest of Orthodox Church authorities, he undertook a translation of Pope's *Essay on Man* (written 1733–1734) in 1753. The archbishop Ambrosia, to whom Shuvalov sent Popovsky's manuscript in 1754, wanted assurance that nothing Copernican would be left in the translation. It was printed in 1757 only after long discussion and with very cautious support from Shuvalov, I. I. Melissino (1718–1795), director of the university from 1757 to 1763, and his predecessor, A. M. Argamakov, and Kheraskov. The Synodal censors had complained in the first instance that the work was "incompatible with the Holy Scriptures." Lomonosov had been pleased with the translation from the beginning, but the church was able to force a number of changes in it. Two years later, Popovsky translated Locke's *Some Thoughts Concerning Education.*[23]

An opening address delivered by Popovsky to inaugurate the Chair of Philosophy at the University of Moscow raised a few eyebrows among his foreign colleagues. Insisting that the importance of philosophy lay in its foundation in logic, he attributed to it certain literary merits as well. Philosophy had to be expressed in clear, contemporary language, and so must be read to Russians in Russian.[24] This was an academic heresy at that time, for most foreigners and many Russians were convinced that the Russian language was not capable of such complex matters. In fact, much to the discomfit of Argamakov, Lomonosov, and others, the languages of instruction at the university were at first Latin and French.

Barsov, who was later to print a definitive grammar for Russia's youth,[25] also read a speech on the opening of the university which typified the feelings of his Russian colleagues. "Learning is everything," he began, and went on to outline the advantages Russians could gain from it. Inquiring minds, virtuous thinking, and an inclination towards the general well-being of all Russians were at the top of his list. But the high priority given to enlightenment by Barsov was of the specifically Russian variety, of the type sponsored by Prokopovich and Tatishchev and by no means in the agnostic direction usually attributed to Voltaire and his followers. In 1760, Barsov demonstrated his adherence to the high-minded principles which were supposed to be maintained at the Land Cadet Corps college and had been expressed in Elizabeth's decree of 1743, that is, that the Christian virtues lie at the very root of proper learning. "Learning is like a weapon," he said, "in that it can be used for both good and evil. One must control it. One must direct the heart through knowledge and keep it virtuous. Knowledge must open the door to virtue. A pure heart is preferred over great minds. But one must be careful here too, for the laws and piousness of Christianity rises above even human virtues. Without devoutness, no learning is truly useful and no virtue is complete. . . ." Almost paraphrasing Montaigne, Barsov was also echoing the words of Melissino, who had said in 1757 that "fear of God, and knowledge of the laws of Christianity are the pre-requisites for Russians who wish to call themselves educated."[26]

D. S. Anichkov (1733–1788) and S. E. Desnitsky (ca. 1740–1789) were other Russian-born professors at the university who hoped to make enlightenment a characteristic, rather than an isolated, phenomenon in Russian society. Their publishing activity, public lectures, and work with students helped create an atmosphere which was increasingly amenable to the fashionableness of learning and letters in the 1760s and early 1770s. In contrast to the Freemasons, and then to the mystics who came after them, these scholars were essentially secular in outlook, and Desnitsky, who had studied under Adam Smith at Glasgow, gave Russians a chance to examine the ideas of a leading theorist of rule by law when he translated parts of Blackstone's *Commentaries on the Laws of England* into Russian. Catherine II, too, read Blackstone and claimed in 1776 that she and the *Commentaries* were inseparable.[27]

An advocate of limited monarchy, in which property owners could share in the government of the country, Desnitsky relied upon Smith's writings for his practical suggestions on the re-structuring of Russian society. He hoped that the Russian state system could be tied together by a firm legal order, and he saw education as a means to create a milieu in which such ideas could be made to work. He wrote about the problem of authority and made a submission to Catherine's Legislative Commission in 1768 in which he outlined his precepts. In contrast to the political thinking sponsored by Peter I and taken up by Tatishchev, he disapproved of Hobbes' absolute reliance upon monarchy and said that Pufendorf dealt too much in the abstract.

Desnitsky held the Chair of Roman Law and Russian Jurisprudence at the University of Moscow for almost twenty years, 1768-1787. Throughout that period, the name of Adam Smith cropped up repeatedly in his writings and lectures, so he contributed to Smith becoming the most widely-read English scholar in Russia during the last quarter of the eighteenth century and the first two decades of the nineteenth.[28] Desnitsky worked hard to foster the principles of rational activity on the part of government. Unfortunately, however, the Pugachev Revolt undermined the tolerance which Catherine and the nobility, recently freed from compulsory service, had for the egalitarian ideas being spread by parvenu scholars like Desnitsky.

In 1769 Anichkov published a work on the natural origins of religion, which earned him the enmity of the Synod and many of his colleagues, and he later worked on a wide variety of subjects using history as a tool for both mathematical and philosophical theory. I. A. Tret'iakov (1735-1776), Desnitsky's companion in Scotland, also used history to analyze the world of ideas. He wrote treatises on the histories of European universities and on the sources of national wealth, for which he has been lauded by Soviet scholars who cite him as one of the first to recognize the character of European feudalism.

The intellectual atmosphere at the university in Moscow had been conducive to political inquiry and literary experimentation before these Russian scholars became famous there. From its first faltering steps, the institution, which was entirely secular and had only Russian students, became a well-spring of patriotic writers and thinkers. Denis Fonvizin was in its first group of pupils, as were the folklorist, I. F. Bogdanovich, and the famous publisher, Nicholas Novikov. Fonvizin was associated with a literary and theatrical circle dominated by Kheraskov, who replaced Melissino as university director in 1763. He and others also attempted their first serious efforts at writing by participating in Kheraskov's student journals of the early sixties. Neither Fonvizin nor Novikov had had any formal education of note before arriving at the university, though they were well read. Nor had another of their eventually well-known classmates, V. I. Lukin. So their years at the university were vital ones insofar as their point of view about enlightenment was concerned, and the first decade of the university's existence, then, was to determine the main direction of Russian political thought and the character of its own "Enlightenment" for the remainder of the century.

The most important associations made by students in Moscow were with the German professors who made up almost the entire faculty during the 1750s, and who for awhile outnumbered the students. The most prominent professors were J. M. Schaden (1731–1797), P.-H. Dilthey (1723–1781), and J. G. Reichel (1727–1778), who taught their audience the integral notions of the German *Aufklärung,* specifically the ideas of Leibniz, Wolff, and Pufendorf. Schaden spent four years before coming to Russia earning a doctorate of philosophy at the University of Tübingen, where the notions of Wolff and Leibniz reigned supreme. Dilthey had been a student of Pufendorf's and used that scholar's legal treatise as a textbook. One of the young men who listened to him attentively in the late 1750s was Alexander Radishchev, whose subsequent enthusiasm for justice and legal order brought him imprisonment in 1790. To be sure, both Wolff and Pufendorf were advocates of absolutism, but they insisted upon a rational basis for it, one in which the ruler had an obligation to govern in the best interests of his state and subjects. They both assigned great importance to duty and obligation for monarch and subjects alike. Pufendorf's influence in Russia was to come full circle, for Blackstone turned to his work for support often.[29]

A particularly active foreigner in Russia, one who contributed more to the dissemination of general knowledge than any other, was G.-F. Müller (1705–1783), who was responsible for selecting most of the university faculty. From the 1730s to the second decade of Catherine's reign, Müller was the doyen of historical studies in Russia and sponsored studies of the empire's peoples and their histories from ancient Novgorod to contemporary Siberia. His bitter debates with Lomonosov in the 1750s over the origins of the Russian state was a catalyst to further historical research and a growing concern among Russian intellectuals for their own past and national awareness. A prolific and tireless worker in the cause of archival collecting, historical source publishing, and research on the nationalities within the empire, Müller also edited magazines and the *St. Petersburg Gazette* from its founding in 1728. The best-known of Müller's editorial enterprises was the first Russian language journal of a general educative nature, the *Monthly Essays* (*Ezhemesiachnye sochineniia,* 1755–1764), which was sponsored first by Shuvalov. In a foreword, Müller wrote that he intended to reach as wide an audience as possible, and that his material was to be simple and useful.[30] Published at a time when Russian literature, education, and printing were still in embryo stage, the journal had immediate success, for its editor did not seek out new scientific information which would appeal only to specialists. Instead, he made available to his readers established, proven information of all sorts. In short, the journal itself was a textbook of general knowledge. Only in the realm of historical, geographical, and statistical data about the Russian Empire did he go beyond his generalist goal. Court pronouncements and several important Russian speeches, including Popovsky's inaugural address, could be found in it.[31]

One feature of the journal was a series of essays on the education of children. In its first year, an article entitled, "Rules for Educating Children" ("Pravila vospitaniia detei"), was translated from the German moralizing weekly, *Der Patriot*. The word "usefulness" was its keynote, but it also urged that sons and daughters be educated with equal zealousness, that harsh punishments be avoided, that good health be a special concern, and that both parents and teachers set impeccable examples for children to emulate. In these ideas, of course, the essay was well in the tradition of Locke, Wolff, and other West European educators. Interestingly, the essay opened by insisting that all mothers with "strong enough constitutions" nurse their own children, which, the author said, was part of natural law.[32] This was to be one of the several practices popularized a few years later by Rousseau's book, *Émile, ou de l'éducation*.

Time and again, the magazine featured translated extracts from the works of Aristotle and Plato, especially the dialogues of Socrates about the duties of citizens, methods of teaching, and the nature of human morals. Typically, an essay on the education of children in the Roman Empire, which was spread over four issues, stressed that Roman pedagogy had as its main objective the training of good citizens, and that a heavy onus lay on parents to set the stage for such instruction.[33] Further notices, all in translation from the ancient writers on the education of children in Sparta, Athens, and Persia, carried similar messages. In each case, virtue, good morals, and patriotism were considered more important than general learning.[34] The journal demonstrated very clearly the importance of neo-classicism to eighteenth-century educational thought.

A study of 1759 followed Locke and Montaigne in its emphasis upon the physical well-being of children. Its Hanoverian author compared children to "young sprouts," or seeds which had to be carefully nurtured from infancy and, as did several other articles, allotted to women the preeminent place in setting standards of behaviour for the child.[35] Indeed, a common theme in the journal's education essays was the high degree of importance attributed to mothers in the rearing of children, and ultimately in the molding of Russia's future good citizens. But there was no suggestion that women receive the same education as men, as we shall see later in one of the items printed in *Monthly Essays* during Catherine II's reign.

The notion that the education process must start almost from birth was another constant to the magazine. An article of 1760 warned that children should not be forced to learn too much too fast and cautioned against parents becoming tyrants over the matter of education; it also said that very small children should not be left to themselves to learn the wrong things. Another writer in that year said that the "youngest child already has a soul," and so must be taught good morals as soon as possible. He disliked especially the practice of turning children over to nurses until they reached the age of five or six and said that it was then that most permanent damage could be done to their character. Man is naturally good, he wrote, but since "small children do not yet have any idea about things which they see for the first time, nor about the consequences of their actions. . . ," they must always be overseen by parents lest they accidentally learn things that will incline them to evil. "Small children . . . are very little different from simple animals," he continued in support of his plea for careful early guidance.[36] In many ways, these were ideas already disseminated in Russia by Prokopovich.

The practical advantages of various scientific subjects were also given considerable attention in *Monthly Essays,* and moral admonition was the main ingredient of a number of articles. Prince M. M. Shcherbatov contributed translations of foreign studies on morality and an original piece, "On the Necessity and Benefits of Civil Law" (1759). In the latter article, the future Imperial Historiographer displayed a Freemason-like regard for individual freedoms, but only if they could exist within the confines of an all-embracing authoritarian state system. Like so many Russians who were attracted to the general principles of the European Enlightenment, Shcherbatov distrusted the natural instincts of humans, whom he regarded as too easily swayed towards violence and destruction unless their passions could be tempered by education.[37]

The *Monthly Essays* was not the only journal which carried items on education during the Elizabethan regime. In 1759, an essay written for the English *Spectator* by Joseph Addison, "On the Effects of Good and Bad Education," was translated for the Russian periodical *Spare Time Spent Usefully* (*Prazdnoe vremia v pol'zu upotreblennoe*). Eulogizing the basic virtues inherent in the "savage nations" as Rousseau had done, the Addison article told Russians that the best way to improve their minds was to contemplate morality and human nature. Another essay of the same year was directed towards Russian mothers, who were urged to allow their daughters access to "enlightenment" and to instruct them in virtuous conduct. The author's aim seems to have been to break the apathy towards ignorance which was so prevalent among provincial noblemen. The "French fop," with his superficial learning and lack of sincerity, also came under attack on the pages of *Spare Time Spent Usefully*. The fop was described as one of the sorry consequences of poor tutoring at home and of the Grand Tour. Other essays urged readers to consult books in order to educate themselves, sang the merits of the natural sciences, and caricatured further the weakly educated young nobleman. Lessons in morality and rules for getting along in society were the chief fare of the journal, but educational questions constantly received attention.[38]

Spare Time Spent Usefully contained many of the same themes which dominated the pages of Novikov's satirical journals some ten years later, but its editorial policy was less consistent. It was the first literary organ to be published and edited at a Russian secondary school, that is, at the Land Cadet Corps College between 1759 and 1761. It contained translations from German, French, English, Italian, and Danish writings, and had original submissions from S. A. Poroshin, Sumarokov, N. Titov, Stählin, P. Baluev, and P. I. Pastukhov. The greater part of the journal, however, was the work of the young cadets and their teachers. Its most common tone was one which was in keeping with the moral-didactic leanings of the literary people of the times.

Along with the student journals sponsored at the University of Moscow by Kheraskov, *Monthly Essays* and *Spare Time Spent Usefully* were a sign of a very important development in Russian cultural history. By the late 1750s Russian society had gained enough educators to serve as leaders in a gradual movement towards a national, Russian-oriented learning programme. The example of Lomonosov contributed a great deal to that process. Scholar, administrator, man-of-letters, and conscious of Russia's intellectual needs, Lomonosov provided the necessary model for young Russian students to emulate. But there were others who developed along with him and contributed to the same process in their own way. A. D. Krasil'nikov (1705–1773, astronomy), S. P. Krasheninnikov (history, botany and zoology), V. E. Adodurov (1709–1780, mathematics and grammar), and Kotel'nikov (mathematics and literature), were all prominent in helping shape a native circle of scholars.[39] It would be wrong to speak of a Russian intelligentsia in the 1750s, but at least a nucleus now existed.

The career of Adodurov is worthy of note, for it proceeded quite differently from that of Lomonosov. Son of a nobleman in Novgorod, Adodurov studied in the Novgorod Spiritual School. In 1726 he spent a year at the Academy of Sciences gymnasium and the next year entered the St. Petersburg university. There he studied under Müller, even though they did not have a language in common. Adodurov's ability to learn was such that he soon earned a position as translator for the major Academy periodicals. Reading mathematics in the same year with the famous Daniel Bernoulli, he progressed enough to be appointed to the Academy in 1733 at the rank of Adjunct-member in mathematics. He was the first Russian to receive such an appointment. While at the Academy, Adodurov used his earlier experience to translate mathematical terms into Russian and, before Lomonosov, he was regarded as the best grammarian and translator in the institution. In 1762 he replaced Shuvalov as curator of the University of Moscow and kept that appointment until 1771 when he gave it up because of illness. Shuvalov, who had been made director of the Land Cadet Corps College by Peter III, thereby becoming by far the most prominent official in Russian education, left the country after Catherine's coup and remained away for fourteen years. Adodurov then proceeded to make the university strongly academic and Russian, bringing to it young professors who had once been in his charge. Among them were Desnitsky, Anichkov, Tret'iakov, P. D. Veniaminov, and S. G. Zybelin.[40]

Lomonosov was not always friendly with Adodurov and argued with most of his Russian colleagues, but he was held in awe by many. Fonvizin called him "immortal" and said that Russia must not forget him.[41] Most of the foreign scholars at the Academy would have preferred never to have heard of him, for he challenged their very right to be there. But by the time of Lomonosov's death, Russia could lay claim to a scholarly community of its own. Indeed, in 1768, the university announced in the *Moscow Gazette* (*Moskovskie vedomosti*, founded in 1756) that native Russians were by then teaching in all of the institution's faculties, and in their own language.[42] The university was well on its way to fulfilling its promise as a wellspring of a Russian intelligentsia.

S. P. Luppov's latest study, this time on the book trade in Russia from 1725 to 1740, indicates that libraries and the book-selling business continued to expand after Peter I died, often despite government indifference. The printing house of the Academy of Sciences was active, providing about half of the nearly forty books printed yearly in the empire. More subjects were encompassed in these books than previously and the percentage of them that was religious fell to less than thirty. Books were distributed more widely than they had been in the petrine era. Several large personal collections were built up and were the main depositories for foreign language items. Even Proko- povich's collection of three thousand volumes had 65 percent secular subject matter. The St. Petersburg seminary library held over six thousand volumes, and the Academy of Sciences holdings increased from just under twelve thousand to eighteen thousand books. Thus, although there was still a long way to go before Russian readers could have access to the variety of titles available then to Western European readers, the era did see a sustained production of reading materials.[43]

Among the books read by Russia's small literate population there were several which are of interest because they demonstrate the main- stream of pedagogical thought and practice as it evolved in Russia during the nearly forty years which separated the reigns of Peter I and Catherine II. The practical bent of Peter's legislation assured that the earliest texts were almost all manuals for use by students of engineer- ing, military matters, and mathematics.[44] There were also a few books and manuscripts which dealt specifically with character-building and pedagogy. While these did not see widespread use, they show that the idea of moral obligation to the community and its leaders continued to be just as important as practical knowledge in the kind of education espoused by petrine educators and their successors. It could hardly be otherwise in a state system where service was the staff of life. In fact, political moralizing was a characteristic, in varying degrees, of all forms of Russian literature.[45] As a tradition in education, it was to reach a culminating point with the publication of Catherine's *On the Duties of Man and Citizen* in 1783. And one need only read Pobedo- nostsev's writing of one hundred years later to recognize political moralizing as a constant in Russian educational theory. For the purpose of this over-view, however, the significance of the didactic trend in Russian writing and thought lies in the fact that it reflected and at the same time helped shape the nature of teaching in Russian homes and schools.

Paramount among the moralizing school textbooks was the *Mirror of Integrity for Youth* (*Iunosti chestnoe zertsalo*), which was first printed in the capital city in 1717, and went through three further edi- tions at Peter's request.[46] A book of sixty-three rules for youth, it stressed respect for parents, elders, and the clergy, with the subtle suggestion that children should be seen and not heard. Its first section

But didn't he earlier suggest that pol. moral- izing began only after Peter

was an ABC text. The second had to do with deportment, and children were also told that they must speak about their rulers only with the utmost deference. Bad servants had to be "humbled, subdued and debased" before those whom they properly "serve, love and defend." Indeed, the general tone of the book had to do with Peter's desire that his nobility behave in a manner which distinguished them from peasants and servants. The *Mirror* even suggested that young noblemen speak to each other about private matters in foreign languages so that their servants could not understand them.

In keeping with Peter's policy, the rules also called for great respect to foreigners and diligence in learning foreign languages and customs. This and other such books were permeated with dictates about the awe one must feel before God. Tatishchev recommended the *Mirror* in his plan of 1736, and in the *Testament* to his own son, and the book was widely advertised still in the 1740s.[47] Its last printing was in 1767.

There was another book printed about the manner in which one must conduct himself at court, which also contained guidelines for the ruler himself to follow. Although mainly moralizing, the book included admonitions of practical value. To leaders of expeditions, settlement groups, and explorers, for example, the book urged that "the glory of God, the profit of the ruler, and the advantage of good people, must always be the aim of your voyages." It advised that rulers gather capable and loyal councillors at court, and that they reward those who rendered good service to the state. Interestingly, it also suggested that the fatherland's best interests are not always served by rigid adherence to "truth," rather in many cases it is best to remain silent if further discussion was to the detriment of the court.[48]

Pedagogical books began to appear and they too mirrored the mixture of pragmatic and religious reminders which characterized educational theory during the first half of the eighteenth century in Russia.[49] A short manuscript prepared during Peter's time, *About Education* (*O vospitanii*), expressed very well the significance which the new order attributed to education. Only by teaching, it repeated directly and indirectly, can the state and church create a virtuous population. A child's friends must be chosen carefully, he must learn to speak Russian properly and he must be well-versed in philosophy. The author of this treatise apparently assumed people to be naturally villainous, and so in need of careful direction: "The source and core of a virtuous and pure life is the exhortation of virtue." But the tone of the essay flew in the face of the traditional Russian, and especially Orthodoxy's, suspicion of the learning process. Using simple but effective aphorisms ("It is better to be ashamed of not knowing, than not wishing to know"), the author made the desire to learn a virtue, as had other practical intellectuals of the petrine era. Freedom of inquiry was an important tenet of the manuscript and prophetically, in the light of Professor Marc Raeff's research,[50] its author warned against the debilitating consequence of corporal punishment in schools.

The most popular of pedagogical books was that prepared by Prokopovich in 1720. The *Primer for the Instruction of Youth* went through twelve editions before 1725 and was used in most of Russia's clerical schools for the rest of the century.[51] Above all a book of moral and religious instruction, it also carried a clear political message. It advocated a paternalistic hierarchy of authority which began with God who spoke to the people through the tsar, to whom all subjects owed absolute obedience. The text was directed more to parents and others who were responsible for the education of Russia's youth than it was to the youngsters themselves. It demonstrated perfectly the tremendous potential for making or breaking the new Russian Empire which Prokopovich attributed to the process of learning. Without good education there was no hope for the new order, Prokopovich wrote, for "whatever a boy is, then that is the kind of man he will be." Education was not a mere matter of learning how to read and to write; it was a total experience in which youth should learn how to learn, how to understand complicated matters, and how to gain useful information from books.

Prokopovich proclaimed that the human disposition was determined during a child's adolescence, and he laid to early education credit or blame for the subsequent behaviour of the student. "How can we be optimistic when a child's education is no good?" he said, adding that the learning process begins with "respect for and fear of God." Books have no intrinsic value or evils in themselves, so a child must be imbued with proper moral and religious attitudes before he can comprehend what he is reading and turn the material to the advantage of himself and of his nation. Books, in turn, must be written simply and clearly so that they can readily be understood. Prokopovich practiced this principle himself by preparing a short and easily remembered answer to the subject of what a sin was in the light of each of the Ten Commandments. James Cracraft has shown recently that this section illustrates very well Prokopovich's "tendency to subordinate piety to the interests of the state." A decree of 1723 called for the reading of the *Primer for the Instruction of Youth* in churches during the most important religious festivals. It was translated into German and

English, and the Russian government even sent four hundred copies to Serbia in 1724 for the purpose of helping to preserve Orthodoxy and Slavic culture there in the face of Habsburg and Turkish pressures.[52]

The *Primer for the Instruction of Youth* had a less well-known predecessor in the *Ifika ieropolitika* (*Philosophy of Ethics*), which was first printed at the Pechersky monastery in Kiev in 1712. It had a scattered circulation and went through at least six further editions, three in St. Petersburg and one each in L'vov (1760), Vienna (1774), and Moscow (1796). The book was abundantly illustrated, as Comenius had advocated, and carried lessons in moral philosophy and ethics. Its 175 pages were filled with brief sermons on faith, love for God, respect for parents and rulers, explanations of the Commandments, and pleas for simplicity, moderation, love for one's neighbours and the truth. It even contained a short section on the value of schools and academies, in which its author said that men without learning are like cattle. The text was well in keeping with the trend towards formal and extensive education recommended in the Ukraine by the organizers and graduates of various Brotherhood schools and the Kiev Academy.

Among the interesting pedagogical books written shortly after Peter I's death was a list of recommendations for the education of the new young ruler of Russia, Peter II. Printed in 1728 under the auspices of the Vice-Chancellor, Baron Ostermann, the book was a plea for a new kind of ruler.[53] No less absolute than his predecessors, Ostermann's prince was to be skilled and trained specifically for his profession, so that he could play a role among the international concert of rulers. Foreign languages, particularly French and German, were assigned first place along with Latin as the vehicles for further and necessary learning. Practical sciences came next. The most important for general knowledge, by which the author meant the things that were intended to assure proper government, were "State history, general politics and military skills." Implicit in this document, of course, is the modern assumption that effective rulers are not made in Heaven, rather they must be taught the techniques of overlordship.

Arithmetic, geometry, trigonometry, geography, and architecture were to be granted some attention, but ancient history and "heraldry, the genealogy of the upper families," were considered especially valuable. "History is the mirror of life," wrote Ostermann, and its basic role as a course of study is to provide a source of moral exhortation and act as a guide for the actions of contemporaries. The young ruler could learn from the glorious deeds of ancient kings, and discover that it is not by chance alone that "well-being results from virtuous acts and harm from villainy." To this end, Ostermann proposed a programme of historical study for which the Academy of Sciences should prepare textbooks. He actually provided the Academy with an outline. Typically, the fate of the Greek republics, the rise in their stead of the Macedonian monarchy, with emphasis on the deeds of Alexander the Great, were to provide eighteenth-century students with axioms on which they were expected to base their own lifestyle. The subsequent perusal of Roman history was to be dominated by the theme of the "destruction of the republic through internecine wars" and the re-establishment of monarchy. The final section of the book would feature the fall of the Western Roman Empire and the survival of the Eastern, Christian section, which was to be connected with Russian history. In 1728, a trial textbook of ancient history which contained this over-all interpretation was printed by the Academy for use by Peter II.[54]

Some years later, a more widely distributed book, Abbé Bellegarde's *The Complete Education for Children* (*Sovershennoe vospitannie detei,* 1747), translated from the original French by Sergei Volchkov, demonstrated a more political turn in Russian notions about pedagogy. The benefits of education are vast, said Bellegarde, for the body can become strong and healthy from it, and the mind will become wise and versatile. That youth must learn how to serve in the ranks with dignity and honour was the message the translator wanted the book's Russian readers to heed. Bellegarde considered education to be a matter for those of rank alone, and he placed honour and loyalty ahead of academic knowledge among the attributes which students should acquire. In this idea, Bellegarde was not far removed from Locke or Ivan Betskoi, who dominated Russian education two decades later. The book became standard fare in the Cadet Corps institutions.[55]

The pleas of Tatishchev, Pososhkov, and the "Learned Guard" to the effect that learning should be encouraged as a boon for everyone had not fallen upon very fertile soil in the 1730s and 1740s. In fact, military and state services seemed to be the only worthwhile functions enumerated in Bellegarde's book, and its exhortations were made in an almost belligerently moral tone. Five hundred and two "rules" attest to the qualities which the translator, who claimed to have made no changes from Bellegarde's version, hoped to see in Russia's future bureaucrats. "Virtue," the book intoned, "is the inclination or movement of the soul towards goodness ... if a man is so inclined he will not move away from the straight path."[56] The text praised learning and criticized luxury and indolence, and its essential political theme was that strong monarchy works far better than any other political system. In contrast to the chaos and lack of decision in other types of government, Bellegarde's text went on, "an autocratic ruler . . . does not recognize anything above him besides God and the law." These, at least, were exactly the lessons preached by Tatishchev, who had said in a final warning to his son that "wealth is the origin of idleness, and idleness is the beginning of all evil."[57] Unoriginal enough to seem even then a tired cliché, that type of admonition was nevertheless something of immutable value in the minds of its eighteenth-century users.

The books available to parents and educators in early eighteenth-century Russia were limited in quantity and did not offer much in the way of encouragement to general learning. The *Domostroi* remained a widely-read item, and the newer guidebooks often served more as complementary teaching aids than efforts to break new ground. The closest work to the pedagogical labours of Locke, Comenius, and other Western European thinkers was still Prokopovich's *Primer,* and it gave pride of place to the politically didactic value of schooling. Others concentrated on character-building in a religious, moral sense, or, as in the case of the Ostermann text, were totally utilitarian in outlook.

The misfortunes of Russia's educational development during the first half of the eighteenth century were due largely to the extremely cautious attitude which the state held toward all matters of learning. In the first place, no freedom was granted to teachers as far as actual subject matter and interpretation was concerned. The regulations under which the Academy's gymnasiums and university operated stated quite clearly that school curricula must avoid anything which might be constructed as "inimical to the Orthodox-Greek-Russian Faith, the form of government, or Good Manners." Teachers were ordered to submit to the Chancellor outlines of everything that they taught. In the second place, the main incentive for Peter's reform, that is, that education was to have a practical end, forestalled the evolution of any real enlightenment in educational institutions. As Vladimirsky-Budanov aptly put it in his classic study on the Russian state and professional education (1874): "From the very first years of the eighteenth century, Russian legislation demonstrated clearly that the state recognized no other purpose in education other than to train one for a particular profession . . . the state concerned itself with instruction and not with enlightenment."[58] And the government attempted to supervise all schooling, whether state, church, or privately conducted. With the exception of those young Russians who were sent abroad for study, "enlightenment" remained a matter of self-education.

It wasn't only the interference of the state which militated against learning in Russia. The Church remained hostile to broad education, and many Russians tended to regard it as a social exercise, so that even among those who read widely the degree of actual comprehension of new ideas and sentiments tended to be shallow. Furthermore, as national consciousness grew in Russia, cultural notions from the West were regarded by many as a threat to Russian civilization — a secular temptation by a devil hitherto feared mainly by the church. Few of the Russian nobility were inclined naturally to continue their education beyond an elementary stage, and few outside of the nobility ever had the opportunity to do so.[59] Nevertheless, since education remained a criterion for important advancements in state service, many of its proponents were those who wished to achieve higher status. Such achievement was not easy, as Robert E. Jones has pointed out in his recent study on the emancipation of the Russian nobility, for good education was a very expensive proposition.[60]

After the 1750s an increasing number of Russians turned to education in general, and the discipline of history in particular, to prove their nation's merits. Lomonosov's diatribes against German historians in Russia and Voltaire's denigration of pre-petrine Russia stimulated this development. There were other Russians who advocated further educational progress because they were embarrassed about their nation's backwardness in comparison to the West. The fact that position on the Table of Ranks could be improved upon as one reached the higher stages of education was an incentive to those of lower gentry who had ambitions for themselves or for their sons. Professors of the academies were given a place in the ninth rank, and some government translators on the tenth. Students at the University of Moscow could count their university years towards promotion on the Table.[61] The same situation assured that the nobility would go to great lengths to maintain their monopoly on higher education facilities.

Peter III's Manifesto of 1762, which freed the nobility from compulsory service to the state, was explicit in its insistence that the nobility must continue to educate themselves and their offspring for the general good:

We hope that in return for this act Russian nobles, realizing what

great concern we have shown toward them . . . will continue to serve
Us loyally and zealously . . . and will educate their children attentively
in useful knowledge. . . .

The Manifesto went on to provide means by which less wealthy
nobility could send their sons to the Land Cadet Corps, and it
threatened them with the "wrath" of the emperor if they failed to
educate their offspring properly. Once a nobleman was educated, the
Manifesto allowed that he would "assume his rank in accordance with
his dignity and reward, and subsequently may enter and continue his
service as indicated above."[62]

When Catherine II came to the throne in 1762, the subject of
education had been discussed at great length, but the only detailed
proposal for the reorganization of educational facilities in Russia had
not been prepared until 1761, when Nikita Panin (1718–1783) presented it to Elizabeth. Many more were soon to follow. Education as a
consolidating force in society had been a constant theme of the
Monthly Essays and was to continue to be for the first few years of
Catherine's reign. Its emphasis had been on morality and good citizenship, rather than on general learning. To a certain extent the magazine
served as a forum in which the old petrine utilitarian view of education
and Prokopovich's concern for loyal and Orthodox subjects could
reappear in more modern pedagogical terminology. That Catherine
was aware of the long road ahead of her in matters of education can be
seen in a paper which she prepared on a myriad of subjects in
1761–1762, before Elizabeth's death. The notations showed that she
was worried about the inefficiencies of Imperial Russia, and they
foreshadowed the *Nakaz* of 1767. Musing in one place that it would be
quite simple and worthwhile to transplant an educational facility for
girls like that at Saint-Cyr in France, she also admitted that if peasant
fathers were able to keep one of their sons out of the army if they
happened to have several, then the stay-at-homes would never gain an
education. In all likelihood referring to the Garrison schools, she said
that the best instruction available to peasants would be that offered to
recruits. "Domestic education in Russia is like a muddle trickle," she
wrote, and wondered "when will it become a torrent?"[63]

Catherine II and Betskoi:
Ideas and Practice to 1775

Catherine II was a usurper of the throne of Russia and, while she was by no means unpopular and came to power in a swell of enthusiasm at least in St. Petersburg, she was well aware that consolidating political control is often more difficult than its initial achievement. Her educational policies throughout the 1760s were determined by a combination of factors, not the least of which was a sincere respect for the benefits of good education. She was conscious too of the potential advantages of favourable publicity at home and abroad; and she was convinced that education was a means whereby her new subjects could be persuaded to respect her laws. Since Peter I's schools had deteriorated so badly that by Catherine's time there was once again no real school system in Russia, she had to begin afresh in her hope to formulate an organization that would simultaneously enlighten and make loyal citizens out of her subjects.

Peter III's manifesto of 1762, in which he granted "freedom and liberty" to the Russian nobility, had urged, as we have seen, that the nobility continue to educate themselves and their offspring. At the same time, it expressed an optimistic view of progress to that date in the spread of learning in Russia. The emperor was quite frank when he said that Peter I had forced the nobility to become literate against their will. The task of convincing noblemen of the "great advantages enjoyed by enlightened states over those people who live in ignorance and sloth," was difficult indeed. But it was accomplished, for now "manners have improved; knowledge has replaced illiteracy; devotion and zeal for military affairs . . . [and] noble thoughts have penetrated the hearts of all true Russian patriots who have revealed towards us their unlimited devotion, love, zeal, and fervour."[1]

Catherine knew better. She recognized the foibles of the gentry and the enormity of the task facing those whom she made responsible for the moral education of Russian children. Sometime in the 1770s she wrote in her diary that "idleness and sloth" were still the chief vices of the Moscow nobility, and that they were governed only by:

. . . their whims and fancies, they set aside or largely ignore the laws, and thus never learn to command or else turn into tyrants. The inclination to tyrannize is cultivated here more than in any other inhabited part of the world; it is inculcated from the tenderest age by the cruelty which children observe in their parents' actions against their servants, for where is the home which has no traps, chains, whips, and other instruments to penalize the smallest mistake on the part of those whom nature has placed in this unfortunate class which cannot break its chains without committing violence? . . . the vulgar gentry, who were much more numerous than I had ever realized. . . .[2]

The new ruler saw the gentry as the greatest opponents to any of her educative programmes, and at the same time as the ones most in need of a centralized training system. She did not intend to allow the future school administration of the Russian Empire to evolve any further without clear guidance from her.

Furthermore, Catherine's earliest edicts demonstrated that order and stability were uppermost in her vision of the new Russian society. In July, 1762, she issued a series of decrees which were intended to correct abuses in the practice of commerce, urged serfs to fulfill their duties to her by staying on their masters' estates, and asked nobles to be kind to their servants. In short, she proclaimed the corporate responsibility of all groups in Russia to further the well-being of the entire community. Her viewpoint was a cameralist one, which had it that in order for the state and its components to prosper and flourish the government had to regulate all aspects of the national life. This attitude was to be carried over into her planning for education.

Thoroughly versed in the writings on education produced in Western Europe, Catherine was especially familiar with the work of Comenius, Locke, and Fénelon, each of whom she studied carefully before becoming monarch. Common to those writers, and to most of their colleagues among educators, was the assumption that the first purpose of schooling was the inculcation of virtuous habits into youngsters. They also recognized the value of good teachers and the overall advantages to society in having a well-educated citizenry.

Fénelon's *Traité de l'éducation des filles* (1687) came into Russia in the original long before its translation in 1763. It was well-enough known to prompt Fonvizin's use of Fénelon's name in his play *The Minor* (*Nedorosl'*, 1782) to contrast an intelligent well-read girl, Sofia, with a pampered poorly educated daughter of provincial nobility. Starodum encouraged Sof'ia to read Fénelon as a source of virtue and wisdom. Locke's *Some Thoughts Concerning Education* was translated into French and German for the first time in 1695 and 1708 respectively, and many times afterwards, and Russians had ready access to it in those forms before it appeared in Russia. In a less direct way, Locke's ideas permeated Russian educated groups because so many of their teachers had been instructed themselves by Christian Wolff, who had read Locke and agreed with him on a number of fundamental points.[3]

Fénelon's study was more than simply a treatise on instruction for girls. It represented his entire philosophy of education. In contrast to Locke, who made education a branch of natural history, and Rousseau, who saw in it a means to create a new world, Fénelon looked to education as a sacred human responsibility. Religion, he said, was the groundwork of all education. His plea for the training of girls was part of an argument for the inculcation of virtue, morality, and love of work in all youth. Virtue was the same for adults of both sexes, he insisted, but women were the ones who had to provide daily examples for children to emulate.[4] Differing as they did on detail, Fénelon and Locke agreed that reason was the infallible guide to all learning, and that children's brains were like blank tablets which must be carefully nurtured from infancy,[5] for it was in those years that their adult characteristics were formed. This latter belief was exactly that espoused by Prokopovich.

In his *Thoughts,* Locke was concerned with the education of sons of gentlemen, said next to nothing about girls, and showed preference for private tutors over state school systems. But that work also had broader implications and illustrated its author's concern for character-building and the nature of the learning process. He and Fénelon were adamant in their insistence upon proper example-setting, the French priest accentuating the role of mothers and the English philosopher seeing in the male tutor the great builder of his nation's well-rounded gentlemen. These notions were to appeal to Catherine, but they had their roots in Russia already, in Prokopovich's *Primer.*

Locke and Fénelon believed that good moral conduct and Christian principles were the paramount blessings of schooling. Indeed, Locke had placed "learning" last among his five components of education. The others, in his order of preference, were physical education and health, virtue, wisdom, and breeding. Quite aware that his avowed priorities might raise eyebrows among exponents of knowledge, he wrote: "You will wonder, perhaps, that I put learning last, especially if I tell you that I think it the least part. . . . Learning must be had . . . but as subservient only to greater qualities."[6] Written in the form of letters to his friend Edward Clarke, this part of the *Thoughts* may have warranted clarification in England, but it would have needed none in Russia.

Assuming that men should be instructed according to their social rank, Locke did not insist that education should be granted to everyone. He had little use for the traditional formal training by drills and memorization, preferring a method that would allow young gentlemen to form good habits from proximity to a carefully selected tutor who had "eminent virtue and prudence." Learning should be made easy and pleasurable, and punishments should not be harsh or even necessary. Locke was especially effective in popularizing the idea that knowledge was not innate; rather it was based upon impressions gained through the senses. He helped undermine the strictly utilitarian viewpoint held by classicist writers, and set many educators to thinking that taste and good behaviour were indicators of one's moral character and worth. Locke and many who came after him, including Addison, Steele, and others whose works were translated into Russian for the *Monthly Essays,* tried to find a median between a coldly rational outlook on education and an emphasis upon the passions.

Locke had a predecessor in Europe for many of his ideas, and that was Comenius (who in his turn was preceded by Montaigne), several of whose works were translated into Russian on Catherine's orders.[7] Comenius was the inspirer of much of the pedagogical thought in Europe during the eighteenth century. In his *Great Didactic* (1628–1632), he preached that one's temporal life must be such that he is prepared for eternity, a preparation that can only result from a proper education. The assumption that man was a "teachable animal" and that his good or bad habits were formed early on in life were points basic to the *Great Didactic* and to Locke's work. Comenius's assumptions that learning was made easier and more effective if children had a desire to learn prompted him to call for less punishments and a readily comprehensible syllabus. Teaching aids, like drawings, would encourage pupils to use their senses. Textbooks and methodology should be consistent, useless knowledge eliminated, and progression from one class to another logical. These methods all would stimulate in the children an appreciation of the importance of schooling. Thus, long before Locke and Rousseau, Comenius advocated methods which fostered learning by experience and sense impression.

Comenius went on to say that the young of both sexes must be educated in common, that is, away from home, and that they should learn the same essential things. Learning, virtue, and piety were the order of his recommended subjects, each of which was to be imparted through a very carefully thought-out and uniform methodology.[8] There is a remarkable similarity in tone between the writings of Comenius and Prokopovich on the importance of rearing children properly from infancy. In fact, Prokopovich's *Primer* reads in part like a synthesis of Comenius's *School of Infancy* (1633), where it was said that child training must have a Christian purpose and that their souls will be lost unless they receive a good education. Responsibility for the close supervision of a child's life before he or she reached the age of six was relegated in both books to parents, with the warning that the basic character which the youngster would retain for the rest of its life depended upon their efforts.

Russian educators from Prokopovich to Betskoi continued to be interested in Comenius, and even late in the nineteenth century (1893) the Ministry of Public Instruction recommended his work for every library of the Middle Schools and teachers institutes in the Russian Empire. The Holy Synod assigned the *Great Didactic* in that same year to clerical seminaries as a basic text.[9] In the eighteenth century, books by Comenius, Locke, and Fénelon had lots of company in Russia. About thirty-five studies on pedagogy were translated from Western languages into Russian during the second half of the century, and about eighty monographs on moral training were translated at the same time.

By no means dependent upon foreign writings alone, Catherine had capable Russian advisers on matters of education. Ivan Shuvalov's proposals for the organization of a national school system, which he had brought to Senate in 1760, failed to attract any great attention, but there were individuals at court already active in developing a philosophy of education for the Russian Empire. One of these was Count Nikita Panin,[10] to whom Elizabeth I had assigned the task of educating Catherine's son Paul, in 1760. Panin was given absolute authority over the direction of the Grand Prince's education to the extent that he was responsible in his actions only to the empress. Catherine was to give him similar leeway for a while after she came to the throne. In preparation for his duties, Panin submitted to Elizabeth in 1761 a prospectus in which were outlined his views on learning in general, and on the training necessary to future rulers in particular.

Although an earlier plan had been commissioned in 1728 by Ostermann for the edification of the Grand Duke Peter, Panin's was Russia's first carefully thought-out guide to kingship. It incorporated most of the progressive principles epitomized in the works of Locke, Fénelon, Comenius, and Leibniz. Paul's curriculum included moral

Can't the same be said of Prokopovich?

and religious training, to which were added mathematics, history, and foreign languages, above all French and German. The social graces were to be touched upon, and the course of study was to end with discussions on the practice of statesmanship. Panin adopted the Lockean idea of visual experience as opposed to rote learning and memorization. He advocated as well a paternal rather than dictatorial attitude on the part of Paul's teachers and suggested similar behaviour on the part of pedagogues throughout the country. Such preferences were not new to be sure, but this was the first time that they were written into an actual working report in Russia. Coupled with Panin's claim to Elizabeth that he hoped to develop Paul's moral and virtuous qualities so as to create a kindly and peace-loving monarch, whose sole interest lay in the well-being of his subjects, these ideas make the document one of the most important Russian expositions of the eighteenth-century notion of enlightened despotism. As David Ransel points out in his study of Panin, that statesman preceded Betskoi in attempting to bring modern educative ideas to bear on schooling in Russia.

Heeding the advice of his friend, the patriotic playwright and poet Sumarokov, Panin insisted that Russians be educated in their own language. Indeed both were later to criticize Betskoi for giving priority to the French language in Russian schools. One of the men whom Panin appointed to tutor Paul was the officer and writer, S. A. Poroshin (1741-1769), who was well-read in Western enlightenment literature but nonetheless an intense Russian patriot.[11] Intent upon instilling in the young prince a firm patriotism, a respect for the Russian people, and an awareness of the main events in his nation's history, Poroshin tried to dissuade Paul from the current belief that Peter I, whom he praised, had solved all of Russia's problems by imitating the West.

The Metropolitan Platon was another of Panin's appointees, and in 1763 he began to instruct Paul in matters of religion.[12] The nature of Platon's contribution to Paul's learning can be summed up by a reference to his essay, "A Word about Education" (1765). Education, he wrote along with comments about the value of religion, "is a preparation for virtue." It is an evangelical science, which must first teach students a fear of God and then prepare them to be honourable citizens. In this, he followed Panin's objectives closely. Platon had his own ideas about the art of teaching and learning, saying that "learning, in order to be effective, depends not so much on wit and eloquence as it does on the purity and chastity of the teacher's heart." He became the director of the Moscow Academy in 1775 and insisted that his teachers set good examples in order to bring proper moral education to their pupils. Later he widened the school's curriculum and demanded that Russian replace Church Slavonic and alternate with Latin as its main language of instruction.

Throughout the first decades of Catherine's reign Platon's energies were directed towards countering the lingering suspicion which Russia's churchmen had of education. Quoting the Scriptures in "A Word about Education," he showed that proper instruction would complement religious orthodoxy by giving youth the means to comprehend the ways of the church. Just as Catherine was to do often, he cited Proverbs (1.7), "The fear of God is the beginning of knowledge." Although he did not bother to add the subsequent phrase from the same verse, "but fools despise wisdom and instruction," his meaning was clear enough. Schools and the church necessarily complement each other, he wrote, for both have as their goal the creation of virtuous men.[13] In this, Platon was repeating the message of *Spiritual Regulations.*

Poroshin, Platon, and Paul's other tutors differed on one major count from N. I. Novikov and some progressive enlighteners of the 1770s and 1780s, with whom we will deal in the next chapter. They rejected out of hand the political ideals of the French Enlightenment. "Noxious weeds sprouting among healthy plants," is what Platon called the notions of the "so-called Encyclopaédists." This comment was made in 1786, in a report sent to Catherine responding to her order that he examine the publishing activity of Novikov to see if his work clashed with "our Orthodox and civil obligations." It does, however, represent a consistent frame of mind. As a matter of fact, most of Novikov's work was roundly applauded by Platon, probably to Catherine's discomfort, but the implications of Catherine's request for the soon-to-be-opened public schooling system are obvious. Platon's opinions fell neatly into pedagogical tendencies which went back to Comenius, who had called for dedication to teaching and high moral qualities among his instructors. Comenius's citation from the oftquoted Seneca, "First learn virtue, and then wisdom, since without virtue it is dificult to learn wisdom,"[14] represented the essence of Platon's viewpoint and, indeed, a tradition in which the Lutsk Brotherhood, Prokopovich, and Panin were all comfortable. To them, virtue and wisdom meant acceptance of the political and social status quo.

The reliance upon moral regeneration which so characterized the educational attitude of Panin and Platon was mirrored in views held

But distinction from Novikov's ideas is not clear.

by professors at the University of Moscow. It coincided as well with pedagogical practices preached by Ivan Betskoi (1704–1795),[15] who replaced Shuvalov as the main spokesman for learning within high officialdom. Betskoi was known to Catherine as early as 1756, when he advised her that "the arts and sciences are more necessary to us than anything else," and tried to persuade her to side with the clique at court which was inclined to support a French-Russian alliance. Betskoi was living in Europe at that time. Catherine saw him as little more than one of the myriad persons involved in the eternal plotting at court, where her own position was tenuous enough before 1758. In fact, she was warned by Sir Charles Hanbury-Williams when he was ambassador from Britain to Russia, 1755–1757, "to one day appoint Betski [sic] Grand Master of your Gardens, but never let him into your house. He will arrange a flower bed much better than a plan, and will produce a better drawing than a scheme."[16] He also called Betskoi a "conceited ignoramus," but whether he believed his own charges or not, they must be qualified by the fact that they were expressed in the heat of bitter lobbying over political alignments during the Seven Years War. At any rate, Catherine seemed not to give Hanbury-Williams' prophetic statement its full due. Soon after becoming monarch she assigned Betskoi posts as the president of the Academy of Arts and director of the Land Cadet Corps, and she made him responsible for beautifying her cities.

While Panin, Poroshin, and Platon were attempting to furnish the heir apparent with suitable moral and patriotic feelings, Betskoi worked to provide the same for the entire Russian population. Having travelled widely in Europe and having studied Locke carefully, he had already concluded in the 1740s that Russia's future was assured only if its school system could be made to combine the best of secular and spiritual training.[17]

Writing in the 1760s, he repeated Prokopovich's idea that "good or bad morals in every man throughout his lifetime depends upon the quality of his earliest education." Therefore, if youngsters are trained well, the next generation will have good parents. Education must begin by instilling "a fear of God, to establish a praiseworthy attitude in their hearts, and to instruct them in the fundamentals of acceptable morals . . . to make them into upright citizens, and useful members of society."[18] Like Locke, Betskoi saw four dimensions to the educational process, those of physical education, physical-moral, the purely moral, and finally, learning. As for the physical-moral, he wrote that "idleness is the mother of all vices, and hard work is the father of all virtues."

Hardly an original sentiment, but nonetheless an important one when applied to teaching habits. The third part of education, the purely moral, or moral admonition (*nravouchenie*), Betskoi thought so vital that he included some of his own warnings about behaviour in his most famous essay on education, the "General Institutes on the Education of the Youth of both Sexes," which was written into the law by Catherine in March, 1764.

A demand for widespread development of educational facilities, the "General Institutes" epitomized Catherine and Betskoi's idealistic sympathies for learning during the next dozen years. It placed emphasis upon primary schooling, on which "all subsequent education depends, for it is from the first level that the *new order* will arise." Moral training was to be the starting point for proper education, Betskoi's plan stated,[19] for it alone prepared children for any further excursions into the risky realm of knowledge. Betskoi attributed this idea directly to Catherine, who, he declared, preferred the teaching of "gentle manners" to the sciences and arts during the early stages of education.[20] The "General Institutes" also proclaimed that schools were to make people useful to society, and it reiterated Prokopovich's old maxim that the source of "all good and evil is education." Betskoi's eloquent essay was the first call for free and universal education for both sexes to be taken seriously in the Russian Empire.

Like many other Russians and Europeans, Betskoi had read Rousseau's *Émile, ou de l'éducation* (1762, translated into Russian in 1779), in which the author argued that early education should be freed from traditional restraints so that children might be allowed to learn from their environment and from their own natural senses. Rousseau believed in the fundamental goodness of all children, an idea which clashed with the reigning Christian view of the nature of children. The young Émile developed with little restriction until he reached the age of twelve, when he was directed towards useful knowledge like science and geography. At the age of fifteen, his tutor then concerned himself with Émile's moral and social development, which included the learning of civic studies and history. Betskoi and Catherine were intrigued with Rousseau's notions about the role of environment in the educational process and, like Comenius and Prokopovich, accepted the idea that the child was naturally good. But they looked askance at his stress on freedom, which went beyond that advocated by Locke. The empress even included *Émile* among books published by the Academy of Sciences in the 1760s which met with her disapproval because they were "against law, good morals, and the Russian nation itself."[21] She later wrote to Mme. de Bielcke (Bjelke) that she "did not like Émile's education; they thought differently in the good old days, and some people from then have turned out all right."[22] Catherine's opprobrium was hardly unique, for the publication of *Émile* had sparked indignation throughout Europe. Voltaire and the encyclopaedists were infuriated because he was willing to rely upon intuition rather than cold reason, the Church suspected his theology, and statesmen saw in the work a threatening element of individualism. But the book was to gain a wide audience.

Betskoi remained an enthusiast of Rousseau's ideas on education. Having spent a number of years travelling all over Europe where he met many of the leading thinkers and artists of the day, Betskoi had also participated in a salon led by Mme. Geoffrin in Paris. There he became friendly with Grimm and listened to discussions on subjects as diverse as daily events, new literature, the theatre and drama, and contemporary ideas on education. Catherine's mother, Princess Johanna of Anhalt-Zerbst, who had met Betskoi previously, attended the salon in 1758 accompanied by the Russian ambassador. The empress corresponded with Geoffrin for many years and several times mentioned Betskoi, whom the French lady referred to as "mon ami." The pedagogical views of Montaigne, Locke, Comenius, and others were all subjects of conversation and Betskoi was able to make Catherine feel part of the cosmopolitan circle, which also had included her one-time lover and future King of Poland, Poniatowski. In a letter to Geoffrin of 1763, the empress wrote that after dinner she talked often with Betskoi for hours: "for my education, he reads books and I do my needlework."[23] He was by then established "in her house" far beyond his own expectations, and Hanbury-Williams' partisan warning.

Rousseau would have preferred a system of public instruction run by the state, but in lieu of that he insisted that the tutor insulate his pupils as much as possible from their parents and relatives, so that they might not be tainted by the rampant vices of society. He urged that mothers nurse their own children to instill in them a sense of being loved and to restore the natural emotions with which children were born. "When women become good mothers," he wrote in *Émile*, "men will become good husbands and fathers." Like his predecessors, Rousseau put the formation of character ahead of intellectual development. He exhorted instructors and parents to teach by setting good examples in their own behaviour and proclaimed that it was a child's "conscience" which must be nurtured by such example. In contrast to Locke, however, Rousseau denied a child's ability to reason, and insisted that his fictional protégé be guided by experience (example) for his first dozen years; only then should he begin to read books.[24] The "General Institutes" carried the Rousseauian conception of education in principle if not so much in detail. Children in their very earliest years must "be educated to virtue," Betskoi wrote, and added that the "new fathers and mothers can, in their turn, instill the rules of life which they received in the hearts of their children." Betskoi believed that formal education should begin at age five or six, rather than at twelve, but his emphasis on moral training and character-building was the same as Rousseau's. He saw the advantages of keeping children separate from families once the educational process had begun. The first order of business would be to teach children the "fear of God," and then proceed to perfect their characters. There was, of course, a Russian precedent for such ideas in the writing of Prokopovich, but there is little doubt that Betskoi was stimulated from his European experience and by the wishes of Catherine with whom he discussed each part of the "General Institutes" before they were printed.[25]

In keeping with the slowly developing Russian national consciousness of that era, Betskoi also wrote in the "General Institutes" that, "it is well-known that any man in society must know all the strengths and variations of his native language. Without that knowledge, he will not understand the ruler, or the codes and the laws which are issued by the monarch. . . ." Only after they learned to read and write in their own tongue should young Russians take on foreign languages. We have seen that Betskoi was criticized later by Sumarokov and others for trying to educate Russians only in French and German. Poroshin accused him of trying to be a Russian Colbert,[26] but the fact of the matter was that Catherine could not legislate Russian teachers where there were none.

It was Betskoi who refined in Russia the notion that schools could manufacture the new Russian man. He was convinced, as was Catherine, that the Russian family was not capable of fulfilling the state's demands for education, and so he decided that parents must cede control over their children's upbringing to his schools which, in turn, he hoped would remain autonomous from government.[27] Foundling Homes for orphans and illegitimate children were sponsored by Betskoi, himself an illegitimate son of Prince I. Iu. Trubetskoi, to serve as models for the regeneration of Russia's youth. Assisted by Barsov, Betskoi began working on a plan in 1763 for a teaching programme for orphans in Moscow. Approved by Catherine in 1764, the "General

Plan for the Moscow Foundling Home" called for the reading of Cicero, Seneca, Plutarch, Marcus Aurelius, Pufendorf, and Locke. These were all proponents of an ordered society in which everyone had a designated role to play. Cicero, the Roman statesman and orator, was a favourite of Betskoi's for his stress on civic responsibility. The laws of the land, "rules for civil life," and things Russian were also recommended. "The main purpose of our education system," Betskoi announced, "is to produce healthy, strong, cheerful foster-children who are able to serve the fatherland in art and trade, to create in them wisdom and heart so that they will not only be useful to themselves, but good Christians and true citizens." A similar institution was set up in St. Petersburg in 1770.[28]

Betskoi's intention to produce a new generation of morally and religiously indoctrinated youngsters was part of a larger hope that Russia could have a stronger middle, or "third class" of people, as he called it in the "General Institutes." Indeed, he opened his submission on the Foundling Homes with the enthusiastic prediction to Catherine that "Peter the Great created people in Russia; your Majesty will give them souls." The homes for waifs, with their accompanying maternity hospitals, were a product of this ambition in that they were designed to save the lives of infants who might otherwise be discarded, and then to shape the mores of their young lives. Like Catherine, who was swayed in this direction by Montesquieu,[29] Betskoi believed that the road to Russian prosperity lay in infusing into its society an enlightened, loyal and economically aggressive class which was not encumbered by the same limiting traditions which characterized both the nobility and the peasantry. Like Locke and Rousseau's, Betskoi's conception of *tabula rasa* did not assume that individuals were born with no peculiar qualities of their own. He recognized that each child had its own innate talent, and he hoped to shape their attitudes and direct their best traits in the interest of the entire Russian community.

Children raised in the Foundling Homes were declared free persons on graduation and were granted passports: ". . . these graduates and their progeny will become free; they will make up a third estate within the state." Betskoi served as the director of the Homes and was assisted in governing their affairs by a council of unpaid trustees who met with him on a weekly basis. He saw his job as a paternal one and made a conscious effort to appear as a father to the foundlings rather than as an official. To act as the friend of Russia's youth and to instill in them a sense of trust and security was Betskoi's understanding of his task as mandarin of Catherine's school systems. He expected the same dedication from his teachers and from the headmistress of the Homes who, he said, must be an "honourable and wise woman."

After spending two years in the hands of wet-nurses and four more in a general group made up of children of both sexes, the children at age seven were assigned to a schedule which included only one hour per day in school. Reading, writing, and religion, with some dancing and weaving, were the extent of their early studies. From the age of eleven to fourteen, they continued the basic lessons which they had begun four years previously, but at an accelerated pace, with arithmetic, geography, and book-keeping added. Girls at this age were also taught preliminary house-keeping skills. Subjects usually deemed important to nobility, like dancing, social manners, and the French language were ignored. During their final four years, girls specialized in the domestic sciences and boys concentrated upon learning skills according to one of three categories. Some were encouraged to study for entrance to university, others were assigned to trades for which they had shown some aptitude. The third group was made up of those who were considered capable only of simple labour or domestic work. By the time he or she was ready to leave the institution, the illegitimate child or foundling, who may have been brought there by an anonymous supplier in return for a two rouble bounty, was aged nineteen or twenty. During that long period the student had not left the premises and had been visited only by a sponsor or members of his immediate family, if he was fortunate enough to have either one. In theory then, the Homes graduated free persons fully trained to take their place as part of the new order of Russian citizens.

The "General Plan for the Moscow Foundling Home" also demonstrated Betskoi's concern for the high mortality rate among infants in Imperial Russia, for he made the matters of health, cleanliness, and physical exercise important components of his charges' upbringing. For reasons of nutrition, Betskoi seconded Rousseau's plea for breast-feeding by mothers or by wet-nurses in the case of orphans. The degree of his worry was illustrated by the fact that he included an entire diet for growing children in the "General Plan": well-baked bread, soup, fish, porridge, with water or kvass to drink. Alcoholic beverages were not to be consumed by the children. But it was fresh air and physical activity that he prescribed most strongly. Infants must not be swaddled, children should not be dressed too tightly, and they should be made to wash often. Time for play was to be included as a regular part of their daily schedule, and all children were to be urged to participate in games and walking.

The Foundling Homes survived Betskoi to become a permanent social service in Russia, but their academic side was of only slight significance. Their importance for education lies more in the fact that they represent Betskoi's attempt to put into practice ideas that he had been dwelling upon since reading Comenius, Locke, and Rousseau. Typically, moral education was assigned a clearly dominant place in the Homes' curriculum. Betskoi's innovation is represented by the fact that he assumed that the best atmosphere for the inculcation of morality was one in which exercise, play, and a loving relationship between teachers and pupil predominated. He forbade corporal punishments and demanded that his teachers show, in terms of their own behaviour, a serenity, piety, and reasonableness which their students could readily emulate. He believed that absolute silence and fear of punishments in the classroom were not at all conducive to learning, and so he insisted that his teachers instruct the children in an open, relaxed milieu. In short, the Foundling Homes and his "General Plan" for them embody Betskoi's experiment in progressive teaching methodology. A few years later, in 1766, he published a collection of extracts from foreign authors who had expressed ideas similar to his own, and added his commentary to them. The *Brief Manual, Collected from the Best Authors with Several Notations about the Education of Children from Birth through their Youth* had five printings before 1771. That its size grew from eighteen pages to forty-eight suggests that Betskoi was constantly reading and thinking about pedagogy.[30]

Of all Betskoi's general ideas about education, the one that met with the least resistance was his assumption that all Russian schools must be centralized. But he also hoped that they would remain free from government interference and would have a corporate existence of their own, responsible to him, a board of directors and, of course, to Catherine. The Foundling Homes were granted quite a few privileges in both administrative and financial matters. In fact, the Homes operated a savings and loan bank which proved lucrative. Nonetheless, although Betskoi's active campaigns for funds from the private sector were particularly successful in the case of the Homes, in the long run he found that he could not rely upon Russia's philanthropists to make his system work. He had to depend time and again on Catherine's good graces. So his projects eventually were to lose their relative autonomy from government, and when the teaching programme of Russia's public school organization was worked out in the 1780s, the idea of state control was included as one of the basic precepts in the compulsory textbook, *On the Duties of Man and Citizen.* As was so often the

But surely Rousseau cannot be regarded as a neo-classicist.

case in Russian didactics, examples from ancient Greece and all its real and mythical glories were used to rationalize Catherine's educative proposals. In trying to explain to young students that patriotism was a natural part of the learning process, the text gave the fundamental neo-classicist view of an ordered life:

> The Greeks considered education of children to be a concern of the state. The supreme leaders were concerned with them and their education. They never left this to the discretion of parents alone, despite the fact that many of them understood very well their responsibilities to educate their children. This was a duty not only to themselves and their families, but to society in general. Those who were entrusted by the government with the task of education strove to arouse in young people an attentiveness to the advantages of the fatherland. They explained to them the usefulness of state institutions, taught the young people to notice their excellence, honour, and get the feeling of all the advantages which everyone in the fatherland could enjoy.[31]

Twenty years after the publication of this textbook in 1783 Alexander I was to found his educational reforms on exactly such presumptions.

There was another project from the early 1760s which had significance for the development of education in Imperial Russia. It originated in 1759 when V. V. Krestinin (1729–1795), A. I. Fomin (1733–1799), and others established the first historical study group outside of Moscow and St. Petersburg. Archangel's Society for Historical Research (*Obshchestvo dlia istoricheskikh issledovanii*), which remained in existence for about ten years, had as its initial aim the collection of ancient documents. Members of the Society were very much aware of the discrepancies between educational facilities in the provincial areas and those in the large urban centres. So they proposed in 1764 the establishment of a school system which would suit the needs of Russia's growing merchant class.

Krestinin's submission called for elementary schools to be set up in the empire's towns. They would be open to children of all classes, who would be taught writing, arithmetic, and the Orthodox catechism — Prokopovich's was recommended. Complementing this beginning would be a gymnasium in which merchandizing and navigation would be taught, along with all the qualities of good citizenship. In the subsequent year, Krestinin proposed to Catherine's Commission on Commerce that a school specifically for merchants be opened. In each of the two projects, the suggested curricula were an interesting combination of professional and general training. So much importance was attributed to education as a national as well as an individual need, that Krestinin requested that expulsion from school as a disciplinary measure be forbidden.

In the first instance, however, the proposal for a gymnasium began with the admonition: "there is a need to teach in this gymnasium the means to be a good merchant, and to be a good citizen."[32] Knowledge of Russian law and history were the keys to the latter aim, and Pufendorf's book on the duties of men and citizens was to be compulsory reading. In this, then, Krestinin's proposals foreshadowed those adopted by Catherine and Iankovich in the 1780s. In recognition of his efforts on behalf of learning, Krestinin, a merchant himself, was appointed as a corresponding member of the Academy of Science in 1786.[33]

Krestinin's ideas about education, which changed little after the 1760s, were published in the capital city during the late eighties and showed him to be in step with current feelings of the state about the purpose of education — if not with Catherine's growing reservations about the extent to which learning should be carried. However, the only action taken on his requests had come indirectly, when a magistrate from Archangel petitioned the Senate in 1765 to institute that part of Krestinin's plan which called for the teaching of the catechism in all Russian towns. The Senate responded by asking Catherine to open a small school in Archangel, to give it wide publicity so that other towns would follow suit on their own, and to adopt for it Prokopovich's *Primer*.[34]

The year 1765 saw another proposal of a school for merchants, also sent to Catherine's Commission on Commerce. Although its author is unknown, the ideas in it suggest a knowledge of Krestinin's efforts. This detailed project called for a school in St. Petersburg for one-hundred and twenty sons of merchants from all over the empire. It was to be administered by a director and a committee of four "notables," which would be responsible for finding teachers, funding the institution, and examining its graduates. Pupils would be enrolled at the age of nine, in three groups of forty, and their fathers would have to provide evidence that they were of the merchant class. The first group, aged nine to twelve, would be taught Russian, writing, drawing, religion, French, geometry, and elementary natural history. The second class, ages thirteen to fifteen, would have German, English, and dance added to their curriculum, along with a more advanced study of Russian grammar. Those in the third class, ages sixteen to eighteen, would undertake the basic sciences, history, and geography. Special instruction in art, trade, and accounting would fill out their programme.

Thus, by the time they finished, the young merchants-to-be would have had a wide practical and general learning. Even during their language instruction, teachers would have been required to teach from books which had to do with commerce. Arithmetic, history, and geography were to be handled in the same fashion, that is, courses had to include information on the trade, resources, and banking systems of foreign countries and of Russia. The proposal reflected Betskoi's aversion to strictness and harsh punishments in schools, called for moral education to be combined with religion, and emphasized the importance of physical fitness and health. Although it was not acted upon, the report represented in detail and intent the progressive attitudes which existed among many of those Russians who were committed to finding a way to educate their nation. But it was not until 1772 that a school for merchants was actually founded by Betskoi in Moscow for one hundred students. This marked an important precedent, for since the petrine era the seminaries, Cadet Corps colleges, and garrison schools had increasingly drawn their pupils solely from the castes which they represented. By the time of Catherine's coup, there were no established teaching institutions catering to the needs of town dwellers. Even the new school for sons of merchants was made possible only through the financial assistance of the consistently philanthropic Prokofeus Demidov, to whom Betskoi turned often for funds. The school thrived, but its curriculum was somewhat less ambitious than that described in the proposal of 1765.[35]

Catherine's own ideas on the value of education were expressed publicly first in the *Nakaz* (Instruction) which she prepared as a guideline for the deliberations of her widely-publicized Legislative Commission of 1767. It was published in nine languages other than Russian before the end of the eighteenth century. Openly dependent upon Montesquieu, Beccaria, and others for many of the ideas in the *Nakaz,* Catherine mainly paraphrased passages reflecting her own views (and Betskoi's) in the nine clauses concerning education. She began the section with the assertion, "The Principles of Education are the Fundamental Principles which Prepare Us to be Citizens," and then went on to tie the *Nakaz* to Betskoi's "General Institutes" by citing from the latter document directly. "An Instruction to every private Person . . . [and] a general Rule of Education" shall be:

It is necessary to instill into Youth the fear of God, to settle their hearts in laudable Dispositions, to teach them the essential Rules which are suitable to their Situation, to kindle in them the Love of Industry and the abhorence of Idleness as the Source of all Evil and Error, to teach them a proper Behaviour in their Actions and Convention, Courtesy, Good Manners, Compassion for the Poor and the Unfortunate, and an aversion to everything Audacious, to teach them private Economy in all its minute parts, and as much of it as is useful, to deter them from Dissipation, and particularly to ingraft in them a habit of Decency and Cleanliness, as well in their own persons, as in what belongs to them. In a word, to endow them with all those Virtues and Qualifications which belong to good Education, by which in our time they may become true Citizens and Useful and ornamental Members of Society.[36]

The *Nakaz,* then, was another link in the chain of semi-official eighteenth-century Russian educational statements which began with Prokopovich's *Primer* and was to end in 1783 with the publication of Catherine's *On the Duties of Man and Citizen.* Even though it carried Locke's and Rousseau's call for a total education which included spiritual and moral instruction, it also encompassed the pietist idea that all people should be trained to fulfill their divinely assigned roles in human society.

The framework within which Catherine's ideas on education were propagated was stated elsewhere in the *Nakaz,* where she said that a civil society "requires an Establishment Order, in which there is one part to direct and command, and another to obey." Her interpretation of "parts" was also quite clear — "The Sovereign is the Source of all Powers Imperial and Civil."[37] For all of Catherine's enlightened commentary, the section of the Legislative Commission which had to do with education was dominated by V. T. Zolotnitsky (1741-1796), who was committed to a system in which each social class received a different training. Youngsters from the lesser ranks, he said, need only be taught subjects which bred character and love for work. As a matter of fact, the *Nakaz* embodied Catherine's rationalization of absolute monarchy, and its brief references to education were part of her formula for the preservation of autocracy.

Its practical failings notwithstanding, the discussions and reports engendered by the Legislative Commission provide us with a wealth of information on the attitudes of large cross-sections of Russian upper society. In his recent study of the Russian nobility in the eighteenth century, Robert E. Jones shows that most nobility of the provinces were in a relatively poor financial position and recognized that education was one of the means out of that situation. Their problem was compounded by the fact that parish schools had almost disappeared by the 1760s, although some informal instruction still existed in a few towns.[38] Reports which various provincial groups of nobility submitted to the Legislative Commission in 1767 demonstrate that education had become a clearly accepted stepping stone to higher office. Jones cited a report from Vereia, which carried a typical request that:

> for the benefit of the fatherland, the empress build state supported schools in every town for the education of poor nobles in foreign languages and other studies that are useful to society . . . Although various schools for the children of the nobles have been established by Her Imperial Highness and now exist in St. Petersburg and Moscow, it is well known that most of the nobles are not wealthy and, being poor, are . . . unable to send their children there; and so the children of these poor nobles, living with their fathers and receiving no education, come to their majority ignorant . . . and can do nothing but enlist as common soldiers.[39]

The question of education as it was discussed at the Legislative Commission has been treated succinctly by Paul Dukes, who suggests that the only unanimous sentiment discernible from the myriad of reports which touched upon education was the recognition that Russia simply had too few schools and teachers. The Senate called for schools to teach sons of merchants subjects which would help them follow in their father's footsteps; a Ukrainian submission requested additional monasteries and convents to instruct children of both sexes in religion and morality; the Academy of Sciences recommended widespread elementary schools and promised to submit an exhaustive plan on the matter. The *dvorianstvo* seemed concerned with education, particularly because they were the class required to have it as one of their service obligations. The most common Ukrainian complaint was the continued lack of facilities equal to those available to Russians.

In 1768, Catherine established a School Committee as an adjunct of the Legislative Commission. On it were T. von Klingstedt, Baron G. F. Ash, honourary member of the Academy and Doctor-General of the Russian army, Jacob Ursinus, a delegate from Dorpat, and its chairman, Zolotnitsky. Together they drew up plans for a tripartite public school organization, that is, a system with elementary, secondary, and higher school levels. All but Zolotnitsky advocated that there be no class distinctions within the system. They agreed that it be compulsory for boys and voluntary for girls. Even after the Legislative Commission itself withered, the School Committee continued to submit ideas to the Senate and to Catherine, including in 1770 a proposal from Klingstedt for compulsory village schools. His *trivial Schulen* resembled in many ways the elementary public system which finally was brought into existence for Russia in 1786. There was little real unanimity on the Committee and Ash and Ursinus compiled submissions that tended to contradict those from von Klingstedt and Zolotnitsky, but it served as a useful focal point for preliminary discussions of school reform.

Foreign tutors came under attack from the clergy and from the Academy of Sciences, yet they remained the only means for educating sons and daughters of provincial gentry, who did not even have the opportunity of sending their children to garrison schools. The church resented the fact that most tutors were not of the Orthodox faith and taught in non-Russian languages, and the Academy said that "foreign teachers . . . undoubtedly bring us more harm than benefit because by far the most part of them are worthless. . . ." Both bodies proposed that existing regulations about qualifications should be enforced before any such teachers be hired. The Academy report also recommended that a code of educational principles be compiled, and a governing agency of nine people, preferably well-known scholars, be organized to administer education. The School Committee successfully countered this idea, perhaps in order to protect their own positions, and suggested that the Senate might serve as overseer of schools. All in all, however, these scattered expressions of concern are of interest only in that they help reveal the extent of educational deprivation in Russia, for nothing constructive came from them.[40]

The first years of Catherine's reign saw so many direct proposals made to her about education that Grimm remarked in 1762 that writing about education was the "rage" in St. Petersburg. Even before those which came from the short-lived School Committee, ideas were put forward by the University of Moscow professors, Dilthey, Barsov, and Schaden, by statesmen, Panin and Betskoi, by officials, bureaucrats, educators, editors, and theologians, Teplov, A. P. Mel'gunov, Müller, Poroshin, and Platon, all between 1762 and 1764. So it is hardly surprising that Catherine paid little attention to reports made to the Legislative Commission. A theme common to most of these presentations was succinctly expressed in an anonymous paper written in the early 1760s. It outlined the practical and intellectual framework in which all of Catherine's educative planning took place, that is, that its purpose was to "inculcate in youth from their very first years a fear of God and a love for moral virtue, . . ." so that they might become "worthy citizens."[41] A general comment on the papers submitted by Betskoi, Müller, and Dilthey, this essay may well have been written by Catherine herself, and for her the phrases were much more than repetitive clichés. They represented a specific and apparently attainable goal.

Although the overall attitude carried in the many propositions was like that stated above, there were some differences in approach. State-Secretary, Ober-Curator of the Synod and member of the Academy of Sciences, Teplov, who gathered most of the submissions, emphasized in his "Opinion about the Provinicial Schools" (1763) the teaching of morality to both sexes. But he also gave to the sciences a priority which did not appear in the other papers. Of working class origins, he was sent to study in Europe at government expense and did not share the disdain for scientific or vocational education which was held by many of the nobility. He and Müller thought that institutions of instruction should be divided into three types, military, civil, and commercial, Dilthey's plan of 1764 included a detailed system of schooling which embodied the principles asked for by Catherine. In contrast to almost all other submissions, his "Plan for the Establishment of Schools for the Spread of Knowledge and the Correcting of Morals" was the only one which went beyond theory to touch upon the real problem of Russia's educational system. It was Dilthey who warned that in order to have an educated citizenry, Imperial Russia must first find qualified Russian teachers. Furthermore, he saw the destructive potential of the rapidly increasing reliance upon untrained foreign tutors, and even hinted that the institution of serfdom itself was a debilitating factor in the evolution of enlightenment in Russia.[42]

Disagreeing with Betskoi's opinion that boarding schools would solve the problem of poor early instruction at home, Dilthey suggested that institutions be established in which domestic servants would be trained to better educate the youngsters who were often in their charge since infancy. The young Russian nobleman, Dilthey began, had his earliest learning experiences at the hands of illiterate serf guardians (diad'ki), then he was turned over to badly trained tutors. Schools outside their homes were managed by poorly-qualified administrators, who were given useless directives from the Chancellory. So the first eleven paragraphs of Dilthey's "Plan" outlined a system which would enable serfs to be educated as teachers. Two pedagogical seminaries were to be founded, one in Moscow and the other in St. Petersburg, in which two teachers and one rector would instruct one hundred serf boys in Latin, French, German, Russian, arithmetic, history, and geography. They would also learn how to speak properly about God, the fatherland, and morality.

Dilthey went on to delineate a middle and upper education, and the establishment of two new universities, one for Dorpat, the other for the Ukraine, at Batorin. Like Klingstedt, he saw merit in the European *Trivial* school organization, and he suggested that for Russia they be divided according to rank, that is, schools for nobles, for merchants, "and for other classes." Except for the pedagogical seminaries, he did not include serfs in his public schools. Even in the gymnasiums, which Dilthey included as the upper part of his programme, the nobility were to be kept apart from pupils of other classes. His conclusion called for the establishment of twenty-one *Trivial* schools and nine gymnasiums, the latter institutions designed specifically to prepare students for university. The main thrust of Dilthey's scheme fit into Catherine's thinking about education, although the recommendations about educating serfs had ominous implications for the nobility. He acknowledged the primacy of moral lessons, which he felt could be passed on to the pupils by means of courses in ancient history taught in the Russian language.[43]

Moral education remained the dominant theme of each of the various reports commissioned by Catherine, and on which she based her decisions about school reform. It was mirrored in Betskoi's "General Institutes," which set all the changes in motion. More than any other document of eighteenth-century Russia, that decree embodied the Enlightenment ideal of education as something distinct from instruction and training for service. In Russia, however, the word "Enlightenment" was always qualified by the pragmatic assumption that it included only "right thinking," and that was typified by a notation, perhaps made by Teplov, on a scheme of 1764 for a state gymnasium: "Of what value is it to the citizenry when a man has an intellect strengthened by science and talent but, wasted from his youth by many harmful examples to his heart, is made into a pernicious official or [unworthy] citizen of his fatherland?"[44] An unsigned French-language document in the same collection cautioned the empress against giving too much attention to the arts and sciences, lest "on néglige par là de former le bon et le vrai *Citoyen*."[45]

Catherine also had direct advice from foreign sources. Daniel

Dumaresq, who came to Russia on her invitation in 1764, was an eminent English educator who contributed suggestions about school reform and brought to her the ideas of another Englishman, Dr. John Brown. One of England's main opponents of Rousseau's ideas on education, Brown imagined children to be naturally sinful and easily swayed towards vices. In his *Sermons on Various Subjects* (London, 1764), Brown advocated extensive training in virtuous habits with the specific goal of making children into good citizens. In sharp contrast to Rousseau, Brown said that youth might have to be taught "salutary prejudices such as may create a conformity of thought and action with the established principles on which his native society is built." In a short statement carried by Dumaresq to Catherine, Brown insisted that the cornerstone of Russia's educational organization should be autocracy and orthodoxy, a view well in line with Catherine's own expectations. The fact that he also called for an extensive education for young women, because it was upon females that youngsters of both sexes depended in their early years, was equally in keeping with her thinking about school reform. Brown criticized European school systems for having no *raison d'être,* and he said that the Russian Empire had a golden opportunity to create the ideal educative institutions, in which nothing would be taught that did not have a "real benefit for the entire empire."[46]

Thus, Catherine and Betskoi had the antidotes for those of Rousseau's ideas which met with their disapproval, specifically the belief that children should be left to their own devices to learn from experience. Their answer was to allow the environment to work its wonders on Russia's youth, but at the same time made sure that they monitored that environment. *not a good summary of their position*

Other European discussions over education intruded upon the complicated planning going on in St. Petersburg. It was also in the early sixties that attempts were being made in France to organize a public schooling system to fill the vacuum left when the Society of Jesus (Jesuits) was ordered out of the country. The first official act against them and their monopoly on schooling came in 1762, and the final royal order commanding them to leave France was issued two years later. One of the men responsible for this action was Louis-René de Caradeuc de la Chalotais (1701–1785), who put before the parlement at Rennes an *Essai de l'éducation nationale, ou plan d'études pour la jeunesse,* in February 1763.[47] The essence of his proposition was that educational activities should be a state prerogative and must be taken out of the hands of the church and private individuals. The year before La Chalotais's essay appeared, an anonymous pamphlet, which H. C. Barnard attributes to Diderot, *De l'éducation publique,* was printed in Amsterdam. La Chalotais spoke highly of it, though he was by no means a *philosophe,* for its author insisted that education should be secular and that its purpose was to create useful, loyal, and skilled citizens. He took exception to the pamphleteer's opinion about the crucial matter of who warranted an education. Diderot, if he was in fact the author or collaborator of *De l'éducation publique,* advised that education should be extended to everyone; La Chalotais hoped that it be limited to the upper classes, to prevent too much wasteful mobility within the various ranks of society. Interestingly, he was congratulated by Voltaire for his suggestion that it was unnecessary to educate the poor. Neither man wanted the lower classes to be discontented with their lot in life.

La Chalotais also recommended that ethical "Truths" be taught in schools in the place of religion, and that the "Truths" be used to assure the training of good citizens. He went so far as to urge that nationalist indoctrination replace religious instruction. Diderot, who certainly agreed elsewhere with La Chalotais's plea for state control of education, lay teachers, more science, and a practical syllabus, expressed his feelings directly to Catherine in the 1770s. La Chalotais's opinions about education also gained a wider Russian audience after 1770 when his main pedagogical treatise was translated and published in St. Petersburg. The axioms carried in the book corroborated the viewpoint already held by most Russian educators and were best exemplified by his comment, "if man is not taught to be good, then he will inevitably undertake evil. The mind and the heart cannot take a holiday."[48] Both Diderot and La Chalotais insisted that women be allowed to benefit from education. La Chalotais cited Fénelon in his plan for state-directed girls' schools, and Diderot said that they should be taught exactly those things which were taught to boys. Thus, Catherine had this set of ideas to dwell upon as she studied Dilthey's proposals and those from others.

During the discussion which took place after 1767 at meetings of the Legislative Commission and in reports presented to it, the strongest arguments for improved educational facilities usually were based on two assumptions. In the first place, many assumed that education would improve the level of competence in the service ranks, and secondly, that enlightenment might temper the bestiality of the peasantry and make them less likely to rise up against the nobility. Both arguments had a practical, state-oriented end.[49] It was in Catherine's

His own evidence disputes this!

time that the idea gradually developed that there was more to education than simply training professionals for state service.[50] Krestinin's proposals are evidence enough for that. Although the realities of Catherine's schools did not mirror her idealistic stance on the importance of learning, there were certain essential characteristics of her programme which revealed a great deal of progress since Peter's era. Peter had introduced the idea of state schools, and that was one of his most lasting contributions to the civilizing process in Russia. But his schools had been a means to a very practical end which had little to do with learning. Pre-petrine institutions produced clergymen and Peter's turned out officers and bureaucrats, but Catherine hoped to mold her subjects in a much broader manner. She felt that general education (*obshcheobrazovatel'nyi*) would serve her needs much better and the "General Institutes" of 1764 carried a direct criticism of Peter's narrowly technical programme. Her educational presumptions included the belief that the greater the number of people who were educated, no matter their class, the better it would be for her empire. In this, at least, she shared an opinion with the Freemasons and with Grimm, with whom she kept up a constant correspondence. Yet her concern was also practical, for she knew very well that it would take more than a system of education to bring modern civilization into Russia and her scepticism was revealed in one letter to Grimm in which she asked why there were always "scoundrels" among educated people.[51]

Catherine struggled with the problem of a public education scheme for a long time before an actual school system was promulgated. Specific institutions were opened in the 1760s in a somewhat disorganized manner. As early as October, 1762, new engineering and artillery training centres were decreed, and one for young artists and architects was affixed to the Russian Academy of Fine Arts, which was founded in 1757 but only began to function seriously in 1763. The curriculum for the latter school was a complete one, including history, geography, and languages, and pupils began their study there at the youthful ages of five or six. Inspectors were appointed by Betskoi from among established artists, who sent regular reports on student progress to him. Catherine even issued orders for the establishment of facilities to provide instruction in Russian grammar and Orthodoxy to newly converted children in the Kamchatka area.[52]

While in the process of re-organizing the Slobodska-Ukraina in 1765, the empress called for an expansion of the syllabus at the collegium in Kharkov. In a decree of July 1765, she said that, "to the present sciences taught at Kharkov Collegium, add the French and

German languages, mathematics, geometry and drawing, and especially engineering, artillery and geodosy." A sum of 3,000 roubles was provided for this effort.[53] One result of this effort to bring a broader and secular education to the Ukraine was a personnel crisis at the collegium, which will be discussed in a later chapter.[54] All in all, the only original scheme with some lasting significance to emerge from the early years of Catherine's reign was the founding of the Educational Society for Noble Girls at the Voskresensky Monastery in 1764, and a complementary institution for daughters of the bourgeoisie in the next year. That institution and other projects for educating young women are also the subject of a separate, later chapter.

While the education of girls was being overseen by Betskoi and sponsored by Catherine, the remnants of her educational inheritance were slowly given some order. The Land Cadet Corps college, of which Catherine made herself Commander-in-chief in 1765, was reinvigorated in 1766 by Betskoi. He brought to it his principle of isolating children from the corrupting influences of family and existing society so that their education could be controlled enough to produce a new moral type of dedicated officer and bureaucrat. This he intended to accomplish by lowering the entrance age drastically, from thirteen to five. Betskoi also increased enrollment to 800. Rigorous social and physical standards were set for the young men. Corporal punishments were still not allowed, but the spartan existence forced upon the boys made the learning process a difficult one. They were instructed in grammar, religion, language, natural philosophy, world history and geography, and some mathematics. Certain social graces, like dancing and drawing, and the martial arts of riding, fencing, and vaulting were also part of their course of study. The physical education dimension of the school so impressed Diderot, who visited it with Catherine in 1773, that he cited it in his refutation of Helvétius several years later.[55]

Betskoi's plans for the Cadet Corps college were contained in a *Discourse* which he printed in September 1766. Opening it with the remark that "an army without discipline is like a body without a soul, and in order that that particularly vital power will always act in war it is necessary to institute schools to teach obedience, . . . *whoever commands obedience, then has command*," he went on to say that the Cadet school must act differently than any other educational facility in the empire. "The pupils must know exactly in what way their learning can be applied to military affairs and to their civil duties," he wrote. The young cadets must learn foreign languages, the technique of making reports, the laws of the fatherland, the history and deeds of great generals. In short, their education must be practical.

Cadets must learn how to observe, to listen, and to make immediate use of what they see and hear. They should lose privileges, or be fed on bread and water, if they failed to follow the regulations of the school. Betskoi also said that their subjects should be taught in Russian, particularly the sciences, history, and geography, but this was one area where he had to act contrary to his convictions. French remained the language of instruction because there were not enough Russian-language teachers available with the necessary qualifications. He quoted from Montaigne to support his opinion that schools could serve their purpose without too much emphasis on theoretical data, and from Montesquieu on the value of law. For civil law, he recommended that pupils read Pufendorf.[56] The exclusiveness of the school and the natural comraderie which evolved among its students tended to insulate its graduates from their own family setting and from less wealthy nobles whose fathers could not afford such schooling for them.

It was in the *Discourse* and in the law which instituted the changes in the Cadet school that Betskoi outlined his version of the ideal teacher. Since he believed, in the tradition of Montaigne, Comenius, and Locke, that learning was the least important component of education, and that character-building was the the most important, he saw that teachers were by far the most vital cog in the educational machinery. "If the teacher will act with good judgement, and instruct their charges with love and kindness," then the pupil will develop his natural talents far better than if his instructor tries to browbeat him into memorizing information. The ruin of real education, Betskoi continued, is pedantry: "If one must select from the lesser of two evils, then it is better to take the teacher who has some deficiencies in learning than a pedant, who is so unbearable by his haughty conduct as to warrant only laughter."[57] Acting upon his own advice, Betskoi placed the teaching responsibilities of his youngest cadets in the hands of a woman, Sofia de la Font, Headmistress of the school for girls.

A companion institution, the Imperial Corps of Pages, which was begun by Elizabeth in 1759, was also designed for especially selected sons of the nobility. Aside from acting as errand boys for the court chamberlains, these youngsters were supposed to be given a full academic course of study and, at the same time, learn the nuances of court procedure. However, when they were joined by Alexander Radishchev in 1763, the entire programme was run by one ill-suited Frenchman, Morambert, and very little general learning was achieved.[58]

Access to quality education remained a very difficult matter for many of Russia's gentry who wished to provide their offspring with skills to further their position in the imperial service. This was particularly true of those who lived outside the main centres of the empire's cultural life. An example can be seen in letters of instruction prepared in 1772-1773 by a landed gentleman from Smolensk, M. G. Lebedev, who decided to send his son to a Jesuit school in Polotsk. A practical man, Lebedev asked that his son be instructed first in the German and French languages, and then turn to sciences and mathematics.

He was not in the least interested in the arts, history, geography, or other courses which the school was able to provide, and he insisted that his son be rigidly disciplined. Lebedev had the right and the means to hire a private tutor, and there were schools of sorts in Smolensk. Moreover, he was of the Orthodox faith, but he knew that only in Jesuit hands would his son receive an education from which the boy might gain some practical advantage.[59] Lebedev's action was not unusual, and it illustrates as well the lengths to which Catherine was willing to go in order to gain an educated population. In 1769 she had allowed the Jesuits to return to Russia and organize schools for Catholic youngsters. Thus, even before the first partitioning of Poland (1772), when a large Polish district with its own educational system was absorbed by the Russian Empire, there was relative tolerance and provision for sectarian instruction.

Other reports which had come to the Legislative Commission reflected the imbalance in availability of educational facilities. A submission from Chernigov complained in 1768 that there were far too few institutions of learning there for even sons of the nobility and none whatsoever for girls. And in 1773, a report from the Governor of Astrakhan to Count Nikita Beketev said that, although there were five hundred pupils in his district ready for school, all sons of soldiers and merchants, or orphans, there were too few teachers, books, or instruments. He requested above all instructors who could speak the native Central Asian languages.[60]

The empress was perfectly aware of the demographic obstacles which lay in the way of her school projects. She could not have expected the gentry to greet her schools for girls with much enthusiasm, for they had no desire to send their young daughters off to expensive boarding schools to learn things which most thought were unnecessary. Catherine was also conscious of the fact that there were not enough teachers to fill all the positions needed to bring a semblance of education to areas outside the Moscow and St. Petersburg districts. Betskoi's correspondence with P. S. Saltykov, governor of Moscow, indicates that officials were sometimes unwilling to co-operate or too caught up in red tape to put his policies into practice.[61] In 1776, when Catherine asked Grimm to return to Russia, she revealed a pessimism about the dearth of learned and experienced people in her empire who could make the system work. "If you would agree to remain with us, then you and I together might be able to accomplish something of great benefit to the state."[62]

A vain attempt to lure Jean Le Rond d'Alembert (1717–1783) to Russia in 1762 to be her son's tutor prompted a letter from her in which she accused d'Alembert of refusing to serve mankind which he professed to love. "I owe to you," she continued, "that I have the education of my . . . son so much at heart, and I think you so necessary to it, that perhaps I press you with too much earnestness."[63] Some Russians were not happy with their sovereign's attempts to bring in foreigners, no matter their reputation, to educate future Russian emperors, and Fonvizin accused both d'Alembert and Diderot of being charlatans pedalling enlightenment for financial return. But two of Europe's leading *philosophes* were persuaded to come to St. Petersburg, for Grimm and Diderot journeyed there together in 1773. They spent hours in conversation with Catherine on the merits of her educational projects, and Grimm prepared a detailed written prospectus for it. During his second visit to Russia in 1777, Catherine urged Grimm to take on the post of minister of education, but he excused himself on the grounds that he could not speak Russian. In turn, he recommended to her Baron Karl von Dalberg of Würzburg, who had set up reforms for the University of Erfurt. Catherine ignored the suggestion.[64]

Of all the foreigners who either came themselves or sent proposals to Catherine on educational matters, it was Diderot with whom Catherine met most often, usually three times a week, and with whom she had open discussion on practically any subject which came to mind. Education seemed to be the most consistently recurring topic on their agenda. In his first two weeks in St. Petersburg, Diderot accompanied the empress to the Smolny Monastery and to the Academy of Sciences. His overall admiration for Catherine's efforts on behalf of education was one of the sentiments he retained even though they eventually became quite disenchanted with each other. A letter which he sent to his daughter from The Hague in April 1774 explains that his return to Paris was to be delayed somewhat because Catherine had entrusted him with a variety of educational tracts which he planned to translate and publish there. They were plans for her education reforms which she hoped to publicize in Europe. Thus, Diderot was knowledgeable about Betskoi's projects and approved of them. To Catherine he exclaimed in another letter that her work to create honest citizens and defenders of their fatherland would surpass that of the Egyptians and the Greeks.[65] Even allowing for considerable poetic licence and practical flattery, Diderot's praise for Catherine's plans was probably sincere. For her part, Catherine undoubtedly was more amused, and eventually irritated by Diderot than her own letters would suggest. But his mind was at her disposal, and he served as another valuable publicity agent in Europe. His custom while in St. Petersburg was to write out for her his opinions on matters which they discussed. These memoranda have been published in a single volume by Paul Vernière, and it is from that collection that the subsequent information is taken.

Aside from Catherine, Diderot's closest associate in Russia was Betskoi, who co-ordinated the arts and letters side of Catherine's court. In his circle could be found many of the cosmopolitan figures of St. Petersburg, among them Doctor Clerc, Catherine's translator and a professor at the Academy of Fine Arts; Anastasia Ribas, Betskoi's daughter, and Mme. de la Font of the Smolny school; her daughter Sofia; and others. Diderot was especially delighted with the Smolny organization and saw in it the ideal means for the training of "mothers, wives, and honest and useful citizens."[66]

On public schools, Diderot called for a far-reaching programme with a school in every large village, compulsory attendance, and free tuition for those who could not afford to pay. His assumption that parents must give up their traditional authority to the school administrators was well in keeping with Betskoi's thinking. At the public school level, Diderot saw no need for frills, writing that "pure and simple instruction in science and morality" would suffice. The main fault of the new education projects, Diderot told Catherine in one of his notes, was that they catered to too few people. There must be some way left open so that capable students of any class could obtain early training and be allowed to rise to the top on the basis of merit. Diderot went so far as to suggest that the office of Chancellor should be open to competitive challenge, but added hastily that this was not an attempt at democracy because the empress would still retain the final decision on appointments.

Even at the Corps of Cadets, an institution which he admired only slightly less than the school for girls, Diderot found a debilitating lethargy among students because their programme lacked competitiveness. He did not object to the fact that instruction was given in

French, a subject of considerable rancour in some quarters. Instead, he recognized that the cadets were not learning French well enough to follow the extensive course of study that was laid out for them. In a Rousseau-like tone, he said that the children should be given more freedom during their first few years at the school. Having to stay in the same institution for fifteen years, always observed by the same masters, contributed to the apathy and indifference which he observed among the students. He claimed to have told Betskoi that "the vice is the lack of emulation." There was no variety in their lives, not enough incentive to achieve excellence, and insufficient reward for special accomplishments.

A final memorandum revealed plans for a full publication in Russia of the *Encyclopédie,* which would be sold around the world by subscription. This note was really directed to Betskoi and promised full cooperation and "glory to all concerned." However, even though Diderot told his wife as late as June, 1774, that "everything is arranged between the minister [Betskoi] and me . . . ," nothing much came of the project.

The submission from Diderot with which Catherine was most concerned was his "Plan of a University for the Russian Government," which did not reach her until 1775, after its author had returned home. "To educate a nation is to civilize it," he wrote, ". . . [education] mollifies dispositions, makes duties clear . . . inspires love of order, of justice and of the virtues. . . ." The object of education, Diderot continued, is to provide "for the sovereign, zealous and faithful servants; for the empire, useful citizens." Such notions, which were commonplace in the eighteenth century, were reflected quite clearly in Catherine's own public schooling statute which was finally made law in Russia in 1786.[67] But she did not build a university.

There were some practical results of the new regime's interest in education by the early 1770s, and there were developments which foreshadowed the subsequent attention given to teaching methodology. An important event in the history of Russian pedagogy was the preparation of a short book, *Teaching Methods (Sposob ucheniia)* in 1771 by Barsov and Kh. A. Chebotarev. Commissioned by Melissino at the Conference of the University of Moscow, it was the first handbook for teachers to be used at the university, the gymnasiums and the privately-run *pensions.* The initial issue was printed in Russian, Latin, German, and French; an edition of 1790 appeared only in Russian and Latin. Although later texts receive more attention and the handbook for instructors published by Catherine's commission on public schools in 1782 is often treated as the first text for teachers in eighteenth-century Russia, the 1771 book contained all the main requirements for teachers which later ones maintained.

In fact, preliminary work on teaching methodology had begun at the university during its first years of existence. Popovsky and Schaden, who came to the institution in 1756 to be rector of its gymnasium, were put in charge that year of gathering together the various principles of education as they were discussed at the Conference.[68] They appeared eventually as *Teaching Methods*. Much of the collection was based on the ideas of Comenius and accentuated once again the great responsibilities which teachers had, for they were the models after whom students would fashion themselves. "Without an education themselves, no one can teach others, and a teacher who does not demonstrate integrity, virtue, immaculate morals and wisdom can do more harm than good to those whom he teaches," *Teaching Methods* began, and went on to say that teachers must answer clearly and reasonably all queries put to them by pupils.[69]

Russia's first pedagogical seminary was established at the University of Moscow in November, 1779. Called the Baccalaureate Institute, it had a three year programme designed to train teachers for the university, its gymnasiums in Moscow and Kazan, and the *pensions*. It was financed by the university and through private endowment. Barsov, Chebotarev and D. S. Anichkov were regular lecturers to the future teachers, and works by John Locke, Comenius, and the abridged version of Rousseau's *Émile* were printed in Russian specifically for use in the school. By 1782 it had thirty students.

Already well-known for his Russian grammar, which was printed in 1771, Barsov began in the late seventies to campaign for the preparation of a national history. He and Chebotarev compiled archival material which was used by Catherine as the basis for her own textbook history of Russia, serialized publicly first in 1783.[70] They also helped Melissino form the Free Russian Assembly (*Volnoe Rossiiskoe sobranie*) at the university in 1771, which aimed to improve Russian language and literature, to popularize history, and to translate works "for the edification of youth." N. I. Novikov was one of their colleagues in this venture, as was M. M. Kheraskov, Fonvizin (later) and a number of other Russian patriots. In 1779 Chebotarev delivered an interesting speech at the university in which he equated the love of learning with patriotism. He said that good teachers and competent instruction are essential for the very survival of a people and, like Barsov, he implicitly criticized the French-language orientation of

Betskoi's schools. He then went on to advocate the building of libraries, the creation of textbooks, the printing of journals, and the establishment of any other forum for the dissemination of knowledge.[71] Chebotarev and Barsov were among those who were at the same time patriots and believers in knowledge for its own sake. By the 1780s, there were very few Russians with any intellectual background who did not advocate the re-organization of the national educational system. And the provincial gentry clamoured for the expansion of tuitional facilities, if only for the opportunity to provide means for their children to find worthwhile places in the bureaucracy. There was, in fact, very little divergence in opinion over the necessity of education even among those whose political viewpoints varied considerably. It remained only for the state to decide upon the nature of the pedagogical instruction which it planned to issue.

In spite of her constant if eclectic efforts on behalf of education during the 1760s and 1770s, which were quite remarkable in the light of the serious nature of Russia's domestic and foreign problems during those years, things did not go well for those who had been optimistic about Catherine's educative strategems. The dearth of good teachers was the most formidable obstacle against a workable system and ruined Betskoi's plans to carry out instruction in Russian. Financial stringency was another, although Betskoi was reasonably successful in raising money by private subscription, without which most of his schools would not have survived.

Writing with some trepidation, Betskoi complained to Catherine in 1775 that none of his teachers, in this case in the Foundling Homes, "manifest reliable wisdom, not one of them comprehends the very purpose of the institution, none of them understand its spirit. They only worry about their own personal advantages. . . ."[72] To a certain extent, Betskoi was already worried about his own career, for he prefaced this letter with a series of abject apologies and excuses. The fact that Voltaire wrote in that year that her "schools [will] endure for all time," did not encourage Catherine very much.[73] When she pleaded with Grimm in 1775–1776 to administer her school system, she explained that Russia simply did not have people qualified to make her projects work, and she admitted that, in spite of her autocratic powers and good intentions, she could not do it alone. Grimm was asked to map out for her a comprehensive plan "for young people from ABC to university." Catherine was so anxious that the task be completed that she claimed that if need be she would attempt it again herself by searching through the *Encyclopédie*.[74]

Voltaire had written Catherine with enthusiasm because he had read an outline of her educational ambitions printed in Amsterdam with a preface by Diderot. *Les Plans et les statuts des différents établissements ordonnés par Sa Majesté Impériale Catherine II pour l'éducation de la jeunesse* had publicized in Europe a universal school system which she ordered for the provinces in November, 1775. Part of a complete re-organization of the provincial structure of her empire, the new proposal called for a Major school in each of the fifty provinces, to be supervised by local Boards of Public Assistance. Once again academic accreditation was required of foreign teachers and some efforts were made to centralize the private schools. There was no coercion involved in this public schooling scheme; rather Catherine relied upon the good will of parents to make it work. There were fees included, so access was limited to those who could either afford tuition or find sponsors.[75]

The same old problems prevented this new project from ever really working. Even its simple curriculum of the three "R's" and the catechism failed because of the lack of Russian teachers and the apathy with which it was greeted by provincial noblemen who wanted more elitist institutions. What enthusiasm they might have had for public-style schools had been dampened considerably by the Pugachev rebellion of 1773–1774. Nor were sufficient funds given to the provinces to make the Boards of Public Assistance effective. In fact, the Boards were allotted only 15,000 roubles, which they could invest, to cover the "care and supervision" of public schools, orphanages, hospitals, poorhouses, houses for "indigent incurables," madhouses, and institutions for delinquents. Catherine recognized these problems, but did nothing to alleviate them. Her appeals to Grimm for help ring a little hollow in that light. Nevertheless, she did write Grimm again in 1780 saying that she had examined the national education programme of Austria and saw from it that what Russia needed most of all were normal school teachers who could train instructors.[76]

As we shall see in the next chapter, there were prominent individuals in the Russian Empire who were strong advocates of universal education. However, it seems that no single person had the administrative or pedagogical expertise to direct the nation's energies into a systematic teaching organization. Certainly, there was no one Catherine would allow to do so. Betskoi, in whose honour the Senate stamped out a state medal in 1773, proved to be incapable of the task. It was not until 1782 that a suitable individual could be found to put the educational affairs of Russia in order, and he had to be imported from the Austrian Empire.

V

The Intelligentsia and Schools

Catherine's willingness to allow a broad spectrum of ideas to filter into Russia from Western Europe, her patronage of writers, journals, and literary societies, and her constant activity in the name of education stimulated discussion about enlightenment and its potential for Russia. Since Catherine herself spoke so often about schools, and Betskoi reaped as much publicity as he could out of every grand opening, it was inevitable that the nature and purpose of institutionalized education held a central place in such deliberations. Although there seemed to be a consensus to the effect that Russia desperately needed some kind of systematic instruction in order to modernize, the means to achieve that end varied according to the experiences and political sentiment of their exponent. The very existence of an intellectual maelstrom which included pietism, agnostic *philosophes,* and Freemasons, the outbreak of political and ideological revolutions in America and then in France, and the peasant holocaust of the 1770s in Russia, meant that persons who thought at all took their presumptions very seriously. Thus, even when their weighty words about education sound like mere clichés to our ears, they were expressed as strongly-held convictions.

The purpose of this chapter, then, is to try and sort out some of the advocates of education during Catherine's reign. Interestingly, conclusions reached by very different people tended to coincide even when their premises conflicted. Although there were still a few critics of formal, centralized educative programmes, none of them could sway policy made at court. Indeed, Catherine's basic principles met with the approval of almost everyone in the literate sectors of Russian society. It was the rigidity of Betskoi's boarding school philosophy and the predominance of bogus foreign tutors, in a sense the two extremes of Russian education, which received the most criticism.

Of all the European teachers who came to instruct at the University of Moscow during its early years, the one who accomplished the most specifically for schools in Russia was Schaden. Teacher of rhetoric, Latin, and philosophy at the university, he also served as rector and teacher of rhetoric at both university gymnasiums from 1756. He was especially interested in pedagogy. In 1768, Schaden wrote an introduction to a new translation of Comenius's *Orbis Pictus* (1635), an abridgement of the *Janua Linguarum Reserata* (1631) which had outlined a method of teaching languages through the vernacular and by means of illustrations and object lessons. Comenius had stressed the use of everyday experience as an educative tool and so the Russian translation was timely in that it corroborated notions expressed in Rousseau's *Émile*. Schaden insisted that education be utilized to turn youth into better adults and advocated Comenius's methods because he saw in education the way to a prosperous and stable society. He cited Rousseau to that effect as well, but he cautioned that the idyllic form of education granted to Émile and copied so enthusiastically throughout Europe would not be suitable for Russia. Schaden chastised Rousseau for isolating Émile from society and accentuated the obligation which parents had to instruct their children carefully in their early years.

Schaden also published a rhetoric textbook in 1769 and, as we have seen, helped to compile the *Teaching Methods* of 1771. In that same year he printed an essay on rules for education and the best means for employing art in the classrooms. A speech delivered at the university in 1773 reiterated his faith in visual aids as teaching devises and at the same time carried an explicit disagreement with Betskoi's insistence that children should be taken away from their homes at an early age in order to be instructed properly.[1] In effect, Schaden was following the emphasis laid upon parental responsibility by the author of that essay, "Rules for Educating Children" which had been featured in *Monthly Essays* in 1755.

Similar attitudes about pedagogy and the role of the family in education were shared by several Russians who were enrolled in the initial class at the University of Moscow. One of these was Denis Fonvizin (1743–1793), who attended Schaden's *pension* when he was still a boy and years later served as secretary to Nikita Panin. He was imbued with German rationalism while at the university, and his work bears witness to a propensity of the intelligentsia for an education system built on simple virtues, character-building, and patriotism. He was also an astute political essayist who urged that Imperial Russia adopt a series of immutable laws so as to safeguard both autocracy and enlightenment. Virtuous atttitudes on the part of the people and powerful moral leadership on the part of the monarchy were his answers to the nation's difficulties. Above all, he warned that rule by favourites, corruption, and excessive luxury were destroying the state.

In his *The Minor,* Fonvizin lampooned the type of education received by sons and daughters of provincial nobility at the hands of foreign tutors. One of his characters, Starodum (Mr. Conservative), saw no need for formal education at all, but at least he had been trained at home by his father (as Fonvizin himself had once been) in simple Russian morality, something that he could not have gained from the best of foreign tutors or from Betskoi's hygenic boarding schools. Fonvizin's real complaint was directed at the superficiality of foreign-derived education as it was practiced in Russia and at the crude ignorance on the part of so many of the tutors as he portrayed them in the person of Vral'man (Mr. Humbug). Vral'man was catered to by the family of his young charge, who were satisfied with him because "he does not drive our child." Neither of the parents were able to read. They felt it shameful that girls were learning to do so and an expensive nuisance that their son was obligated to gain an education.[2]

In a paper which remained unpublished during his lifetime, Fonvizin went so far as to predict that further debilitation of the office of autocrat would lead to revolution. In 1783, just as Russia's educational facilities were undergoing major re-organization again, he submitted a series of political "Questions" to the journal, *Companion for Lovers of Russian Words* (*Sobesednik liubitelei rossiiskago slova*), of which Catherine was an editor. To the final of twenty-one queries, "In what consists our National character?," the empress, who answered them all herself, replied: "Sharp and quick conception of everything. Exemplary obedience and the root of all virtues given to man by God." By that time Catherine put obedience above all other civic virtues and that preference was to show in her school reform. Fonvizin, however, whose character Dobroliubov had said in *Brigadir* (1769), "it is true that education determines everything," still gave first priority to moral virtue.[3]

By far the best known of Fonvizin's colleagues during his student days at the university was Nicholas Novikov (1744–1818), who also caricatured the kind of education which was available to Russians in the 1760s. In his satirical journals especially, Novikov flailed the pomposity of Russia's noblemen and the favouritism which was featured at court. In one journal, the *Truten* (*The Drone*), an article of 1769 carried bitter complaints about gentry who hired foreign tutors so that young Russians could be instructed, and badly at that, in the ways and languages of Western Europe. He implied that most of the important teachers, especially domestic tutors, were criminal escapees from France or political exiles with no academic training.[4]

It was not until the 1780s that Novikov wrote his main essays on the principles of education. By that time he was a leading Freemason whose word was esteemed among Russia's intelligentsia, and was predominant enough as a publisher that in our century the 1770s have often been referred to as the "Novikov decade." His attitude during that era was Rousseauian in that he spoke against the rigid structuring of learning and asked teachers to concentrate on real knowledge which children could comprehend through their own senses and experiences. He insisted that only through education could youngsters attain "social and civil virtues." Familiar with the works of European educators, Novikov also praised Russia's own Lomonosov and recommended equal access to schooling for women. But his ideas were not quite so original as a recent Soviet study on education claims.[5] It is difficult to calculate Novikov's actual contribution to education in Russia, for Catherine's later programmes did not include his ideals. However, the facts that his publishing houses produced more than a thousand books and that his journals were very popular during the time in which education was so widely discussed, imply that his opinions were an important ingredient of the deliberations.

In 1780, Novikov wrote an essay for the masonic journal, *Morning Light* (*Utrennii svet,* 1777–1780), which he entitled, "Moral Admonition as a practical Precept." Making a strong case in it for writers to act as teachers and "to be useful" along with being entertaining, he went on to say that moral admonition, or ethics, "is the science which directs us . . . [it] is the first, the greatest and for us the most useful study." Ethics must be taught to youth, as much as possible under the aegis of the church.[6] In this latter assumption, Novikov unconsciously followed the lead of Prokopovich, and even of Lomonosov, who also had assumed that the Church was better equipped spiritually than the state for imparting learning to children.

The essay expressed a theme which characterized the journal since its inception. Novikov had used its pages to publicize two charity schools, St. Catherine's (1777) and St. Alexander's (1778), which he helped open, intending them to serve as agencies for educating children of Moscow's poor. In them, reading, writing, and the catechism were offered to day and boarding pupils, with some arithmetic and grammar added later. In general, their purpose was to fulfill the Freemason ambitions for improving society by instilling proper moral notions in the nation's youth. Religious study was the starting point of their syllabus. In a foreword to the first issue of the magazine in 1777, Novikov told readers that all profit engendered by its sale was to go to the charity schools, "a light, agreeable burden which can hurt no one and can do great honour to the country and to humanity."[7]

Morning Light was a perfect example of the growing belief among Russia's intellectuals that classical antiquity might provide solutions to contemporary problems, and it included translations from Plato, Seneca, Cicero, and others. It was founded only a year after Novikov had formed a Masonic lodge of his own in Moscow, having disassociated himself from what he believed to be a less sincere one in St. Petersburg. Members of his lodge were hostile to the immorality and superficiality of court life in the capital and turned to the great classical philosophers in reaction against the hard rationalism and secularism which they saw as subversive forces coming into Russia from Western Europe. Novikov and Kheraskov were the intellectual leaders of the University of Moscow, and they helped Professor J. G. Schwarz (1751–1784), who was brought to Russia as a tutor in 1776 and then took a teaching post in the university gymnasium. Schwarz, who lectured in philosophy and philology, collected financial contributions from wealthier Freemasons for much of their educative and publishing activity. He may well have hoped primarily to use the services of Moscow's Masons to spread the gospel of his own Rosicrucian Order, but the outward consequences were the same as if he had been promoting learning for its own sake. Schwarz gave public lectures at the university, organized seminars to train teachers, gathered around him a circle of devoted students, and was associated with Novikov's vast publishing enterprises.[8]

A much more pivotal Novikov essay on education appeared in 1783, when he was beginning to fall out of favour with Catherine. "On the Upbringing and Instruction of Children" was not so idealistic as his earlier writing on education, and its thrust was towards usefulness and good citizenship. "Love of order, moderation, and true love of their country" were among the vital lessons to be conveyed to children, "for everything depends upon each person being educated in the virtues appropriate to his calling and station in life." Apparently no advocate of social mobility here, he presented a picture of proper upbringing with which Catherine could have no quarrel. The best education, he wrote, will inculcate in Russia's youth an "inclination to virtue, a habit of order . . . a patriotic feeling, a noble national pride, . . . contempt for weakness and . . . ostentation, . . . men and women must be educated according to their sex, and each particular class of society must be taught to fulfill its proper function." Novikov's argument for education was typically masonic, for he believed that enlightenment would preserve and not destroy the existing political structure. In a fully educated society, he said, "the laws will be universally obeyed . . . and citizens of every class will be true to their stations in life."[9]

Like Locke, Rousseau, and so many of their contemporaries, Novikov assumed that a child's mind was a *tabula rasa* which only needed to be shaped meticulously from youth. The essay mirrored Rousseau's feeling, so famously expressed in *Émile,* that the student's "heart" should be trained before he received intellectual instruction. Novikov also insisted in his essay that some forms of rational control should be maintained over the diffusion of "useful knowledge and the general welfare," a phrase which formed part of the subtitle of the piece.

Repeating in more detail the message of his 1780 essay, Novikov wrote that the ultimate aim of pedagogy, which he deemed a "special and subtle science," is to "educate the children to be happy people and useful citizens." The degree of knowledge which a child should be granted depended upon the social class to which he or she belonged, "for the benefit of the state and his own contentment." The message of the essay, then, was very clear. The lower sectors of society should not be taught too much, lest they become dissatisfied with their lot in life. A less obvious feature of the essay was the surprising absence of references to the needs of the Russian Empire for technology or experts of various kinds. To be sure, professional qualifications may have been an implied concern in Novikov's writing on the purpose of education. Nevertheless, he and others of the Russian intelligentsia concentrated on ethics, civil obligations, and patriotism. This emphasis marked quite a change from the utilitarian demands put upon education in the petrine era.

Novikov did not limit his efforts to preaching about proper instruction for children. In 1772 he published the first extensive dictionary of Russian writers, and between 1773 and 1775 he printed a multi-volume collection of historical documents, *Drevniaia Rossiiskaia Bibliofika* (*Ancient Russian Bibliophilia*). In an introduction to the latter collection, which had a second printing in the eighties, he wrote that the great merit in seeing the deeds of one's ancestors lay in the fact that "their morals and customs will help readers to improve the present."[10] In 1785, Novikov founded the first Russian language journal specifically for children. In an introduction to the *Children's Learning, for the Heart and Mind* (*Detskoe chtenie dlia serdtsa i razuma,* 1785–1789), he bemoaned the fact that Russian children seldom, if ever, read things in Russian. They did not know their own language as well as they knew German or French. But the essence of the journal was the moral and civil advice which it offered to readers.

"In the first place," Novikov wrote, "there will be moralizing pieces [in the journal], that is, those in which you can learn your duty to God,

. . . and to the Ruler." Only in this way can Russia's youth become "good citizens of their Fatherland." Physics, natural history and geography were also to be included, and historical tales were to be the carriers of much useful information.[11] Nicholas Karamzin, also a former student of Schaden's *pension* and one of Russia's most prominent defenders of enlightenment during the last years of Catherine's reign, followed Novikov's reasoning to the letter when he helped A. A. Petrov edit the journal for him in 1787–1789.[12]

The opinions expressed in *Children's Learning* and in Novikov's earlier satirical writing reflected a general anxiety among Russia's thinking population. The predominance of foreign instructors prompted a quite legitimate fear that young Russians were growing up alienated from their own land and people, a trend for which Betskoi was often if unfairly blamed. An interesting example of this concern appeared in the form of a booklet, *Testament, or Lessons for Children of Both Sexes,* printed by S. V. Drukovtsov in St. Petersburg, 1780. In a Novikov-like manner, the *Testament* denigrated the harsh aspects of serfdom, if not the institution itself, and criticized the tendency of Russia's *dvorianstvo* to copy all things French. Drukovtsov urged children to learn Russian first, to be kind to their servants, to avoid all forms of gossip, and to be careful about extravagant spending. The little book, which praised simple values and patriotism, represented well the groundswell of support for moral regeneration which grew in pre-French Revolution St. Petersburg and Moscow.[13] Its author, along with Novikov and Fonvizin, also represented the kind of unstructured resistance which prevented Betskoi's allegedly Western leaning boarding schools from gaining across-the-board support among Russia's intelligentsia.

While Novikov and Fonvizin wrote extensively on education as one means for correcting some of the fundamental weaknesses of their society, the professionals in education worked much more directly on improving the level of learning standards in Russia. There were a great many active teachers, translators, and textbook writers who constantly added to the work initiated by Lomonosov, but the efforts of N. G. Kurganov (1726–1796), F. V. Krechetov (1747–n.d.), and A. A. Prokopovich-Antonsky (1763–1848) represent a good cross-section of enthusiastic practitioners of the discipline of education.

Kurganov, an already established pedagogue when Catherine came to the throne, remained active throughout her reign. A student of Magnitsky's in the 1730s, he went on to study at the Naval Academy where he eventually became a professor of mathematics and astronomy. He succeeded Poletika as its inspector in 1771. In the Lomonosov tradition, he also mastered languages, literature, history, and geography. In fact, Lomonosov considered Kurganov to be one of the best young Russian scientists.[14] In the 1760s Kurganov produced atlases and textbooks, one of which, a Russian grammar, remained in general use until the 1830s. The grammar was expanded in the 1770s to a broader study of the Russian language. Added to it were folk tales, anecdotes, and ancient axioms, which made it one of the first collections of Russian folklore for popular reading. For our purpose, however, its importance lies in the tone set by Kurganov in the foreword, which carried the emphasis upon national consciousness so characteristic of native-born educators. "Writers who have been blessed by God with talent and virtue, must as much as possible practice what is useful; and sacrifice all their efforts to the good of the fatherland...," he intoned.[15] But more in the style of pedagogues from an earlier time than those of the 1770s and 1780s, he saw education as a great social equalizer and constantly crusaded for a serious programme of instruction that might provide the nation with a necessary professional class. Above all, he wanted to eliminate the caste basis for education which he recognized as the main barrier against a system based on merit.

Similar but even more extreme notions were expressed by Krechetov, who in 1784 submitted to Senate a plan for a national school administration which would enable all people in the Russian Empire, male and female, to become literate. The next year, he organized a "Society of Good Deeds" of some fifty persons mainly from the middle echelons of society for the purpose of advocating education for the broad mass of the Russian people. He and his colleagues were more radical in their outlook than most of the intelligentsia because they hoped that education would provide a vehicle through which Betskoi's somewhat abstract "third class of people" could achieve equality with the noble and clerical estates. General knowledge, free typographies, and the wide dissemination of books were among the proposals which they had in common with other intellectuals. But Krechetov's activities, which included the editing of a popular knowledge magazine and his advocacy of representative political bodies, earned him a prison sentence in 1793, just one year after Novikov fell victim to the same fate.[16]

An equally active but more typically conservative proponent of expanded educational services for Russia was Prokopovich-Antonsky, a teacher of natural science in an elitist *pension* founded by Kheraskov at the University of Moscow and graduate of the Moscow Baccalaureate Institute. He was also a regular contributor to Novikov's *Children's Learning*. Prokopovich-Antonsky was well established in the pedagogical circles approved of by Catherine and posed no threat to the status quo in the way she assumed that Novikov and Krechetov did. Yet his basic views on education, which were contained in two valuable essays, "A Word About the Beginnings and Success of Science" (1791), and "About Education" (1798), were not much different from theirs. Prokopovich-Antonsky's tone in the latter piece mirrored Betskoi's assumptions of the 1760s, long after Catherine had become wary of flowery idealism. He spoke in them of education as the means to regenerate the human spirit in Russia, to create a new class of people. In both papers he singled out moral training and character-building as prerequisite to intellectual instruction. But the theme which prevailed in them was that all schools must pay more attention to things Russian. He insisted that the Russian language be given precedence over those of other countries. By this time, he was General-Inspector of Kheraskov's *pension* and an outspoken critic of events in France. His hostility to things French was not so much a product of the revolutionary era as a consequence of his familiarity with the ideas of Lomonosov, Barsov, Chebotarev, Sumarokov and Kheraskov.[17] Prokopovich-Antonsky had no intention of excluding things foreign, rather he wished for a better balance in school programmes between Western and Russian knowledge. The entire purpose of education, he wrote in 1798, was to build a community in which each member recognized his or her obligations to the state, family, and society:

> Fortunate is that nation whose ruler learns wisdom and virtue in his early youth, who has been inspired by the rules of truth and the love of man, and whose thoughts, will, and actions are directed towards love for his nation and its welfare. Fortunate is that government where each class of person values the duties of his rank, . . . and carefully avoids everything that might interrupt the calmness of his society, that might destroy its order and structure. Fortunate is that family whose father is educated in the rules of honour and fear of God.

Written when optimism about Paul I as a progressive monarch was fading, this essay represents well the feelings of those who foresaw their hopes for enlightenment being dashed. In the essay, Prokopovich-Antonsky challenged Rousseau's notions about freedom in education and the good qualities of the so-called "natural man," but he was firmly convinced that man must have the freedom to learn and that the state must provide its subjects with the means to become acquainted with all the cross-currents of European Enlightenment. He followed the example of other intellectuals who were appalled by the horrors and irrationalism of the French Revolution and used the rationalism of his century to provide an explanation of the merits of his and other monarchies.

Like Tatishchev and Shcherbatov,[18] Prokopovich-Antonsky worried that the ever increasing demands for luxuries and the prevalence of bad moral habits were undermining Russia's mental and physical health. Firm and good instruction in schools would call a halt to this development, for education was both a physical and moral experience. History proves that those states which fall into intellectual apathy and dissoluteness were always destroyed. Citing Bacon and Rousseau, and drawing analogies to classical times, he said that teachers had the most crucial role in training young Russians to be good citizens.[19] Both sexes and all Russian classes had to be trained properly; they must learn to love their fatherland and to obey the rulers and laws of their society. These were creeds which were built into Catherine's public school curriculum of 1786. Prokopovich-Antonsky concluded his plea on behalf of education by warning his readers that students must also be taught to respect learning for its own sake, but by the 1790s the Russian court preferred loyal to learned subjects if a choice had to be made between them.

Novikov was best known among intellectuals for his vast publishing enterprises, and Fonvizin for his poetry, translations, and drama. Although Fonvizin was a bureaucrat of some importance, neither man contributed anything immediately constructive to Catherine's decision-making about schools. Nor did they participate to the same extent as the professionals did in the actual instruction of youth. But there was one person who was close to Catherine personally, who played a vital role in the administration of her educational apparatus, and who at the same time continued to speak out in support of ideas similar to those of Novikov and Fonvizin. That person was Catherine Dashkova (1743–1810), daughter of Count Roman Vorontsov.

Well-educated and widely-travelled, Dashkova met with and admired several of the most famous *philosophes* in Europe during the 1770s; she was also an unreserved supporter of rational absolute monarchy. Her first published statement on education appeared in the *Companion for Lovers of Russian Words,* which she edited together with the Empress and O. P. Kozodavlev in 1783. "Thoughts on the True Meaning of Education" ("O smysli slova vospitanie") was in the first instance a scathing denunciation of the prevalence of ill-trained French educators in Russia.[20] Novikov and Fonvizin had focused on this problem already, and it was to become a common theme for Russian writers to dwell upon in the 1790s. In 1790 Alexander Radishchev's notorious *Journey from St. Petersburg to Moscow* carried an account of a Frenchman in Gorodnya who could neither read nor write, but was given a good job as a tutor and kept it for a year before being found out. Friends who had advised him to apply for the position in the first place had told him, "you speak French, that is enough."[21] Plays by Ia. B. Kniazhnin, above all *Chudaki (The Eccentrics,* 1790), also caricatured the vulgar emulation by Russian provincial nobility of French customs and language.[22] In neither case was the French Revolution a factor in the author's revulsion for the imitation of French habits. Even foreign observers had long since noted the awkward presence of poorly trained European tutors in Russia. In 1757, a member of a French delegation to Elizabeth's court wrote that he was astonished and chagrined to find that in many noble houses there lived "fugitives, bankrupts, debauchers, and not a few women who, because of the local passion for things French, undertook the education of children." The British ambassador, Lord Cathcart, wrote home in 1768 that Catherine II had instituted boarding schools because of the "strange low French people who have made themselves necessary in all families."[23] Even after the turn of the century the situation was remarked upon by English friends of Dashkova, who spoke of the tutors with whom they had contact as "unprincipled adventurers," and claimed that "every house of consequence has an outcast Frenchman to instruct the heir apparent."[24]

Dashkova's article of 1783 included a series of axioms which together summarize her vision of the purpose of education: that is, teaching should be based on examples rather than solely on the written word; schooling should begin earlier and end later in the life of young Russians than it did then; emphasis should be on the training of "beautiful minds and hearts" rather than on external skills; character and a sense of order should be part of the lessons taught to pupils. Thus, her basic interpretation of the proper educational system was quite typical of the progressive thinkers of her time, but it did not coincide with schools as they were actually structured in Russia.

Although Dashkova had been involved in Catherine's coup of 1762, perhaps in a leading role, her two long trips abroad after 1769 were in part a self-imposed exile from the court where she was no longer on good terms with the empress. She was, after all, the only Vorontsov who had not been a strong supporter of Peter III. Her older sister, Elizabeth, had been Peter's mistress, so it was inevitable that she was disliked in some circles. Nevertheless, on her return from Edinburgh in July 1782, where her son Paul had been the first Russian to graduate from the university there (1779), Dashkova's reconciliation with Catherine was so complete that she was appointed the new director of the Academy of Sciences.

The fortunes of the Academy had reached an especially low ebb under Dashkova's predecessor, Serge Domashnev (1742–1796),[25] who in eight years had brought that institution to near ruin by his inefficiency and probable dishonesty. In November 1782, A. A. Viazemsky and Dashkova's brother, Senator A. R. Vorontsov, joined members of Catherine's newly convened Commission for the Establishment of Public Schools, P. V. Zavadovsky, P. I. Pastukhov, and F.U.T. Aepinus to form a special tribunal to investigate Domashnev's activities. They recommended his dismissal and agreed to Catherine's suggestion that Dashkova replace him.

By dint of thirteen years of hard work, intense interest, and careful expenditure, Dashkova was able to increase enrollment, set up new study programmes, and improve the library. Three public courses, on mathematics, geometry, and natural history were started. Given free of charge and in Russian, they provided access to learning for children of impoverished gentry and for young subalterns from the army. When she took charge of the Academy its teaching section had in it only seventeen pupils and twenty-one artisans, but she raised their numbers to fifty and forty respectively.[26] Yet Dashkova's position at the Academy had some ominous overtones. It had been administered by its own Council from the late 1760s and, even though councilmen were chosen by the empress, it had enabled scholars to play a part in regulating their own affairs. The Council was abolished in 1782 and the Academy became an agency of the government in a more direct sense than it had been previously. Eventually, after the French Revolution caused Catherine to regret some of her earlier advocacy of *philosophe* ideals, the institution lost whatever academic autonomy it had once enjoyed and became a censoring sounding board for the court. Dashkova was gravely disappointed by this development and she retired in 1794.

Dashkova's efforts on behalf of learning earned for her, and so to a certain extent for Russia, an international respect. On the recommendation of Benjamin Franklin, with whom she began to correspond in 1781, she was elected unanimously to the prestigious American Philosophical Society of Philadelphia. She was the first woman to be so honoured. A few months later, Franklin, whose works were the first American ones to be translated into Russian, was in his turn elected by acclamation as a foreign member of the Russian Academy of Sciences.[27]

Dashkova's ascendancy in 1783 had coincided neatly with Betskoi's fall from grace. She had never thought very highly of him herself and described him in her memoirs as a doddering sycophant. That impression of Betskoi was fairly widely held. Diderot, whose relationship with Catherine was orchestrated by Betskoi in the 1770s, spoke of him rather sardonically as "something between a waiting-maid and a prime minister." Even Dashkova's essay of 1783, with its hard words for the predominance of French in Russian schools, was an implicit attack on Betskoi. Catherine had approved that article, and her last demonstration of favour for Betskoi, perhaps a swan song, was in October 1782 when she appointed him a Cavalier of the Order of Holy Apostolic Prince Vladimir, 1st Class. In announcing the Order, which was created in September of that year, Catherine praised Vladimir for bringing enlightenment to Russia; so it was appropriate that Betskoi be the first recipient.[28]

During one of her conversations with Catherine, Dashkova proposed to her that an Imperial Russian Academy be opened, the purpose of which would be to study the Russian language, literature and philosophy. The empress agreed with enthusiasm and the new organization was ordered into existence. It replaced the Free Russian Assembly, and Dashkova was named its first president. The Russian Academy included as members all the leading literati of contemporary Russia. They prepared manuals for versification, grammars, books on rhetoric, and most importantly, the first *Dictionary of the Russian Language* (1789–1794). The Russian Academy was assigned a permanent secretary, Ivan Lepekhin (1740–1802), a soldier's son who had attended the Moscow university gymnasium and later graduated from the university in Strasbourg. Although he was by training a doctor of medicine and a specialist in natural history, Lepekhin's work with the *Dictionary* enabled him to bring naturalist principles to the study of language, which in turn helped consolidate the methodology for teaching Russian in schools. Thus Lepekhin and his colleagues continued the work begun earlier by Lomonosov, Popovsky, Kurganov, and Barsov, which made it possible and normal to express the new learning in Russian.

Claiming to have felt humble and undeserving amongst the scholars whom she addressed at the Academy of Sciences, Dashkova may have been silently delighted by her power over men. The Imperial Russian

Academy also took over the work of Catherine's Society for the Translation of Foreign Books (1768–1783), and in 1784 Dashkova had it publish a translation of one of Henry Kornelius Agrippa's lesser essays which suggested that noble women were superior to men.[29] Catherine apparently was not pleased that this work was printed without her prior knowledge, and its translator hastened to assure her that he had done it only out of curiosity without any idea that it might be printed. Interested in the occult, and the author of *On the Uncertainty and Vanity of the Sciences* (1530), the most sceptical book of the sixteenth century before Montaigne, Agrippa was not considered proper reading in eighteenth-century Russia.

Not to be outdone by Dashkova or Novikov, Catherine prepared thorough instructions, which she described immodestly to Grimm as "beautiful," for the education of the princes Alexander and Constantine and sent them to Prince N. I. Saltykov in March, 1784. Containing ideas which resembled those she had expressed often twenty years earlier, the instructions included entire passges from Montaigne, Comenius, Locke, and Fénelon. Still intrinsic to her pedagogical overview was the value of moral training: "Language and knowledge are the essence of a lesser part of the education of their Majesties. Virtue and morality . . . must be the main part of their training. When virtue and good morals are impressed upon the souls of children, all else will come in time," she wrote in reference to the initial subjects which her grandsons were to master.

As usual, first among the lessons to be learned was the fear of God; then came languages, and an entire series of practical precepts, like military sciences, rules of government, and a complete knowledge of the history, geography, and laws of Russia. But it was more important, Catherine went on, for the princes to gain a love of knowledge than to memorize a wealth of data. Moderation in clothing, food, drink, play, and speech was to be encouraged and their lessons were to be conducted in a rational, kindly way. Citing Locke, she wrote that "children find it difficult to be diligent, but to teach them through fear is unnecessary and harmful, for they cannot learn when their paper is quivering with fear." She also asked that special attention be given to physical exercise, recommended that they use a *Russian Primer* that she herself compiled in 1781, and told Grimm that her lengthy "Notes on Russian History" had been prepared primarily for use by her grandsons.[30] She still at least sounded like Betskoi.

Catherine had read further on the subject of education during the 1770s. Before working out the instructions to Saltykov, she read C. A.

Helvétius's work, *De l'ésprit* (1758), which had shocked the French church by claiming that morality should be treated as a science and taught in schools like any other subject. This pragmatic view of a personal quality that the Christian fathers had always assumed to be innate already had its Russian precedent and was to be integrated into the Catherinian school system. The empress allowed parts of *De l'ésprit* to be translated into Russian by Dashkova.[31] Even more important was the Helvétius assumption that everyone is endowed at birth with the same faculties, and the environment alone is what creates differences in people. Persons who are subjected to exactly the same educational influences will grow up with very similar characteristics. He carried the *tabula rasa* concept further than Locke had done. Ignoring the effect of heredity, Helvétius attributed all the vices of mankind to faulty education.

The essays of Madame Genlis on the moral education of children had also become popular in Russia by the 1770s, and Catherine knew them well. Most of Genlis's works were translated into Russian in the 1780s, and a number of them appeared in Novikov's *Children's Learning* while Petrov and Karamzin were its editors. Between 1775 and 1780, Catherine often turned to a book written by the Marquise d'Epinay in 1774, *Les Conversations d'Emilie*. Typically the author had stressed the development of character in children rather than concentrating on factual data. An associate of Rousseau and Diderot, and for eight years Grimm's mistress she conducted a salon over which Grimm presided. So d'Epinay was very much a part of the circle of *philosophes* with whom Catherine liked to be associated in people's minds. The empress spoke highly of *Les Conversations d'Emilie* in letters to Grimm, who had sent it to her, saying that it was "very useful." She then ordered its translation into Russian. D'Epinay's book had two printings in Russian and in 1786 Catherine still proclaimed it as the best general guideline for the upbringing of children at home.[32] Ironically, that was the very year that her new public school system opened and, as we shall see, its syllabus was in many ways an antithesis to d'Epinay's formulations. It was in 1784, that Catherine contributed financially to Basedow's *Philanthropinum,* and for that Grimm constantly referred to her in his letters as the "Normalschulmeisterin."

Because of the French Revolution public statements and writings in the name of universal education were much more constrained in the 1790s than they had been in the early years of Catherine's reign. Indeed, public statements of many kinds involved considerable per-

sonal risk, as Novikov, Radishchev, and Krechetov found out. But
there were still prominent personages who continued the campaign for
improved education and for an expansion of the new school organization which Catherine opened officially in 1786. Among them were
A. F. Bestuzhev, I. P. Pnin, V. V. Popugaev, and Nicholas Karamzin,
each of whom hoped that more facilities for educating Russians would
prevent rather than cause revolution. They assumed that a child's ideas
could be directed in whatever way educators wished, and so saw in
Russia's youth the potential saviours of the status quo. "General education is the science through which children are taught to be useful and
pleasant within the family and in the fatherland," wrote Bestuzhev
(1761-1810) in 1798. He went on to quote Montesquieu in support of
his contention that children must be trained to fit into existing society
and to the "laws of government." Of all Montesquieu's political orders,
republicanism, despotism, and monarchy, Bestuzhev said, "monarchy
is without doubt the best and the most complete," but only through an
extensive educational system could that fact be brought to the attention of Russia's youth.[33] This does not mean, however, that Bestuzhev,
Karamzin, Popugaev or Pnin were reactionaries. In fact, it was in
Bestuzhev's home that a future Decembrist was raised. A generation
later than Novikov and Fonvizin, Bestuzhev and the others respected
the ideals of the Enlightenment and were trying to put some kind of
rational order into the intellectual chaos which they saw around them.

    Nicholas Karamzin (1766-1826), who was a good friend of Proko-
povich-Antonsky, was one of the most prolific belle-lettrists in Russia
during the nineties. Throughout his work the idea predominated that
villainy and insubordination of the type released by the French
Revolution were best combatted by enlightenment, which, he said, "is
the palladium of good behaviour."[34] He strove to prevent the government from reacting against education, to the extent that he was the
only public defender of Novikov when that man was imprisoned for
alleged subversive activities. Karamzin's ode for Novikov, "To Mercy"
("K milosti"), was an epistle to intellectual freedom in which he even
dared speak of man's civil rights. Karamzin abhorred the very idea of
revolution and said that if men were given the means to pursue normal
and peaceful human desires, they would remain gratefully loyal to the
throne. He prepared an important essay in 1793 entitled, "On the
Sciences, Arts and Enlightenment," in which he wrote that "education
quenches the thirst of rulers and slaves alike," and helps to create
"better men and citizenry." An attack on Rousseau's 1749 defamation
of the sciences and the arts, the essay was intended to counter the

inclination of many Russians to cite Rousseau against enlightenment or to blame the new learning for the French Revolution. Rousseau would have opposed the French Revolution anyway, Karamzin claimed elsewhere.[35]

More famous for his conservative, monarchical viewpoint and vilified by most radicals of the nineteenth century for his support of autocracy and serfdom, Karamzin was nonetheless one of Russia's men-of-letters who spoke out in favour of improved standards of education in the face of rigid government restrictions and stifling bureaucracy. And his ideas in that regard were exactly like those of Novikov, with whom he kept up a sporadic correspondence until 1816 and who is usually lauded as part of the liberal intelligentsia of the period. Some twenty years after Kurganov had done, Karamzin wrote that Russian writers should try only to be useful and not criticize each other. His aim as a reviewer in his own *Moscow Journal* (*Moskovskii zhurnal,* 1791–1792), was to be constructive and to bolster Russian writers so that they might gain confidence in a milieu dominated by West Europeans. For that reason he insisted that foreign domination of Russian pedagogy be ended. In a semi-autobiographical story of 1802, Karamzin's hero was-born "to a wealthy family . . . was taught in French, played the theatre for ten years and by the age of fifteen had no ideas about the duties of man and citizen." In another piece he expressed dismay that a French teacher had advertised a school in Paris where young Russians could go and learn Russian."Only in Russia can good Russians be made," and "we Russians are not barbarians," he wrote in angry reply.[36]

During the first two decades of Alexander's reign, Karamzin and his disciple, V. V. Izmailov, were among the most vociferous admirers of the new monarch's educational reforms, and they had nothing but contempt for the repression of schools undertaken during the 1820s by members of the Ministry of Public Instruction, Prince A. N. Golitsyn, A. S. Sturdza, and M. L. Magnitsky. In 1798 Karamzin called enlightenment a "moral bridle" that would eventually pave the way to Russian greatness. He said too that only education separated great people from wild people, and that enlightened subjects would be more likely to obey laws than unenlightened ones.[37] This was the same argument made early on in the century by Prokopovich, Kantemir, and Tatishchev, who did not have the cataclysm of civil strife and revolution to shape their thinking.

A contemporary of Karamzin's, I. P. Pnin (1773–1805), was an editor of the *St. Petersburg Journal* (*Sankt-Petersburgskii zhurnal,* founded 1798), which featured co-editor Bestuzhev's article on education.[38] Although Pnin's most important publication on education, "Essay on Enlightenment as it Applies to Russia," did not appear until after the turn of the century, the journal carried translations and essays that supported freedom of speech and pleaded for a greatly improved system of education. Pnin repeated Karamzin's notion that learning was a soothing force in society because it prompted people to respect existing laws and the political system. He used history ("since Rurik's time") to justify his position. Pnin's open hostility to despotism and his support for freedom in intellectual pursuits were obviously sincerely felt, for it was risky to make such sentiments public while Paul I governed Russia. Karamzin showed his displeasure only in private correspondence. Later, Pnin was to echo Radishchev's condemnation of serfdom, but he recommended that full education be available only to nobility. In fact, Pnin's liberal bent can only be seen as such within the context of the reactionary nature of the Russian state.[39] The author of a recently completed doctoral dissertation made a comparison between the educative views of Pnin and V. V. Popugaev, with interesting results. Both of them, according to S. C. Ramer, wanted "to use education to transform the moral values of the population and create a new type of citizen." In this attitude, they were a product of the mainstream of educational theory of their times and of practices with which Betskoi experimented. But in order to obtain some political stability in Russia, Pnin hoped to eliminate in youth a desire for social mobility. Ramer came to the conclusion that Pnin saw in a centralized education system a means to "legitimize a hierarchical society and eradicate social mobility by teaching everyone to love the estate to which he was born." Popugaev, whose "About the Popular Well-Being" (1801–1802) was typical in that it placed emphasis on moral education as the basis of proper enlightenment, wanted maximum possible social mobility, and in that sense he was an heir to traditions generally associated with Radishchev's name.[40]

Men like Pnin provided the corpus of thought behind the school reforms undertaken by Alexander I after 1802, and both the moralizing theme and the all-encompassing respect for authority remained as the dual props of Russia's national system of education. Besides the numerous Russian writings from state officials, nobility, and clergy which supported the traditional conception of learning, certain foreign works were translated which gave the official version some credence. Among them was a translation from Thomas Hobbes, the philosopher of power, which appeared in 1776.[41] Like Bossuet, Hobbes believed that there must be a supreme ruler in each state, but he justified this belief in rational and secular terms. His ideas, which were cited liberally in Prokopovich's apologia, "The Truth of the Monarch's Will," had been antecedents to those of Pufendorf, Peter I's favourite. The German, Christian Furchtegott Gellert, was another of those writers whose works were translated by Catherine's Society for the Translation of Foreign Books. His *Moralische Vorlesungen,* which appeared in a Russian version in 1787, had already been used by such important educators in Russia as Schaden to instill a moral philosophy in the students of his Moscow *pension.* One of these students was Karamzin, who later said that Gellert's fables were almost his sole reading during his school days, and that Schaden had "instructed us, his little pupils, in ethics according to *Moralische Vorlesungen.*"[42]

Novikov and his educated contemporaries were continually involved in literary and intellectual disputes with one another, the Academy, and the various university faculties. Members of the Friendly Learned Society (*Druzheskoe uchenoe obshchestvo*), which was opened in 1782 by Schwarz and Novikov, competed to a certain degree for young readers with the Free Russian Assembly, 1771–1783, and the Society of Lovers of Russian Learning (*Obshchestvo liubitelei Rossiiskoi uchenosti*), which was inaugurated at the University of Moscow in 1789 by Melissino. Their differences had often to do with personal pride, conflicting interpretations of the purpose of Freemasonry, religious factionalism, and bitter arguments over literature. The presence of such societies and of literary-scholarly factions within them added an intensity to the intellectual atmosphere in the university and, to a lesser extent, in the schools and *pensions.*

The Friendly Learned Society was dominated by Moscow's Freemasons, who hoped to promote general learning and moral development. The Masons also helped sponsor the Baccalaureate Institute. Schwarz was made its Inspector and organized the gathering of funds to send young scholars abroad for further study. Karamzin was a translator with the Friendly Learned Society in the 1780s, and Prokopovich-Antonsky was one of the first to benefit from its scholarships. It was this group that was responsible for Novikov's *Morning Light.*

The expressed purpose of the Society of Lovers of Russian Learning was to "assist the dissemination of science in Russia and its influence on the general national enlightenment."[43] Its charter called for a number of translations of the "best" foreign books in the natural sciences, economics, philosophy, history, geography, politics, and religion. The group was also asked by Melissino to prepare textbooks in order to assist youth in their normal development and to maintain a library. While most of these philanthropic groups worked well within the official guidelines for education, they also made available to many Russians who were past school age the rudiments of contemporary thought.

The progressive intelligentsia played a very important role in keeping alive in Russia the principle that there was merit to universal education, especially after the ideas of the *philosophes* were so discredited by the French Revolution, which for many Russians appeared as a natural consequence of too much learning. In fact, the backlash against education had a foothold in Russia already in the 1770s following the Pugachev outbreak. But the intelligentsia had help in their advocacy of education even from arch-conservatives. Shcherbatov, once a prominent speaker in Catherine's Legislative Commission, the Imperial Historiographer and powerful proponent of *dvorianstvo* rights, also gave a high priority to education among the tasks of government. He once wrote that a "little enlightenment leads only to greater illusions and to a spirit of insubordination," in opposition to Novikov and the Freemason desire to bring education to the peasantry. Nevertheless, in his *Journey to the Land of Ophir,* Shcherbatov described a utopian society in which his own class, the aristocracy, was the leading force. Like his harshly polemical *On the Corruption of Morals in Russia* (1786–1787), the work was not available for publication during his lifetime, but it included the idea that each class should have its own schooling system and that it be free and compulsory. Shcherbatov supported the idea that every Russian should be educated only so far that he or she be capable of performing well a specific role in society. But he also believed that the laws of the Fatherland should be taught to all classes. Thus he was another of those who saw in schooling the means to pacify society. Shcherbatov was not enamoured with Betskoi's school projects because he felt that they were not structured well enough to suit the complete needs of the state. As far as he was concerned, Betskoi was merely another courtier, a man "of small intellect" who established educational institutions only to please Catherine, and so failed to make them work properly.[44]

Almost all of the individuals mentioned above were part of the state service in one form or another, but the man who earned a reputation in many circles as the greatest teacher of Imperial Russia was neither a servitor of the state nor a member of the two official estates, the nobility or clergy. While putting his recollections to paper in the 1830s,

F. P. Lubianovsky remarked that the peasants of the Kharkov district still remembered G. S. Skovoroda (1722–1794) as a "wise and honest man, who taught us goodness and the fear of God." A few years later, A. Khidsheu wrote of the continuing popular image of Skovoroda as a teacher of all men.[45] Interestingly, however, Skovoroda never played a part in Catherine's educational programmes and, in fact, after 1766 purposely remained aloof from her institutions of formal education.

The most outstanding graduate of the Kievan Academy in 1750, Skovoroda travelled through Central Europe for three years. There he came into contact with ideas disseminated by German pietists, whose attack on rationalism and emphasis upon religious fundamentalism, practical preaching, and Bible study made a lasting impression on him. Returning to Russia in 1753, Skovoroda spent thirteen years in and out of positions as a private tutor, a teacher of poetics at the Pereiaslavl seminary, and a master at the collegium in Kharkov. His constant intransigence in the face of rigid academic tradition and learning by rote finally cost him his post at Kharkov in 1766.

The immediate bone of contention had been a manual on good behaviour prepared by Skovoroda for a course on civics requested of the school by Betskoi.[46] In spite of such official sanction, the Bishop of Belgorod objected to sections of the textbook and insisted that it be changed. Skovoroda refused and left the school to become an itinerant preacher of morality and good sense. Carrying little more than a copy of the Old Testament, he travelled throughout the Ukraine talking whenever and wherever people would listen to him. He became a legend in his own time and his fame was such that he became known as the "Russian Socrates." Catherine visited him in 1787 on her way to the Crimea and invited him to come and live in St. Petersburg. Skovoroda politely declined the invitation.

Skovoroda's rejection of formal pedagogy was the result of a series of run-ins with school authorities, which led him to conclude that "true" learning was really a higher cognition which could not be attained by normal empirical methods. He believed that true knowledge was spiritual and that the job of schools was to encourage the natural talents of each student. His ideas were much like those of Betskoi, but the two men differed sharply on the means to reach a mutually-desired end, that is, a well-rounded, religious, and useful citizen. Skovoroda believed that the place for proper education was in the home, where parents could guide their children in ethics and common sense. In this and in general teaching methodology, he was closer to Schaden and Novikov than he was to Betskoi.

Essays, speeches, plans, and eventually, a real school system did not provide much that was practical for the thousands of parents who still felt obligated to give their children a sound foundation in the three "R's" and morality at home. Old texts like Prokopovich's *Primer,* and even the *Domostroi,* were still used in the 1770s and new ones appeared. In the later books, a doctrinaire political scheme tended to overshadow the religio-moral sense of earlier ones. A few of the books are worth mentioning. Abbé Bellegarde's treatise on the duties of Christians and citizens was translated in 1743 and reprinted in 1762, 1770, and 1780. Barsov demonstrated the variety of his interests by preparing in 1768 a short primer of church and civil life, and A. A. Artem'ev translated *Of Virtuous Souls or Moralizing Rules for the Benefit and Instruction of Youth* from French in 1777. The eighties saw a number of essays and tales from A. D. Baibakov, who wrote the kind of story so characteristic of Novikov's journal, *Children's Learning,* which had its own in-resident hero, rather suggestively named Goodheart (*Dobroserd*).[47] The year 1782 saw the publication in Russian and German of an illustrated book, *Golden Mirror for Children* (*Zolotoe zerkalo dlia detei/Goldener Spiegel für Kinder*), which was a collection of items from different sources with accompanying prints. It was supposed to be used by parents as a basis for moral admonitions ("*nravouchenie*") to their children. The very young and the illiterate could learn from the pictures. Tales of vices were included along with those about honesty and respect for elders, so that readers would be sure to "remember . . . about the obligation to hate vice."[48]

A great many of these and similar items were printed by Novikov's typography; indeed, it was the Freemasons who provided an intellectual atmosphere uniquely conducive to an educational system which concerned itself with ethics. Much has been written about the Freemasons in Russia, particularly on those in Moscow where the young Karamzin, Ivan Dmitriev, A. A. Petrov, and others learned at the feet of Novikov, Schwarz, Schaden, and A. M. Kutuzov. The Freemasons of Russia were committed to improving society by leading exemplary lives themselves and by sponsoring education and morality in others. Far from being radical in the tradition of French Freemasonry and certainly not atheist, they rejected the institutionalized piety of official Orthodoxy.

Concerned too with the dignity of the individual, they fostered an intellectual commitment to making the lot of the peasantry more palatable. And their dedication went beyond rhetoric, for they opened libraries, organized schools of their own, and built hospitals, hoping that the gentry might change their habits and that the serf/peasant might learn to be content with his lowly station. They seemed to have believed with sincerity that happiness was a matter of the heart and not of material possession. Such notions were to be at the very core of the enlightened conservatism fostered during the next century by Karamzin.

Citizenship books were still being prepared in the last decade of the century. Elie Bertrand's treatise on the foundations of general morality and the responsibilities of man was translated from the French in 1796, and August Witzmann printed several short essays on the duties of honourable men.[49] The two most interesting of such books were a *Children's Book (Detskaia kniga)* published first in 1770 and in its third edition by 1780, and a *Russian Primer for the Instruction of Youth (Rossiiskaia azbuka)*[50] written in 1781 by the Empress herself. In the first two weeks after its printing, Catherine's primer sold 20,000 copies in St. Petersburg alone. In many ways these latter two items reflect the sum of the state and Orthodox versions of Russian society and its political and spiritual life. Above all, they characterize Catherine's ambitions for her school system. Thus, they warrant some self-explanatory extracts.

The *Children's Book,* printed in back-to-back French and Russian, included simple definitions of those things which the author felt Russia's youth must know. In a foreword, the author suggested that parents were failing in their duty to educate their children, adding that, "this indolence is inexcusable!" Using the question and answer method, he outlined forty basic topics, among them, man, the soul, temporal things, God, Christ, world, land, sea, natural law, illness, justice, prayer, church, human law, clergy and nobility, lower estates, and so on. Each topic was the basis of a lesson. Locke's essay on children's education was referred to several times.

The best way in which to show the character of the book is to illustrate from it:

Lesson I: Q: What are you?
                   A: I am a man.

                   Q: What is a man?
                   A: It is an animal that can reason.

Lesson XI: Q: What is an Empire, or Kingdom?
                A: It is a large country of which one person is the
                   master.

                . . .

Lesson XIX: Q: Who is the first king?
                A: God.

                Q: Must one obey the monarch in everything?
                A: Yes. If not, it is against the law of God.

                Q: Why did God make kings?
                A: To govern the people, defend them from their
                   enemies, and to create well-being.

                Q: What is a republic?
                A: It is a country which has many masters.

                . . .

                Q: Is domination by one sovereign better than that
                   by a republic?
                A: A hundred times better, because one sovereign
                   answers to God who is the sole master of all.

                . . .

Lesson XXIX: Q: Who are the nobility?
                A: They are persons who are distinguished from the
                   others by birth or duty, or by the grace of the
                   prince.

                . . .

                Q: What are the qualities of a good domestic?
                A: Fidelity, discretion, propriety, activity, and always
                   affection.

                . . .

                Q: What is a poor person?
                A: One who has no means on which to live, and does
                   not know where to get it.

                Q: Do poor people serve a purpose?
                A: Yes! They make the rich people practice com-
                   passion and charity, and so attract to them the
                   eyes of God.[51]

Catherine's *Russian Primer*, which was prompted by her reading of d'Epinay, had somewhat the same tone as the *Children's Book*, but she mixed in it questions, answers, and pithy clichés about life and learning. Opening with a careful outline of the new and old Slavonic alphabets, Catherine voiced the Rousseau-Lockean notion of learning, that is, that all children are born knowing nothing, so that it is the responsibility of the parents to start them off in the right direction. Man is also naturally inclined to good, she said, so parents must set a good example in order to take advantage of this natural good beginning.

Some of her political expressions were taken directly from the *Nakaz* of 1767. Two of her favourites, "All citizens are equal in that they are all subject to the laws," and "Freedom is the right to do everything that the law allows," mirrored the "Enlightened Despot's" regard for law. But the law rarely had contradicted her wishes since she first adopted these fine words from Montesquieu. Among the questions and answers section was the query, "What is a good citizen?," the answer to which was, "he who fulfills to the letter all civil obligations. . . ." Plato, Aristotle, and Confucius were cited as authorities on man and his relationship to the state. The book ended with two meaningful rules, no's 116 and 117: "Whoever says what he wishes, then will hear what he does not wish to hear"; and "Whoever does not know how to be silent, will not be heard."[52] Although superseded in schools by a primer prepared a few years later by Iankovich de Mirievo, Catherine's book remains an interesting sign of her concern for her subjects' morality — even though it was originally intended solely for her grandsons' use.

The individuals whose ideas on education were touched upon in this chapter do not in any sense of the word represent schools of pedagogical thought. Their opinions on politics, society, and education varied considerably. Some of them were close to Catherine, others she put in prison. But they had in common an explicit faith in education as the panacea for Russia's ills. Moral admonition, proper religious instruction, and rules for civic behaviour were touted by all of them as essential components of good schooling, both before and after the French Revolution. The petrine clamour for technological proficiency took a back seat in Russia at the very time that West European educators were experimenting with institutions that might provide their states with the expertise necessary to modernization.

The facts that respected people spoke out on behalf of education in Russia and that books on pedagogy and morality were printed, did not mean that Russians were much closer to an effective school system in the 1770s and 1780s than they had been in 1762. Catherine still sought the means to create a school programme which had built-in mechanisms for control and a more solid foundation than the somewhat erratic — even esoteric — projects undertaken by Betskoi. She found a tentative model by turning to the well-established, multi-national, and autocratically structured Austrian Empire. The key to understanding the merits of her choice lies not so much in the detail of the Austrian system as in the way the Austrian method fared in Russia.

Iankovich de Mirievo and the Austrian Public School System for Russia

A turning point for the better in the doldrums into which Catherine's school projects had descended came early in the 1780s. Her enthusiasm for education seemed to have waned considerably since the first few years of her reign, so that the breakdown of the universal school system which she had ordered for the provinces in 1775 had prompted only her plea to Grimm for emergency assistance. But the fact was that her major preoccupations were the far-reaching attempts to consolidate her administration, including provincial reorganization; the conduct of her first Turkish War, which ended in 1774; and the diplomacy stemming from her concern over the fate of Poland and the implications of the American Revolution. Even a proposal for elementary schools, which took a commission on church estates nine years to formulate under the guidance of Teplov, was simply set aside by Catherine when she received it in 1772. But in 1777 Paul's first son, Alexander, was born, and Catherine soon began to concern herself with her grandson's upbringing. Besides compiling notes herself for textbooks on Russian history and civic behaviour, she opened a Charity School of her own at St. Isaac's Cathedral in 1781.[1] It attracted a number of pupils who were taught in a somewhat haphazard fashion, with no division of classes by age or by previous knowledge. Funds for the school, which offered basic lessons plus history and geography for extra fees, were raised through private subscription and matched by the monarch from her own coffers.[2]

The real breakthrough came in 1782, when Catherine ordered into existence a Commission for the Establishment of Public Schools, and appointed to it an Austrian-Serb, Theodor Iankovich (1741–1814), who was ennobled by Maria Theresa in 1774 for his contributions to educational reform and management in Austria. He then added "de Mirievo," his birthplace, to his name.[3] The appointment was not quite so sudden as it must have appeared to many interested Russians at the time. Catherine had met with Austria's Joseph II in Mogilev in early

1780 and had taken the opportunity to discuss education with him. In May, she wrote Grimm about the conversation and mentioned Joseph's pride and confidence in his Normal School system. A few months later, she asked Grimm to find out from Baron von Dalberg exactly how the system worked, telling him that the Austrian emperor himself (she referred to him as Count Falkenstein) had sent her several copies of guidebooks prepared by the man who had inspired the Austrian school administration, Abbot J. I. Felbiger. Still awaiting the expected information from von Dalberg in August, she wrote again somewhat plaintively, "in the old days they pressured me about the education of the people, but will they ever be educated?"[4]

Her interest was accelerated when both Schaden and F.U.T. Aepinus (1725–1802), who had been a tutor to Prince Paul in 1765, recommended the Austrian system to her. Aepinus gave her a long memorandum in which he spoke very strongly in favour of the Habsburg method of creating teachers. He said that each Austrian province had its own seminary for teacher training and concluded with a plea that "Your Majesty decisively undertake and introduce to Russia the Austrian school system, without any change . . . and to institute three or four teacher's seminaries which could be opened in St. Petersburg, Moscow, Kazan, and Kiev." He added that Catherine should request aid in the form of pedagogues from Austria right away.[5]

Outlined in Felbiger's *Allgemeine Schul-Ordnung* of 1774, the school system of the Western Habsburg empire was three-tiered, open to all religious denominations, and supervised by a central Study Commission in Vienna. All teachers had to be certified by means of state examinations, and all curricula and textbooks were carefully regulated. No deviation from rules set by the Study Commission was allowed. The *Trivial,* or elementary school, provided reading, basic mathematics, and religion. *Haupt* (Higher) schools expanded upon the *Trivial* curriculum and lasted one or two years longer. The latter schools were designed more for the sons of middle class subjects, the former catered to those of the peasantry and artisans. Normal schools, of course, trained teachers. This system had been adopted by means of a special statute for the Orthodox adherents of the Austrian empire in 1776, and it was that sector which was administered by Iankovich before he came to Russia.[6]

Director of Serbian and Romanian schools in the Banat of Temesvár from 1773, Iankovich had been successful in having schools built for minorities in the Habsburg domains, and he had translated into Serbian and Romanian several of Felbiger's manuals. He was

Orthodox and Russian speaking and that coupled with his experience in organizing education for those of his Faith made him the logical choice as the man to bring the system to Russia. Felbiger himself praised him highly. Iankovich had a personal audience with Joseph II in March 1782, and his first meeting with Catherine on 6 September. The next day he was made the director of Russian schools and by law a permanent member of the Commission for the Establishment of Public Schools.[7] Ten days later, Iankovich produced a draft plan for a public school system in Russia which was accepted by Catherine on 21 September For the next four years the Commission worked out ways and means to implement the proposals.

Iankovich replaced Betskoi as the leading personality behind the empire's schooling programmes for the remainder of the century. In fact, Count P. V. Zavadovsky (1739–1812), briefly Catherine's favourite in the 1770s, became her main official liaison with her schools after 1782, and Betskoi was generally ignored after that time. He was, after all, nearly eighty years old and had wanted to retire for some time. Sadly in the light of Betskoi's sincere if not very effective attempts to bring enlightenment to Russia, Catherine became so indifferent to him that his death in 1795 was not noted by the court, and she mentioned it only tersely in a letter to Grimm on the day of her former associate and friend's death. But Betskoi's own philanthropy did not stop with his death, for he bequeathed his fortune of almost one-half million roubles to his education projects. His funeral was well-attended and Derzhavin prepared an ode for the event in which Betskoi's good deeds were recognized.[8]

The Commission was chaired by Zavadovsky, who in 1803 was to become Russia's first Minister of Public Instruction. It met at his home twice weekly until October, 1784, and then once a week at the St. Petersburg Major School until 1787, after which its members were called together less regularly. Aepinus and another member of the Academy of Sciences, P. I. Pastukhov (1732–1799), were also on the Commission but Iankovich was the only one whose chief occupation was Commission work. For the four years which preceded the official announcement of Catherine's public school system, Iankovich laboured tirelessly organizing the writing and translation of textbooks, and training teachers to fill the needs of the programme. Elected to the Imperial Russian Academy in 1783, he also contributed extensively to its *Dictionary*.

The first task set before the Commission was the translation of Western, mainly Austrian textbooks. This work was not to be taken lightly, for the decree which established the Commission outlined its obligation very carefully. Not only was it to render books into Russian, "for the benefit of our schools," but its members were to "examine as well everything in them that needs to be corrected to make them coincide with the laws of our Orthodoxy and . . . with the circumstances of the citizens of our empire. . . ."⁹ As a safeguard, the archbishop of Novgorod was made the final arbiter on the publication of all the Commission's books. All in all, thirty-two such books were produced under the auspices of the Commission between 1782 and 1802.

Its quite remarkable accomplishments in this regard were due in large part to the efforts of the best of Russia's educators from the Academy and the University of Moscow. Among them were Barsov, M. A. Kovalev, who helped Iankovich write a manual for teachers, V. P. Svetov, a teacher at the Academy gymnasium, S. P. Strugovshchikov, the inspector of public schools, O. P. Kozodavlev, graduate of the University of Leipzig and the director of the St. Petersburg Major School, M. E. Golovin and E. B. Syreishchikov, both teachers. The Commission's first book was an ABC primer which Iankovich compiled in 1782. In rapid succession there followed a Russian-language grammar, a short catechism, and two important guidebooks for teachers. Before 1786 texts on handwriting, biblical and universal history, mathematics, mechanics, and natural history were completed. A textbook on Russian history was commissioned in 1783, typically from a German, I. G. Stritter, but it was not ready in the Russian language until 1801. In fact, Stritter, an associate member of the Academy of Sciences, had been given a detailed plan for the history by Iankovich, but Catherine had not been satisfied with it and had the plan returned to the Commission with instructions that it be made to conform more closely to her own "Notes on Russian History" ("Zapiski kasatel'no Rossiiskoi istorii") which appeared in serialized form 1783–1784. So she kept a close watch on the Commission's activity. The first history of Russia to be officially adopted for schools was one written by Iankovich himself and printed in 1799.¹⁰

The year 1783 saw the publication of three books by the Commission which in themselves reveal Catherine's entire educational attitude. The first was a guide for the teachers who were to staff the new schools, the second two were books of rules for students to follow. The teachers' manual, *Guide for Teachers of the First and Second Class of the Public Schools of the Russian Empire* (*Rukovodstvo uchiteliam pervago i vtorago klassa narodnykh uchilishch Rossiiskoi Imperii*),¹¹ was

Russia's first systematic outline of pedagogical method. Iankovich was the author of the manual, which was based in part upon a Felbiger *Handbuch* already translated by him into Serbian in 1776 for use in the Austrian Empire.[12] But the Russian guidebook also encompassed ideas held by the University of Moscow compilers of *Teaching Methods,* a slightly expanded version of which appeared again in 1790.

Iankovich's new pedagogical textbook was divided into chapters on the methodology of group lessons, reading, numbers' tables, and questioning; ways to instruct individuals in learning their letters, writing, and arithmetic; and administrative procedures. These divisions were the same as those in the book's Austrian counterpart. But as was so often the case when an idea, ideal, or system indigenous to Western Europe was adapted to Russian circumstances, the textbook took on specific Russian characteristics. In contrast to the earlier Felbiger/Iankovich Serbian manual, this one practically ignored religion as a subject to be taught in school, was shorter and more precise, and stressed the use of the Russian language in the classroom. The central theme of the *Guide for Teachers* was put succinctly enough in a foreword: "The rank of teacher obligates them to try and make from their students useful members of society, and to do what is necessary to frequently encourage youth towards the observation of their societal duties, to enlighten their minds, and to teach them to think and to act wisely, honourably and decently."

The best known of the Catherinian rule books, *On the Duties of Man and Citizen,* was preceded by a simpler version for the primary class of students. The *Rules for Pupils in the Public Schools* (*Pravila dlia uchashchikhsia v narodnykh uchilishchakh*)[13] was also based on a Felbiger text. The first of its three parts described ways in which a pupil must behave towards God and the Church; the second part outlined the way in which a student should act while in school; the third guided the young Russian on his actions when outside the church and school. "The beginning of wisdom," the book began, "is fear of God." There followed a series of admonitions about hard work, concentration, and absolute obedience. Since one of the objectives of Catherine's early programme was to make education a more fashionable practice in Russia, the students were also encouraged, even exhorted, to respect their school and its teachers, and to speak well of them in their home communities.[14]

On the Duties of Man and Citizen, which was prescribed for the second class by the statute on public schools of 1786, did not represent a new phenomenon in Russia, for Peter I had attempted a similar production sixty years before. But its immediate model was another Felbiger book, the *Anleitung zur Rechtschaffenheit.* The Russian version was printed in two formats, an inexpensive, short version for pupils, and a longer, more costly one with questions and answers for teachers. The text opened with a complicated discussion about virtue and vice, character and wisdom, true well-being and the soul. All ranks of people are capable of being happy and satisfied with their lot in life, "when our souls are good, and free from indecent desires," was its message.

The student's book was divided into four parts: (1) education of the soul (5–47); (2) care of the body (48–71); (3) duty towards society (72–159); (4) how to run the home (160–180). The last two sections, which were much more specific than the first two, overlapped considerably. Besides stressing the importance of a feeling for the brotherhood of man and respect for one's own family, the text said that "a true son of the Fatherland must be attached to the state, its system of government, its authorities and its laws."

The largest part of the book had to do with patriotism. The third section opened with a clear reference to the obligation which all governments had to provide for the well-being of its citizenry. But in order for the state to fulfill its duties properly, citizens in turn must not criticize it or disobey the laws of the land. "Love for the Fatherland is a duty of each member of the government and of each subject," it said.[15] The lower classes must show their patriotism by being particularly obedient and hardworking; they also must be willing recruits for the defence of the fatherland. The soldier must love the fatherland and be brave no matter the odds that he faced. The clergy could fulfill its obligations by educating the people to be true Christians, and to love the fatherland and its rulers. The *dvorianstvo,* who were closer to the monarchy than were members of any other class, must be the models of patriotism in all circumstances and, above all, be demonstrably faithful to the sovereign.[16] As a matter of fact, the basic attitudes sponsored by *On the Duties of Man and Citizen* were almost exactly those emphasized by Tatishchev in his *Testament* of the 1730s.

Interestingly, the book was withdrawn from schools in 1819, when the Archbishop of Tver, Filaret, and the Minister of Public Instruction, Prince A. N. Golitsyn, saw revolutionary ideas in it. They complained that it did not praise monarchy enough and was too neutral about republics. Their charges were not without foundation, especially seen in the context of the French Revolution, Napoleonic Wars, and generally troubled times in Europe of 1819. Written before events in France shook the foundation of all European monarchies, *On the Duties of Man and Citizen* did carry several provocative comments about republics which, though undoubtedly referring to the authoritarian type of republic exemplified by Plato, certainly evoked different images in the nineteenth century. In trying to explain why a subject should be willing to sacrifice himself for his country, Iankovich wrote:

> Some believe that love for the fatherland is a civic virtue more characteristic of a free society or *Republic* than of a monarchy, or that in a republic there are at least more reasons and motives for [such love].

Accompanying this sentence was a footnote which attempted to explain to Russians what a republic was:

> A republic is the name given to a state in which many people, selected either from the nobility or from the common folk, govern. Such a state is called *free* because it is free from autocracy and because the supreme authority is shared by many. A land in which the supreme authority is in the hands of a single sovereign is called a *monarchical* state.

The cause of the decline in patriotism, according to the text, was not in any way the fault of governmental forms, rather it was due to inadequate education. Improved education, it went on, will create "true sons of the fatherland in our time, too."[17]

Even the extremely conservative A. S. Shiskov, who replaced Golitsyn in 1824, twice tried to have the book reinstated, but in vain.[18] It is not hard to see why Filaret, Golitsyn, and others of their mystical leaning saw a clear challenge in the rationalism of the text. The assumption that people must be satisfied with their lot in life permeated the book and its intense patriotism and military spirit suited the national consciousness which developed in Russia during the last quarter of the eighteenth century. But it also held a residue of Catherine's early enlightened spirit. It stated unequivocally that the state, its leaders, and the upper classes had immutable moral obligations towards those below them in rank and fortune. *On the Duties of Man and Citizen* and its companion citizenship and moralizing books served as the catechisms for Catherine's new Russian man.

At the same time that the Commission worked on translations and original textbooks for Russia's youth, it also experimented with new schools. Having as one of their most crucial duties the training of teachers, the Commission opened in December, 1782, a Pedagogical Seminary for twenty students from the Alexander-Nevsky monastery. Catherine allotted 10,000 roubles to the school. By the end of the year its remaining fifteen candidates were already teaching all subjects except mathematics in the capital's minor schools, and a building had been purchased for them near the St. Isaac's school. More aspiring teachers from academies and seminaries in Moscow, Kazan, Smolensk and Tver, about fifty in all, joined the Pedagogical Seminary in 1785. Iankovich acted as their main instructor and school director until later that year, when that office was turned over to Kozodavlev.[19]

Following the Austrian lead, an entirely new methodology for instructing young Russian children was devised, and opportunities for its use were created in the capital city. In the Betskoi system of pedagogy, children had been taught individually and a lot of time had been wasted, at least insofar as school administrators were concerned. So now teachers were asked to conduct classes in a more orderly fashion. They were to begin each session with a lesson for the entire class, and the group of pupils was asked to read aloud together. The teachers then used a blackboard to teach the letters of the alphabet and word tables. The class ended with simple questions directed to the students on matters previously covered. Repetition, clarity, and simplicity were to be the catchwords of the system. Moreover, within schools the teachers themselves were advised that they should meet every Saturday to discuss their own fields of study and those of the others. Recapitulation and discussion were tools of their self-instruction as well. In short, pedagogy was to be the instrument of uniformity, and Betskoi's idea that children should be encouraged to develop their peculiar talents went the way of his other innovations. The teachers' candidates were also instructed in the intricacies of administrative work, or as their Seminary charter put it, they must learn "the duties of a director, a supervisor, [and] how to make tables, lists and simple bookkeeping."

Religious study was an important part of the new teaching programme, at least at the early levels, and the catechism was used for reading and writing exercises. Much in the manner of instruction from the old *azbuki,* from which all letters were learned, teachers repeated catechisms to pupils, for example: "Veruiu vo Edinago Boga Ottsa" ("I believe in one God the Father"), and wrote on the board the first letter of each word, "V, v, E, B, O," for the child to memorize. The teaching method guidebook contained prayers in a table at the end for use at the opening and closing of each class.

but see p. 134

These new methods were given a test at a Major Public school which was inaugurated in the capital in 1782 and announced to the public by notices in the *St. Petersburg Gazette* and in the Commission's own newsletter. Simultaneously, a school with the same programme was opened for Russian citizens of the Lutheran faith who wished to be taught in German.[20]

Between 1782 and 1786 more schools were founded as teachers were trained and funds gathered. In 1783 a new institution got under way in Kronstadt and an old one at Schlüsselburg changed over to the new teaching methods. Catherine called for public donations and gave large sums herself, so that other schools started in Kazan and in Narva. In April 1785, Catherine wrote Grimm that already there were ten *Normalschulen* in St. Petersburg with a total enrollment of 1,000 pupils. Shortly after that, the Pedagogical Seminary became more of a gymnasium to train candidates for university entrance and most of its original functions were taken over by the Major Public school of St. Petersburg. Although Catherine's statement to Grimm was not very accurate, for she was confused in her terminology, by 1786 when the Commission printed its first decree on a programme for the entire empire, there were already nineteen public schools underway in the capital, with forty-four teachers and 2,355 students. There were also 251 pupils in German schools and 517 in *pensions*.[21] Libraries were expanded and the Commission continued to produce new textbooks.

The *pensions* had long been the most accessible of schools for those of Russia's gentry who could not afford to send their sons to the elite Cadet Corps Colleges. They existed in a variety of forms in all major cities, although most could be found around St. Petersburg and Moscow. There was very little control over standards in them and well-to-do families could provide their children with just as good (or as bad) an education by hiring a private tutor. By the 1780s, *pensions* bore a very heavy part of the teaching load in Russia. I. I. Dmitriev reported that in the 1760s he attended four different ones in the Kazan-Simbirsk area and learned something from only one of them. Similar recollections can be found in the memoirs of Fonvizin, Derzhavin, and Radishchev. As early as 1775, plans for the centralization of *pensions* or at least of their curricula were put forward by V. Kh. Gensh, but Catherine had more pressing problems that year and paid little attention to his suggestion.[22]

A special Nobles Pension was created in Moscow in 1779 by Kheraskov, at that time the curator of the university. Open to both nobility and merchants, it had a fee of 150 roubles and was overseen by

Russians, most of whom were associated with the university. Its first students were all well-born, between the ages of nine and fourteen, and committed by their parents to undergo a demanding eight-hour per day course of study. They often took part in the university programmes. Kheraskov hoped that it would prove to be a Moscow version of the Land Cadet Corps College in St. Petersburg, but with a greater emphasis upon Russian language and literature. Foreign languages were given their due, however, along with the laws of God and the basic sciences. Moral philosophy, history, geography, and writing in Russian were part of the curriculum; so were music and dance. Announced in the *Moscow Gazette* (*Moskovskie vedomosti*) in 1778, its original plan had been for only twelve students, but the response was so great that by 1790 its enrollment had grown from fifty to 400 students. By then it had its own building and was generally regarded as a monumental success. Its professors even worked with students to prepare translations and publish them as texts for discussion.[23]

The Moscow university *pension* was one of the few pedagogical experiments of the 1770s in Russia to be founded independently of Betskoi, but it featured some of the characteristics of his schools, above all of Smolny. Pupils at the *pension* took part in theatrical productions and were given practical experience which put them in good stead in a society dominated by officers and gentlemen. In short, they were trained for service, but without the elitist trappings of the Cadet Corps. One of its prominent graduates, who developed a literary bent and who became tutor to Alexander I's children, was V. A. Zhukovsky. Prokopovich-Antonsky taught natural history there after 1787 and edited for the school a journal called *Studies for the Heart and Mind* (*Chteniia dlia serdtsa i razuma*). He was made its General-Inspector in 1791, and Director in 1818; a job he kept for five years.

The overall purpose of the *pensions,* or at least its official version, was printed in the *Moscow Gazette* in 1783. Among the goals called for were the familiar ones, "to instill in the hearts of Russia's youth good behaviour; and through that to make them truly useful students, that is, good and virtuous citizens." Other demands on the schools were fully Lockean: to teach "useful knowledge," so that graduates could fulfill the needs of society, and "to preserve their health and make their bodies strong."[24] That most of the *pensions* were not achieving these ends and, in fact, were run by foreigners for personal gain, was brought to Catherine's attention by an investigatory committee set up on her orders by the Governor-General of Moscow,

Count Ia. V. Brius (Bruce), in October, 1785.[25] It included two members of the Moscow Board of Public Assistance, two appointees of the Orthodox church, and two professors from the University of Moscow (Schaden and Barsov). Their report prompted Catherine to close all the Russian-language *pensions* and transfer their teachers to the public school system. Most of the foreign *pensions* were allowed to remain in existence, but they were told to adopt Iankovich's teaching methods, and their students were examined twice yearly by representatives from the Commission for the Establishment of Public Schools. This procedure was part of an overall centralization policy which saw the Charity schools also being told to conform with Commission practice; so they too lost their autonomy.[26]

Writing in 1849, A. S. Voronov calculated that there were twenty-eight *pensions* in the St. Petersburg area alone by 1780. Of their five-hundred students, only 200 were Russians; of seventy-two teachers, twenty were Russian. Half of those taught dancing and drawing, and the remainder instructed in arithmetic and the Russian language, which suggests that Russian was barely taught at all and certainly was not the lingua franca of the *pension* system. Most of the textbooks were in the French language, although a few were of German origin. Voronov repeated a fundamental criticism expressed by the authors of the 1785 report, that is, that young Russians were learning the "word of God" in foreign languages and from non-Orthodox teachers.[27] That is not to say that there were no good *pensions,* for notable exceptions include those run by the academician, J.-A. Euler in St. Petersburg, and by Schaden and Chebotarev in Moscow. Karamzin and Denis Fonvizin both studied under Schaden and had only praise for him; the poet and friend of Karamzin, I. I. Dmitriev, called Schaden "one of the best professors of Moscow University."[28]

The future and purpose of the *pensions* remained a source of constant concern for the public school commissioners, who had organized the investigation for Catherine in 1785. In the 1790s, Catherine corresponded with the translator-educator-dramatist M. I. Verevkin on the subject. Although Verevkin reported to her that there had not been much improvement in the schools, no further action was taken. Verevkin, incidentally, was a translator of several European textbooks and had been involved in educational matters since 1759, when he had prepared a report on the gymnasium at Kazan for Shuvalov. He was the first director of that school and for a while its only teacher. His leading pupil had been Derzhavin, whose own account of the learning process there was far from favourable. Verevkin also translated in 1792 an important work on the principles of primary education by Robert Dodsley (1703-1764), who was co-founder of the British *Annual Register* with Edmund Burke.[29]

The *pensions* were not the only privately-organized schools in the Russian Empire during the latter decades of the century. Samuel Bentham, brother of the utilitarian Jeremy Bentham, spent eleven years, 1780-1791, in Catherine's service and established Regimental schools in Siberia. Though they did not exist for long, Bentham's schools introduced educational standards to a remote area, and represented an alternative to the Garrison schools, which were abolished by Paul I in 1798.[30]

The Commission for the Establishment of Public Schools also examined the nature of education in the Smolny Institute, the Land Cadet Corps, the Artillery-Engineering Noble Cadet Corps, and individual schools around the St. Petersburg and Moscow districts. Its recommendations in each case were followed closely, so that the first years of the Commission's existence were marked by general change throughout Catherine's educational organization. In short, a reform era culminated, rather than began, with the statute of 1786.

When the Commission finally got around to printing its programme of education for the empire in a widely publicized statute of 5 August, 1786, much of the organizational labour was complete. New teaching methods had been tested, teachers trained, and texts written, so that the new system started out on a stronger footing than had the hodge-podge of plans organized by Betskoi in the 1760s and 1770s. Perhaps most important was the fact that there were now available some very capable instructors who were born and educated in Russia. Iankovich's Pedagogical Seminary and the Major Schools in St. Petersburg had produced 425 teaching graduates by 1801, most of them during the Seminary's first eight years of existence. Quite a few of them were able to gain reputations in their own right. The best known were V. F. Zuev, Golovin, Syreishchikov, J.-F. Hackmann, and F. I. Iakovkin, each of whom helped teach in the school from its first year and at the same time learned methodology from Iankovich.

Zuev prepared Russia's first textbook for natural history, stressing in his foreword the merits of Iankovich's teaching methods and eliminating Latin and other foreign terms. He and Golovin, who wrote six mathematics textbooks for the Commission, were open admirers of Lomonosov and worked to construct a specifically Russian school system. Syreishchikov, secretary to the Commission and a teacher of the Russian language, edited in April 1784, the first pedagogical journal in Russia, *Rastushchii Vertograd* (*The Growing Garden*), which was printed at the Pedagogical Seminary. One of its first important contributors was Kozodavlev, whose long essay on public education in Europe appeared in the April 1785 issue. Zuev was its editor by that time. Syreishchikov also wrote a grammar for use in schools, modelling it after that of Lomonosov. Iakovkin was an accomplished historian who worked with Iankovich to translate and write general histories. He later became a director of the University of Kazan. These men did not all accept the rigidity of the rules for pedagogy set out in the plan in 1786, but they worked within the system as advocates of learning in their turn training new teachers and sponsoring new schools.[31]

The statute of 1786 called for two types of schools, a Minor school of two grades and a Major school of five grades. A Middle level, of the kind within the Austrian system and which Iankovich had included in his proposal of 1782, was dropped. Major schools were to be established only in cities and large towns, while the Minor institutions served smaller towns and neighbouring villages. Major schools prepared teachers for Minor ones. Both systems were technically under the authority of the Commission but were overseen by the local Boards set up already in Catherine's legislation of 1775. Minor schools had only two teachers, who were to instruct in reading, writing, arithmetic, religious history, the catechism, and a smattering of Russian grammar. Drawing was available if there happened to be a qualified instructor in the school. Teachers' salaries were paid by the Boards of Public Assistance, which were also responsible for distributing textbooks: free to poor families, and with a charge to better-off ones. Education itself was to be free and open to all classes, or at least to those who lived close enough to the schools to attend.

The Major schools were divided into four classes, the final one of two-year duration. The first class studied Iankovich's primer, reading, writing, a minor catechism, Biblical history, and numbers. Second year classes learned religion and morality, were responsible for *On the Duties of Man and Citizen,* basic mathematics, Russian grammar, spelling, drawing, and design. In the third year, students undertook the Gospels, a major catechism, a second book of mathematics, universal history, Russian geography, Russian grammar, spelling, and drawing. The senior class was assigned advanced Russian grammar, Russian history, universal and national geography, geometry, mechanics, physics, natural history, and architecture. All Major schools were supposed to have a library, exhibits for the natural sciences, and mathematical equipment. They were also intended to have six qualified teachers. The Minor school curriculum corresponded to that of the first two years of the Major school.

Not surprisingly, the role of the teachers was carefully defined in the statute and their responsibilities were thoroughly spelled out. In the Major schools they were burdened with providing detailed monthly reports to their director on the progress, behaviour, absences (with reasons), and the academic capacities of each pupil. The instructors themselves were subject to rigid rules of conduct, for they were to be the examples after whom the youngsters could model themselves. In a tradition that goes back to the Lutsk Brotherhood, teachers were expected always to demonstrate by their own actions how to behave, to pray with their charges, and to instill in them by means of their own good ways, "piety, good morals, friendship, courtesy, and diligence. . . ." These same virtues, plus "patience" and "satisfaction in their jobs," had been spelled out in much greater detail in the *Guide for Teachers*. The contribution which such pedagogues were expected to make to society was such that Catherine ordered that all qualified teachers in Major schools be assigned a place on the Table of Ranks.

The statute showed that most of the high ideals of Betskoi's 1764 document had fallen by the wayside. The conception of education as something good in itself was not diminished particularly, but the new plan revealed a hard practical concern which had not been so prominent in the 1760s. It also showed that part of the syllabus's aim was to repatriate Russia's well-to-do youth, for there was a complaint in it about the fact that many young people were shipped off to foreign countries by parents who assumed that they would learn more elsewhere.

Nothing was left to chance. Teachers, teaching, and subject matter were to be closely controlled from above. Minor schools were overseen by a trustee elected from town dwellers, who made monthly reports to a Board of Public Assistance. Major school directors were appointed for each district and were responsible to a General-Gubernator. The final arbiter of all educational matters was the Commission and, of course, the empress. The "new order" which was so glowingly but vaguely defined by Betskoi nearly a quarter-century earlier was now quite clearly expected to be one of state servants who would be competent and, above all, politically reliable. Echoing the ideas of Feofan Prokopovich, Catherine made her aim very specific in the preamble to the statute, which also reflected some of Diderot's sentiments:

> The education of youth has been regarded so highly by all enlightened
> countries, that it is assumed to be the only means of maintaining a
> good society; this is inarguable, for the subject of education includes
> pure and wise ideas about the Creator and His Holy Law, and the
> basic principles of unwavering loyalty to the Ruler and true love for
> the Fatherland and one's fellow citizens.[32]

Thus, teaching method was completely revised. The main changes
were abolition of corporal punishment and other brutalities which
students outside of Betskoi's boarding schools often had had to face,
and the institution of mass, rote learning. Rather than attempt to work
with individual students and beat an education into them, teachers
now followed Iankovich's guidance and taught the group as a whole,
having them read aloud and reading to them. The complete mastering
of textbooks was insisted upon and, indeed, became the basis of the
entire educational system.

Even such subjects as handwriting were carefully prescribed in
textbooks, with rules about formation of letters carefully supple-
mented by dicta on how to sit, where to put the hand, how to hold the
pen, and what colour ink to use. The statute said specifically that
teachers must "teach exactly according to the rules. . . ," nothing
"extraneous or irrelevant" was to be taught and only those books
designated in it were to be used.[33]

The aim which Wolff, Locke, and others had for education, that is,
training for citizenship in society, was also the essential ingredient of
the Russian system. But to obtain their goal, the Western Europeans
had opposed excessive memorization and an absolute reliance on
textbooks. So had Betskoi. By adopting the Austrian system, and
employing Iankovich, Catherine went in the opposite direction, choos-
ing to regulate more closely the individual child's reasoning powers.
Furthermore, Catherine ignored the fact that the great majority of her
subjects lived in villages and so could not be served by the town-
oriented school system of 1786. Perhaps, like Locke, she assumed that
by educating the middle and upper sectors of her population, the
benefits of enlightenment would filter down to the lower ranks as far as
it was necessary.

Whether or not Catherine's public school policy can be deemed a
success is a question that can be answered only within the context of
her aims. From Betskoi's plan of 1764, to the *Nakaz* and the statute of
1786, her goals were rarely clearly defined, but she consistently paid
lip-service to the assumption that general education was good for the

state. Moral regeneration was at the same time the consistent goal which she set for general education. Whereas Betskoi's efforts produced certain benefits insofar as the Foundling Homes, Smolny and the Cadet Corps were concerned, he accomplished very little when it came to bringing education to people without wealth. Thus, the 1786 legislation was a breakthrough in that it spread at least limited access to education to all the provinces, enabling sons and daughters of merchants, soldiers, clergy, and even peasants to have basic instruction if they so desired [see Table A]. The introduction of new teaching methods and the preparation of new textbooks raised the quality of instruction, widened the potential audience for education, and gave rise to a system that could truly be called Russian. Once again, however, Catherine failed to follow the Austrian lead and make education compulsory. Nor did the Commission have any dominion over the seminaries, gymnasiums, or universities, and so the educating apparatus in Russia still could not be described as systematic.

The Commission for the Establishment of Public Schools continued to function until 1802 when it was replaced by a Ministry. Only Iankovich served throughout those twenty years. Aepinus retired in 1797, Pastukhov in 1799. Zavadovsky was removed from his post as its chairman by Paul in 1799 and exiled to his family estate, but he was reinstated by Alexander I and appointed in 1803 as Russia's first Minister of Public Instruction. Others who sat on the Commission were A. V. Chrapovisky (1784–1793), F. W. Creydemann (1784–1795), O. P. Kozodavlev (1793–1797), V. N. Zinov'ev (1799–1800), E. K. Kromin (1800–1802), A. M. Rykov (1800–1803), and P. S. Svistunov (1799–1802), whom Paul appointed as Zavadovsky's replacement. Iankovich, Pastukhov, and Svistunov later were asked to sit on Zavadovsky's new council, the Major School Board, and so brought the Commission's experience to Alexander's school administration.[34]

Russia's pedagogical difficulties were by no means over in 1786. Traditional problems remained to haunt the incipient school programme. Catherine never opened up her treasury for the public schools as she did for the elitist institutions. The combined expenditures yearly for the military academies, Army, Navy, and Engineering, averaged about 550,000 roubles; for Smolny about 100,000 per year. Catherine also sometimes underwrote pupils for those schools, and so did other wealthy patrons. But the entire public school system received only 10,000 roubles in its first year from the royal purse. Its best year seems to have been 1788, when Catherine allotted public schools 71,000 of a total 803,103 roubles set aside for education. Even the sum provided to all schools that year represented only 2.6% of the state budget. The empress spent much more annually on the trappings of imperial glory and on gifts, even palaces, for her favourites. The Commission resorted to relying upon profits made from its own investments, which were handled by the Shchukin house of merchants in St. Petersburg. By 1801, it had amassed a capital of nearly 200,000 roubles, which was not very much in the light of the task it was expected to accomplish.[35] The fate of individual schools depended all too often upon the degree of interest and financial support which their administrators were able to attract locally. For that reason, even the Major schools rarely developed their curriculum beyond the elementary stage, that is, reading, writing, mathematics, and catechism; further courses usually cost parents a small sum of money.

It was some time before all the schools called for in the statute of 1786 were constructed; for example, those in Ekaterinoslav, Simferopol, and Tavrichesky districts were not opened until 1793 and 1794. Many were in makeshift buildings or on the estates of local squires, and a few regions simply never obtained their school. Reliance upon local funds often meant an inconsistent rate of supply. Kozodavlev pinpointed an important obstacle to the growth of the system in 1788 when he was lobbying for the establishment of more universities in Russia. In a report to the Commission he noted that enrollment in the third and fourth classes was often very small and that those in the second class had little inclination to proceed further [see Table A]. The reason for this, he said, was the fact that parents saw no future in their children proceeding beyond the first two years of the programme: "We must show the people the advantages of an advanced education . . . when they see that in order to obtain a desirable place in service one must have knowledge of the sciences which will be taught in our universities. . . ," then the problem of enrollment in the secondary schools will be solved. Since his advocacy of more facilities for higher education was all in vain, the dilemma remained.[36]

Administrative difficulties were particularly acute in the Ukraine where Catherine's public schools were sometimes looked upon as a form of unwanted Russian intrusion. To cite but one example of the kind of feeble growth suffered by certain schools: in 1789–1790, a Major school and a Minor one were opened in Chernigov with limited facilities. Three years later an inspector named Martov reported that the school had no library, no barometer for mathematics classes, no animals for the natural sciences classes, and that the textbooks were

Interesting that largest single group is from domestics (handwritten annotation)

Table A

Social origin and numbers of students in the
Riazan Major School, 1788: *

Social rank of students	*Number of Pupils by Class*				*total*
Children of:	Class I	II	III	IV	
Nobility	7	6	2	-	15
Officers	8	5	7	-	20
merchants	5	1	2	1	9
clergy	2	3	1	-	6
bureaucrats	2	11	8	4	25
bourgeois	3	4	-	-	7
couriers, watchmen, craftsmen	5	-	-	-	5
peasants	6	5	1	1	13
domestics	21	18	8	-	47
soldiers and junior officers	10	8	1	-	19
unknown (Father's rank)	1	-	-	-	1
	70	61	30	6	167

*From Beliavsky, "Shkola i sistema obrazovaniia v Rossii v kontse XVIII v," 114.

given out at the pulpit of the local church. Even though eighty-five students from seminaries in Kiev, Chernigov, and Pereiaslavl had been sent to study at the new Pedagogical Seminary in St. Petersburg, and the statute of 1786 had called for Major Schools in Kiev, Kharkov, Chernigov, and Novgorod-Seversk, the first Ukrainian Major school to be put into service was one in Kiev in 1789. A decree of late September, 1782, had allowed for instruction in Latin in the Polish-populated provinces; Greek in those of Kiev, Novorossiisk, and Azov; in Arabic, Irkutsk and other non-Russian languages in appropriate parts of the empire,[37] so Ukrainian reservations about the system as a conscious 'Russification' instrument were perhaps exaggerated. But the fact that it was a highly centralized one and that Russian was its operative language meant that uniformity was one of its consequences.

The success or failure of public schools was often determined by the interest taken in them by local governors or town councillors. Derzhavin took matters into his own hands while he was governor of Tambov (1786–1788), and began by setting up a school for children of both sexes in his own home. Classes for children included dance, led by an instructor whom he had hired to teach his own daughter, grammar, arithmetic, and geometry. Literary discussions at his home were attended by both wealthy and poor patrons. When the potential attendance in class reached unmanageable proportions, around 150 pupils, Derzhavin was responsible for a Major Public School being instituted in his district on a solid financial footing.[38]

Nevertheless, the number of youngsters who passed through the regular public school system gradually increased. By 1801 there were forty-nine Major schools and 239 Minor ones, with 760 teachers instructing 22,220 students [see Table B]. There were by that time forty-eight *pensions,* with 169 teachers and 1,125 pupils. A surprisingly high percentage of the children in public schools were from the peasantry, about thirty-six percent, and clerical schools and seminaries which operated in every substantial provincial town, sixty-six in all by 1800, accounted for about 21,000 students. The various elitist academies had in them another 2,000, so the total number of youngsters actually in school by the turn of the century was just under 62,000. This figure, which was calculated by M. T. Beliavsky in 1959,[39] includes an educated guess at the number of pupils participating in the soldiers' schools, which provided basic knowledge and especially mathematics to a great many children living in regimental districts.

In fact, a 1793 report from a garrison school in Saratov indicates that children there could have, if their parents wished, a wide course of study. Of ninety-nine students in the school, only thirty-six were registered with the government. Others took special subjects or had already completed some basic programme elsewhere. Among the topics studied by a variety of the pupils in the Saratov area were geometry, Russian and political geography, natural and general history, grammar, catechism, and writing. Only eighteen of them studied *On the Duties of Man and Citizen,* which suggests that these schools were less centrally directed than were the public schools.[40] Catherine's remark of 1761, to the effect that the only place where a peasant's son might have an opportunity to gain some learning was in the army, remained a reasonably accurate judgement throughout the century. Beliavsky illustrates his point in this regard by naming a few soldiers' sons who later contributed to the development of Russian science and letters, among them two of the individuals mentioned above as teachers and learned men, the academician Krashenninikov and Zuev.

Table B

Growth in enrollment in Russian Public Schools: *

Year	schools	teachers	students males	students females
1782	8	26	474	44
1783	9	28	654	77
1784	11	33	1082	152
1785	12	38	1282	209
1786	165	394	10230	858
1787	218	525	11968	1571
1788	227	520	13635	924
1789	225	516	13187	1202
1790	269	629	15604	921
1791	288	700	16723	1064
1792	302	718	16322	1178
1793	311	738	16165	1132
1794	302	767	15540	1080
1795	307	716	16035	1062
1796	316	744	16220	1121
1797	285	664	14457	1171
1798	284	752	15396	1405
1799	277	705	15754	1561
1800	315	790	18128	1787

*from: Rozhdestvensky, "Ocherki po istorii sistem narodnago prosveshcheniia v Rossii XVIII–XIX vekakh," in *Zapiski istoriko filologicheskago fakul'teta imperatorskago S. Petersburgskago universiteta,* CIV (St. Petersburg, 1912), 605. According to Beliavsky, the 1800 figure for schools is distorted by the fact that a report to Alexander I in 1801 included *pensions* along with the Major and Minor schools (Beliavsky, 110–12); thus, the difference in number in the table and the text, but the impression of growth remains the same.

One should take care, however, to point out that the increase in the number of students was actually rather disappointing in the light of the number of schools that were built. New schools found pupils readily enough, but their individual enrollments did not seem to expand to any great measure; and the fact that Imperial Russia had a population of forty million in the 1790s makes the number of school children miniscule indeed. Crucial to understanding the sporadic evolution of the public schools in Russia is the above-mentioned fact that attendance in them was not made compulsory. Thus the initiative to take up the state's offer of educational facilities was still left to Russian parents.

The obvious contributions made by Austria to the evolution of public schooling in Imperial Russia should not be allowed to cloud the fact that their differences remained significant. Iankovich brought with him a fundamental plan, a curriculum, and a methodology of teaching. Furthermore, Kozodavlev followed the Austrian lead by basing an entire series of propositions for university reform on reports drawn up by Iankovich's former mentor at the University of Vienna, Joseph von Sonnenfels. But Kozodavlev's quite egalitarian university statutes of March, 1787, were never made into law by Catherine. Catherine's public school system was much more secular in nature than that in Austria, where, even though the state took complete control of education, religion was still taught by priests. In Russia, religion in state schools was taught by lay instructors and was not even included in the final two years of Major school curricula. More important in the long run, however, was Catherine's failure to acknowledge in any tangible way the principles which made Austria's school administration effective: compulsory attendance, accessibility for all classes of people, and a serious financial commitment on the part of the government. Thus, while Austria's new programme had over 200,000 pupils in it by 1780 and became the envy of Europe's educators, Catherine's endured as a reflection of the hardening caste structure which characterized social development in eighteenth-century Russia.

In addition to the proliferation of schools, there was an acceleration in the number of books printed in Russia during the last decades of Catherine's reign. Of almost 8,000 new books printed between 1750 and 1800, 6,800 appeared after 1770, and most of those were of 800 to 1,000 copies.[41] And an increasingly large percentage of them came from the pens of people outside the nobility. Societies like those sponsored by the Freemasons, by Krechetov, and by wealthy patrons throughout the provinces helped disseminate knowledge by opening up their own libraries and conducting reading salons. The number of book stores also multiplied rapidly, increasing in St. Petersburg from one in 1768 to twenty-nine at the end of the century. Translations abounded and foreign literature flooded in at least until the 1790s.

Novikov remarked in the 1780s that some books went through four or five editions, "because they were being purchased by middle class people."[42] Public libraries were also popular with the middle echelons of society, and an increasing number of important scholars, educators, translators, musicians, and writers who earned their reputations during the final quarter of the century were sons of merchants, professional people, minor officials, and soldiers.[43]

The flurry of activity in the book business was due in great measure to Catherine's own policies. In 1783 she allowed the establishment of private printing presses and gave their owners a reasonably free hand in publication. New presses appeared even in private homes in the provinces. Novikov immediately started two printing houses in Moscow and in 1784 joined with fourteen associates to form a Typographical Company. It was by far the largest private publishing enterprise in Russia, but soon came under Catherine's distrustful eye. In fact, in 1786, the very years that her public schools were announced, several of Novikov's books were confiscated, condemned, and burned. Wars with Turkey and Sweden between 1787 and 1792 and the French Revolution brought a halt to the near frenetic publishing business which started in 1783; the wars also forestalled any serious support Catherine may have planned for her new schools.

There was undoubtedly considerable progress made in Russia's educational services, both qualitatively and quantitatively, during the eighteenth century. But soon after the enunciation of her aims in 1764, Catherine had been faced with the dilemma which was to continue to perplex her successors, that is, how to educate Russians on the one hand and to leave autocracy impregnable on the other. Like those who followed her on the throne of the Russian Empire, she solved the problem by compromising her principles on education and by doing her best to see that it could not create disloyal subjects. Thus, schooling tended to remain a preserve for service nobility and bureaucrats, and the masses remained illiterate, kept in place by their own ignorance and supersitition. Peter's utilitarian ambitions had proven their resilience. As Paul Miliukov put it, "the mastering of knowledge and not the development of thinking," still prevailed.[44]

И. И. БЕЦКОЙ.

I. I. BETSKOI

Ѳ. И. ЯНКОВИЧЪ де МИРІЕВО.

F. I. IANKOVICH DE MIRIEVO

И. И. ШУВАЛОВЪ.

I. I. SHUVALOV

S. A. Mad.me la Princesse de Daschkaw,
née Comtesse de Worontzow Dame d'honeur de Sa Majesté
l'Impératrice de toutes les Russies Chevalier de l'Ordre de
Ste Catherine, Directeur de l'Academie Imple de Sciences President de l'Acad.ie Imple Russe. Membre de l'Acad.ie Royales de
Stockholm de celles de Berlin et d'Erlange de la Societé Oeconomique
de St Petersbourg et de la Societé Philosophique de Philadelphie

DASHKOVA

Графъ П. В. ЗАВАДОВСКІЙ.

P. V. ZAVADOVSKY

С. В. де ЛАФОНЪ.

SOFIA DE LA FONT

VII

Educating Women in Eighteenth-Century Russia

To be a woman in Muscovy and in the opening years of Peter I's Imperial Russia was to be illiterate and a virtual slave to father and husband. We have seen that it was some time before Russia's gentry could be persuaded to accept education as a normal achievement for their sons; insofar as their daughters were concerned, most fathers regarded instruction in anything but religion and housekeeping skills as a waste of time and money. That this was a continuing tradition is evidenced by characterizations in plays written during the final decades of the century by Fonvizin and Kniazhnin, who was Betskoi's secretary for ten years.

In his *The Minor,* Fonvizin lampooned the uneducated wife of a provincial nobleman who exclaimed with dismay, "And girls know how to read!" Kniazhnin's play of 1790, *The Eccentrics,* contained a description of what some provincial social climbers believed to be proper behaviour for their daughters. Mrs. Indolent, in describing the merits of her daughter to a prospective suitor, said:

> I must confess that her education is what her birth demands . . . she is removed from all coarseness; and keeping herself aloof from everything, as our dignity demands, she knows neither how to sew nor to weave, leaving such occupations to common people; she dances like a peacock, sings like a nightingale, and, knowing French like a Frenchwoman, she would like to forget her Russian; she retires at three o'clock, rises at twelve, and passes two hours at her toilet.[1]

Both Fonvizin and Kniazhnin used their characters to express serious social concerns and so one must allow for exaggerations, but their caricature of prevailing attitudes towards women was accurate. Indeed, at the end of the century many Russians still would have concurred heartily with the statements made in the *Domostroi* about women's place in society. Harsh on the matter of education in general, the *Domostroi* gave strict advice about the subordinate role of women. "The Wife is always and in all things to take Counsel with her

Husband," was the title of one section in the book, wherein a woman was cautioned to abstain from drinking liquor, "for a drunken woman has no place in the world," and was urged to learn crafts and housekeeping. Guidance was offered her for instructing children and servants, and she was told to avoid all gossip. Women of good society were expected to master the intricacies of conversation but not to engage in conversation with male guests of the home unless enjoined to do so by their husband. In return for their wives' exemplary behaviour, the *Domostroi* directed husbands not to beat them publicly with the lash, rather it should be done in private. Nor was it deemed proper that wives be struck on the ears or eyes, that they be kicked, or beaten with iron staffs.[2]

During the first decades of the eighteenth century, however, there were certain circumstances that made the education of women an increasingly palatable subject for discussion in Russia. In the first place, the practical thrust of the petrine reforms called for a mobilization of all the newly formed empire's human resources. The fact that Peter included women in his decree on Assemblies of 1718 is evidence of that. Furthermore, Peter showed his interest by visiting in 1717 the aging Mme. de Maintenon, who had founded at Saint-Cyr in 1686 the *Maison Royale de Saint Louis,* a school for daughters of impoverished French nobility. In his own country, there were a few institutions already which allowed for the teaching of both sexes. One such was organized as early as 1694 in Moscow, another in St. Petersburg in 1703, both by Lutheran constituents for their own children. A few private schools existed where girls were taught household skills but were rarely shown how to read.[3]

Arguments by F. Saltykov, Werner Pause, Tatishchev, and Prokopovich during and shortly after Peter's reign did not go very far in prompting the building of educational facilities for girls, but they did keep the idea alive. The fact that Russians were ruled mainly by women after 1725 also assured that at least a sympathetic ear was usually available to proponents of women's education at court. In fact, Elizabeth sent an envoy of her own to Saint-Cyr, even though her reign saw little improvement in the growth of educational means in Russia. Shuvalov's plan for national gymnasiums included places for girls, but so little was done for women that Dashkova could write in her memoirs at mid-century with reasonable accuracy that "there were no other two women at the time apart from the Grand Duchess [Catherine] and myself who did any serious reading. . . ."[4]

But the setting for change was being laid. Elizabeth's emissary to

Saint-Cyr was Betskoi, who had a genuine respect for women as thinkers. There is evidence, too, of several *pensions* which catered to girls in the 1750s around Moscow and St. Petersburg. They stressed languages, mainly French, and offered little more than basic training in the domestic arts and lessons on manners and charm.[5] But they, along with various items in *Monthly Essays,* Rousseau's *Émile,* and the growing popularity of pedagogy brought the question of educating women to the fore by the time that Catherine became monarch. In general and for the reason stated in the first education article of 1755, the *Monthly Essays* stressed the advantage of instruction for girls "especially as they themselves will become mothers and they can contribute considerably to society by being good examples to their own children."[6]

In 1762, an article in *Monthly Essays* described a Lutheran school recently opened in St. Petersburg, which prescribed for women a much different pattern of instruction than that for men. Both sexes were to be given fairly broad subject matter, but for women greater value was assigned to religion, history, and languages. The sciences were left mainly to boys. Girls were also expected to learn sewing, embroidery, and drawing, as well as the skills of music and the dance. Boys who hoped to go on to the university were required to learn Latin and Greek. No such suggestion was made for the girls' curriculum, for it was not intended that they should enter into higher education.[7]

Catherine was well aware of the disadvantages faced by a nation with an illiterate population, and she saw a basic contradiction and potential problems in educating only males. Her comments in 1761 about the creating of a Saint-Cyr on Russian soil illustrate her concern and foreshadowed her extensive efforts on behalf of education for women in Russia. As we have seen, she was inundated with proposals for the reshaping of Russia's almost non-existing educative facilities during the first years of her reign. Several of these papers suggested access to schools for women, but her main reference on the subject remained Montaigne, Comenius, and Fénelon. There is no evidence to show that she knew of Saltykov's propositions of 1712, or of Tatishchev's essays on the subject. But she quoted Fénelon and Comenius many times. Comenius had gone so far as to say that "women are endowed with equal sharpness of mind and capacity for knowledge (often more than the opposite sex) and they are able to obtain the highest positions, since they have often been called by God himself to rule over nations. . . ."[8]

Fénelon, whom Catherine claimed to read constantly, had not given women that much credit. In fact, he had made it quite clear that women should not be allowed to govern states, and even suggested that they not be so plentiful at court. Their education, he maintained, should be a matter of instilling in them the desire and ability necessary for hardworking, thrifty homemakers. He was probably partly responsible for Maintenon's similar feelings about the purpose of her school at Saint-Cyr. Fénelon preached there until his exile from France in 1697. Maintenon also urged that girls be industrious and useful to the state. Neither of them approved of theatricals as part of a curriculum, nor did they allow the skills of letterwriting to be taught. In short, they looked upon salon type society as frivolous and wasteful, feeling that such diversions would serve only to make women bored with home life. Book learning was not regarded by either of them as nearly so important as virtue, which they defined as the fulfillment of duty. Thus, from Fénelon and the school at Saint-Cyr, Catherine could find both inspirations and much to ignore.[9]

Catherine also read *Le Magasin des jeunes dames* which was prepared by Mme. Leprince de Beaumont in Paris between 1761 and 1764. Written in the form of a dialogue between a "wise governess" and her best pupils, the work was a monumental textbook for charm. The empress was familiar with the opinions of Brown, Diderot, and La Chalotais, but her main inspiration for education for women came from her own thoughts and from Betskoi.

The earliest agency established by her government which involved education for girls was the Imperial Foundling Home opened in Moscow, June, 1763. The plans for that and subsequent orphanages, which included maternity wards for unwed mothers, called for a uniform education for young children of both sexes. Reading, writing, and the catechism were to be taught throughout, although as they grew older girls were to concentrate on learning domestic skills, boys on manual skills. But an entire chapter in the decree which sponsored the Home was devoted to reasons for giving girls a general education equal to that of boys. Above all else, since children learned first from their mothers, and sons of nobility were often under the care of domestic servants, Betskoi's plan insisted that the girls must develop minds "enlightened by different knowledge in order to lead a useful civil life."[10] In this idea, he was close to Dilthey.

In the same month that the "General Institutes" was passed in 1764, Catherine issued an order which reorganized several of her provinces, and that order mentioned specifically that there be established schools for girls, where they were to be taught reading, writing, and the domestic arts.[11] But it was the "General Institutes" which carried with it the first official recognition that female children must have the same access to elementary education as did males. Betskoi's notion of a new order of people was obviously meaningless unless girls were educated along with boys, and he recognized this: "the new fathers and mothers can, in their turn, instill the rules of life which they received into the hearts of their own children."[12] So the role of women in creating a new society was to be an active one, and all of Betskoi's recommendations about boarding schools and the separation of children from their semi-literate parents' applied as much to girls as to boys. Indeed, the "General Institutes" mentioned the upcoming formation of the Imperial Educational Society for Noble Girls, which had been in the works since 1763.

The commonly-held idea that Catherine's institution for educating girls was a carbon copy of Saint-Cyr was belied from the very beginning by the fact that she sought advice from other quarters before finalizing her project. In 1763, representatives of the imperial court were sent to Vienna, Copenhagen, The Hague, Berlin, Stockholm, Hamburg, and Regensburg to glean information about schools for girls in those areas. Reports came to Catherine from D. M. Golitsyn, V. S. Dolgoruky, the Barons J. A. Korff and I. A. Ostermann, each of whom had examined female training programmes in Europe. None seemed to have interested Catherine very much.[13]

The Russian institution was a permanent one which catered to many more pupils than Saint-Cyr. It had a serious academic library and curriculum, and it followed very closely Betskoi's dictum about isolating girls from their family setting, if not from the grand society of St. Petersburg. Girls entered Catherine's school, which was located at the Voskresensky or Smolny monastery, at an earlier age than they would have at Saint-Cyr, and they remained there for at least twelve years. Catherine was also more concerned with females of the lower ranks of society than Mme. de Maintenon had been. Even Voltaire recognized in 1772 that Smolny was "more than Saint-Cyr," a conviction later repeated by Diderot. The empress replied to Voltaire that her intention was not to create "prudes or coquettes, but pleasant and capable women able to raise their own children and to manage a household."[14] In this instance she was taking exception to his remark that the school might produce amazons.

A short monograph by Nina Nikolaevna Raspopova, prepared in 1864 to celebrate the centennial of Smolny's founding, lists in an appendix those sections of the original regulations for Saint-Cyr and

Smolny which coincide. In structure, they were undoubtedly alike. Saint-Cyr provided for 250 girls whose parents could prove their status as nobles; and that they were poor. The girls had to be healthy, and they progressed in classes of three year duration; each class was identified by a colour. Their course of study was reasonably demanding for that time, but the Russian girls had a decidedly more challenging curriculum:

Saint-Cyr	Smolny
1st Class: reading, writing, counting, basic grammar, catechism and Biblical history.	Basic laws and catechism; elementary reading, writing, mathematics and morality; Russian and foreign languages; Music, sewing, knitting.
2nd Class: same as above, with music and basic history added; geography and mythology.	Same as above, geography, history and some economics.
3rd Class: Basic rules of French grammar; music, religion, design, and dance.	Same as above, grammatical science, historical and morality studies, architecture and heraldry.
4th Class: advanced French grammar, music, religion; above all, their morality was to be perfected.	Law, rules of education, ethics, science, art, household economy.

Saint-Cyr was staffed and operated by nuns and became a monastery in the traditional sense of the word by the early eighteenth century. Smolny was a secular organization in which monks taught only reading and religion, and their numbers never exceeded fourteen. It was structured to accommodate two hundred pupils, to be admitted in blocs of fifty every three years.[15] The first group of fifty were to be girls aged five to six, and their course of study was to be in four stages over a twelve year period. Parents had to agree not to request their daughter's release during that time, assure that they were of good health, and provide some evidence that they were of noble birth. The curriculum of 1764 was preceded by a charge that pride of place be given to religion, followed by the "secular virtues," which encompassed such traits as "courtesy, meekness, temperance, consistency in moral conduct, cleanliness, . . . and modesty." Class supervisors were asked to pay particular attention to the matter of cleanliness and physical education, and to make sure that the young ladies were silent in church. All classes had to adhere to a strict regimen of physical exercise, which amounted mainly to long walks daily, for which special hallways were constructed to serve in case of inclement weather.

The academic programme, as we have seen, was a wide one. But girls were to be taught in a relaxed atmosphere, and play and amusement were encouraged. Catherine was serious about wanting her graduates to be more than the homebound girls desired by Maintenon and Fénelon. Smolny students were expected to learn much more, including sciences. But when Diderot recommended in 1773 that human anatomy be added to the curriculum so that the girls would not be frightened of, or ignorant about marriage, Catherine was affronted and emphatically rejected the idea. Household and general economy were stressed in the third and fourth classes, and arithmetic was to be taught in such a way that the girls would have at hand "those facts which will lead to good order in the household economy." In short, as Catherine wrote another time to Voltaire, the school would produce "wives suitable for our Lords."[16]

In their final years, the young women were expected to take part in the management of the kitchen of the school and to assist in teaching the younger girls. Kept busy almost all the time, for Catherine believed that "idleness is the source of all evil," they also performed, before select audiences, their own plays and those of Molière, Racine, and other well-known European dramatists. Among the royal spectators at these performances were King Gustav III of Sweden (1777) who sent them his portrait, Prince Henry of Prussia (1770), Grand Duke Paul and such foreign visitors as Diderot (1773), Grimm (1777), John Howard (1781), Lord Cathcart (1768), Wiliam Coxe (1773), Nathaniel Wraxall (1774), Lady Craven (1785), and the brother of the Crimean Khan (1772). No such "frivolities" would have been allowed at Saint-Cyr.[17]

A four-man supervisory Board, made up of members from the Imperial Senate or other highly ranked state officials, was assigned to the school and undertook interviews of prospective pupils and their parents. Over the remainder of the century the Board had on it a variety of capable people, with Betskoi its single permanent member until the late 1780s. A headmistress was given "full powers" to manage the affairs of the school, and she was to oversee the work of the teachers and of the supervisors whose job it was to guide the girls in their everyday activities. The top positions in the school were filled by Catherine with care, for she fully intended that its graduates were going to be tempering forces in society. They were to provide the Russian community with a stable moral base capable of countering the ravishes inflicted upon it by the "vulgar gentry" to which she referred in her diary.

The first Headmistress was Princess Anna Dolgorukova (1719–1778), and the Governess was Madame Sofia de la Font (1717–1797), who replaced the haughty and unpopular Dolgorukova in 1766 and handled both positions almost by herself for the next thirty years. De la Font attended most Board meetings during that time, even though the first years were somewhat awkward because Dolgorukova's uncle was a member. Catherine worked closely with her and so did Betskoi, who had been responsible for her selection. According to contemporary witnesses, de la Font seems to have fit very well the criteria set by the empress in a letter to Bielcke, that is, that Dolgorukova's replacement be "neither young, nor Catholic . . . nor titled, without obligations, independent. . . ," have good morals, be of sweet temperament, love to teach, and not to be haughty.[18]

Advertisements for places in the school were sent around the empire in 1764, but failed to attract much attention, so the Board eased its regulations about age and even waived its demands for official noble accreditation and birth certificates. In some cases such documentation, particularly birth certification, was simply non-existent anyway. Only sixteen girls and their parents showed up at the first interview so that it was not until a year later that a full complement of fifty young girls was ready to begin the course of study. And several of those were supported financially by Catherine and Betskoi. A sum of money was banked for each girl, either by their parents or from subscriptions raised by Betskoi, so that they would have an income when they finished their long years of training. Two years later, Betskoi wrote Catherine that he was still not very optimistic about the number of upper nobility who would ask that their daughters be accepted in the school. The first enrollment of 1764–1765 consisted almost entirely of girls from the capital region, daughters of members of the royal guard or court officials. The next two recruitments included many orphans or at least fatherless girls, fourteen in the 1767 group, twenty-one in that of 1770. Only with the fourth induction of new pupils in 1773 was there a smattering of girls from the higher provincial nobility, and the percentage of orphans declined.[19] Over the course of time recruitment from upper nobility became less and less a problem.

In January, 1765, Betskoi organized a complementary school for girls of the bourgeois rank, "for the welfare of society no less demands that all members of the female sex be educated to good morals and to the particular behaviour which suits their rank and skills."[20] They too were divided into four classes, of sixty each, so that final enrollment would be 240 girls. Criteria for admission to this branch of Smolny were more confusing than those for the nobility, whose facilities they shared, but easier to fulfill. The programme of study for bourgeois girls, which was similar to that of their noble counterparts but more oriented towards training good wives and governesses, was less demanding academically.

Catherine took a direct hand in finding recruits for the new section of Smolny, often sending there orphans and daughters of pensioned soldiers or meritorious servants, without much regard to age or previous education. Furthermore, she and Betskoi financed a great many of these girls from their own funds, and Betskoi and several of his friends opened up their own homes to girls for whom there was no space in the school. Young ladies from the noble and bourgeois classes mingled freely at Smolny and there appears to have been very little rank consciousness among its pupils. However, the law of 1764 which formally established the school did make it clear that noble girls were not to be left alone with servants. For whatever reason, this stipulation was not included in the subsequent legislation for the bourgeois division. It is also true that most of the recollections and letters extant from Smolny graduates are the creations of girls who attended the institution during its first decade, and at that time there were few daughters of upper nobility present, so the actual distinction among the girls was less striking than it was later on. The Englishman, William Coxe, reported in 1773 that he saw the senior girls waiting on one-hundred poor women in the hall. Each woman was given a coin and a few yards of linen. "This ceremony," he wrote, "was instituted to inculcate in their tender minds an attention to the poor and a readiness to relieve human distress."[21]

It wasn't until 1767 that the final programme for the Smolny School was worked out, and in that year Catherine issued an ukaz which altered somewhat the direction of Betskoi's original scheme. The rules of 1767 commanded teachers and supervisors to pay more attention to their charges' health, morality, and virtue than to their academic achievement. To the Headmistress was assigned the key role in guiding the girls in manners, decorum, and proper conduct in society.[22] De la Font was given carte blanche in matters of education and behaviour.

Memoirs and letters prepared by former pupils suggest that she served as a real focal point for a feeling of comraderie which developed among girls of all ranks at the school. But the onus on her was very heavy, for she was long unable to find a capable assistant. Nor could she locate a competent teaching staff, so that the number of teachers varied between seven and twelve until 1780. Altogether there were generally about twenty-four instructors, a total which included monks to teach reading, two dance masters, two drawing masters, and four teachers of music. The first Russian-language teacher was not appointed until 1772 and remained the only one for several years.[23]

Betskoi was constantly in attendance at the school, and the girls learned to trust him and count on him for support. He kept Catherine aware of events there and arranged for her participation in Smolny's first graduation, in 1776, which was a major social event for the capital city, with expositions, awards, and ceremony. Some of the graduates were taken directly into service at court, some stayed on at the school because their parents were too poor to take them at home, and others went home to arranged marriages or to positions as nannies. Each girl received a stipend of between fifty and one-hundred roubles, and the Board promised to keep a fatherly eye on their subsequent careers. This remained the general pattern until the mid-1780s. Katherine Anthony's comment to the effect that the girls "emerged . . . entirely penniless and homeless," is simply not founded in fact. The minutes of Board meetings, which have been thoroughly examined by Cherepnin and E. Likhacheva, show the details of attempts by its members to care for the future of their students. In 1776 the empress granted one hundred thousand roubles to the school specifically for that purpose.[24]

Betskoi's concern for the success of the school for girls was noted by the English ambassador to Russia, Lord Cathcart. After paying a visit to Smolny in 1768, he wrote to his superior in London that, "I saw their dormitories and and was present at their supper; nothing can surpass the care or success of Mr. De Betskoi and the ladies employed in this seminary which is but in its infancy. . . ."[25] Catherine was pleased with the progress of Smolny while the first group of girls was still in school, and in her letter to Voltaire of January, 1772, she spoke of their "astonishing progress."[26] She kept in touch with some of the girls of that first group, among them A. P. Levshina, E. I. Nelidova, and Glavira Alymova, each of whom graduated in 1776 and received positions at court.[27] Alymova's short diary illustrates the genuinely high esteem in which the girls held Catherine, Betskoi, and de la Font. She spoke of her own stay at Smolny as one of "Delightful memories! Happy times!"; and Diderot wrote to his daughter that Catherine, "has founded a magnificent establishment for girls . . . these children, who are no higher than cabbages . . . gather around her, embrace her, put their arms around her neck and head. . . . The sovereign of a huge empire? That was not considered either by her or by them."[28] Catherine was still defending the girls in 1778 when she wrote tartly to Grimm that he was being "impolite" and unfair in criticising their coiffure and dress. Nurturing their habits and morals were of greater import, she said.[29]

Catherine's early optimism notwithstanding, by the 1780s there was increasing evidence that she was not satisfied with the academic achievements of girls in either of the Smolny schools. Betskoi, as the chief official of both schools was not in a position to oversee the actual academic programmes of his charges. In fact, his main association with most of his educational institutions came in frequent dinners at his home with Madame de la Font, the Director of the Cadet Corps, Count A. G. Bobrinsky, and the Ribas family, who lived at Betskoi's home.[30] Mr. Ribas was a supervisor in the Cadet Corps, Mrs. Ribas was a teacher at Smolny. Even Catherine was aware of Betskoi's weakness in matters of discipline, and already in 1773 she had written to one of the senior girls not to be afraid of him, for "at his age . . . he usually makes more noise than work. Speak to him and he will agree to anything.[31] His kindness was certainly appreciated by Alymova, who said of him: "This astonishing man, this honourable man earned our respect as a father and defender . . . I loved Ivan Ivanovich with childlike devotion." The childlike element may not have been reciprocated by Betskoi who later asked Alymova, who was much younger than his own daughter, to marry him. In 1782, Betskoi took it upon himself to allow one girl to return home to live with her recently widowed mother, thereby acting out of compassion against what he assumed to be Catherine's wishes. His reputation as fatherly overseer appeared in I. M. Dolgorukov's memoirs, where Betskoi was referred to as "an honourable old man, good, respected as the protector of the school in which my Evgenii was educated. . . ."[32]

The arrival of Iankovich in Russia in 1782 was as much a turning point for Smolny as it was for all other sectors of Catherine's faltering school system. When members of the Commission for the Establishment of Public Schools were asked to examine existing institutions to see if they were serving the purposes for which they had been founded,

Smolny was not excepted. Early in 1783, Iankovich presented to Zavadovsky a detailed report on its failings, with recommendations for its improvement. He noted that languages, and especially the Russian one, were being taught very badly, and that courses were offered by French-language instructors to pupils who did not have enough French to comprehend the lessons. The report differs strikingly from the impression gained in 1773 by William Coxe, who wrote later about the "astonishing purity" of the French language used by the girls. However, he had seen only their public performances.[33] Since almost all the teachers were foreigners and not able to speak Russian, the girls were not proficient in their own tongue either. According to Iankovich, some of the bourgeois girls even had difficulty in writing their own names. There was a sad lack of textbooks in the schools, particularly Russian ones, and there was no ordered academic progression from one class to another. Girls advanced simply according to age. Nor was there sufficient discipline to prevent lateness and absenteeism. Finally, the report stated that far too much time was spent in the school on drama. All in all, there could hardly have been a harsher criticism of Betskoi's management. In its conclusion, the Commission said of Smolny:

> Since the intent and the end of education for girls . . . is to make them good housekeepers, true wives and trustworthy mothers, then it is necessary to make for them such books which, on reading under the close guidance of teachers, can instruct them, (A) in the rules of behaviour towards their husbands, (B) how to act in regards to their children: (1) in times of pregnancy, (2) breast feeding, (3) when to begin teaching their children in youth, (4) how to select their teachers. (C) Rules of housekeeping: (1) the general rules of housekeeping as they are found in the book, *On the Duties of Man and Citizen,* (2) housekeeping in towns, in noble houses, (3) knowledge of all those things which belong to the home, (4) rural housekeeping, (5) garden tending, (6) handling income and expenditures.[34]

The Commission's solution was in theory reasonably simple: all literary subjects to be taught in Russian, more Russian teachers to be hired, textbooks to be prepared, and Iankovich's teaching methods to be adopted. It also suggested that the school direct more of its efforts than before towards inculcating in its charges the ability to be capable wives and mothers, and that moral training remain its essential task. Smolny was now to have seventeen teachers and twenty-two supervisors, whose main duties were to be instructors in the "female skills."

Apparently, the new scheme was not well-received at Smolny, or so Catherine wrote Grimm.[35]

Matfei Pakhomov, whose wife had been the first Russian teacher in the school, became its initial inspector of classes and made weekly reports to the Commission. That meant, among other things, that Betskoi and Smolny's own Board would soon lose control of the school. Betskoi recognized this likelihood but his pleas to have it avoided were ignored by Catherine. Pakhomov's reports included information on the number of girls in each class and absences because of sickness. They also gave an account of the academic progress of each class during that week, even to listing chapters covered in textbooks.[36] Some girls were demoted from the fourth class to the third. So pleased was Catherine with the reshaping of Smolny and with the results of a public examination in March, 1784, that she awarded to Iankovich an Order of St. Vladimir, fourth class. The empress also presented M. E. Golovin, teacher of physics, with a gold snuff-box for his efforts and distributed one thousand roubles among the rest of the teachers.

V. N. Liadov may have been right when he wrote in 1864 that Iankovich's proposed reforms proved to be of little significance, for the teaching remained of poor quality until the end of the century.[37] But there were some clear-cut changes. The new programme of study for Smolny was a simplified version of its original one and resembled that which was soon to be announced for the national public school system. The primary group studied the short catechism, reading and writing in Russian, French, and German. In the second class, biblical history, geography, mythology, arithmetic, and drawing were added. Two new additions came for the third class: physics and natural history, and two more for the fourth section: architecture and geometry. Smolny's traditional subjects — needlework, domestic economy, music, and dance — were given apart from regular class hours. Heraldry, a field of study assigned to noble girls in 1764, seems to have been discarded in 1783. The bourgeois division was assigned the same subjects, except for architecture and geometry in their fourth stage, and its pupils concentrated more on the Russian language.

The Commission report had recommended as compulsory reading in the school, *On the Duties of Man and Citizen,* which had little to say in it about women. It did point out that the term "true son of the fatherland" was a title of honour that could apply equally well "to people of both sexes."[38] The single most consistent element of the book, however, was its paternalistic view of society, so that when the family was described in it, women were given a role almost as subservient as that expressed in the *Domostroi.*

In order that Smolny's new teachers could carry out the task assigned to them by the Commission, another text was written especially for young ladies. *The Pocket, or Memory Book for Young Girls, Containing Rules for the Fair Sex,* was prepared and printed in Moscow, with an introduction by A. A. Barsov. In it were descriptions of the duties of wives and mothers, lessons on hygiene for growing children, ways to educate youngsters and to select proper instructors for them, information about housekeeping and diet, especially in the homes of nobility and guards officers, rules of gardening, and so on. Readers were urged to keep in good health "or offend God," to refrain from drunkenness, and to act always as a tempering and moralizing catalyst in society.[39] "True bliss exists in a calm soul and in performing our duties," was a dictum taken directly from *On the Duties,* but a special admonition was deemed necessary. "Honourable women must have the same virtues that men do: friendships, proper souls, and equally observe their duties."[40]

That women were considered particularly susceptible to the evil temptations which the author presumed to be all around them was demonstrated in the advice: "Shame is such a feeling from which it is possible to gain great benefit. It directs us from evil and is the truest preserver of feminine honour." Finally, girls were warned to ignore the passions of love, the "complaints of our hearts," and to memorize the basic "prudence and frugality of domestic science."[41] The old 1717 text, *Mirror of Integrity for Youth,* had been assigned reading at Smolny since 1764, but the *Memory Book* replaced it.

This book was fully in line with Fénelon's thinking. An article in the supplement to the *Moscow Gazette* of 1784 carried a similar message. The author of "Instructions from a Father to his Daughter," claimed to recognize women as equal in ability to men, but assigned to them the role of guardian of human morality: "Girls who cease blushing lose their most innocent charm. Shyness is evidence of extreme sensibility, which in our own sex is a sign of weakness . . . but in you it engenders charm."[42] By the 1780s, then, even though the traditional resistance to the idea that girls should be educated had been broken down considerably, the official version of a woman's role in society appeared to have come full circle. Except for the matter of wife-beating, the attitude towards women expressed in this article and in the *Memory Book* was not too far removed from that in *Domostroi* and was far indeed from the Agrippa book published by Dashkova.

Needless to say, such moralizing was hardly unique for the 1780s, but its import for Russian education lies in the fact that it marked the end of Betskoi's dream of providing equal instruction, with an academic bias, for boys and girls. In fact, *Memory Book* opened with remarks by Barsov to the effect that girls need not trouble themselves with courses other than languages, diction, art, history and geography, and a study of the morals and customs of their own people. The Commission was able to fill the complement of teachers needed at Smolny partly by taking them from existing schools. Within a few years, however, Iankovich's teachers' seminary produced a group of well-trained young Russians, many of whom had had previous experience at the University of Moscow, so that the academic level of the school showed some improvement. That is not to say that suddenly the institution began to graduate bona fide female scholars, for inertia operated to keep many of the academic recommendations on paper only. The only part of the institution that did not change at all was the place of de la Font in it, and she was finally given a governess to assist her in 1786. However, the balance between noble and bourgeois girls at Smolny went through a major transformation. By 1791, the bourgeois section had been so inundated by girls of noble standing for whom there was no room in the nobility section that by the end of Catherine's reign there were 368 noble girls in attendance and only 135 of the lower order. The practice after 1791 was to transfer bourgeois pupils to the Foundling Home in St. Petersburg when their place at Smolny was requested for a girl of noble birth.[43] This practice would have met with the disapproval of Betskoi, but he had stopped attending Board meetings in 1789.

This new trend illustrated an important change in the attitude of Russia's nobility towards the school. In its first years, Smolny had been regarded by noblemen with very little enthusiasm. The wealthy could find suitable tutors, some had not wanted to expose their daughters to foreign influences or lose them from their own homes for such a long period of time, and not a few in the 1760s still considered education a frivolous occupation for females. Prince M. M. Shcherbatov spoke for many in the 1780s when he denigrated in private the claim of the school to have produced accomplished young ladies. He insisted that Catherine ignored Smolny after founding it,[44] a statement that has often been quoted but is, perhaps, the least accurate of contemporary generalizations about the institution. While Comte de Ségur's observations cannot be taken in themselves as refutation of Shcherbatov, his astonishment at the number of well-read women in St. Petersburg when he arrived as French ambassador in 1785 is worth noting. Claiming that it was the female sex which had led the way in bringing enlightenment to Russia, Ségur wrote: "One sees already a large number of elegant ladies, young girls remarkable for their graces, speaking equally well seven or eight languages, playing many instruments and familiar with the most celebrated poets and novelists of France, Italy, and England."[45] Ségur was writing of the situation in the capital city, for there is no doubt that the level of education among provincial ladies was still low. It was provincial society that was caricatured by Fonvizin and Kniazhnin. At any rate, there had been considerable progress since the days described by Dashkova.

The fanfare which accompanied public ceremonies at Smolny, the obvious pride which Catherine had in it, the attention given it by Grand Duke Paul, and the fact that several girls were taken directly into court service after each graduation made the school increasingly fashionable. The fact that many Russians worried about an apparent decline in the morality of upper society, especially in the capital city, gave impetus to the idea that such schools would protect their daughters from evil "Voltairean" influences. Educators continued to support it for reasons like those expressed by V. I. Lukin in 1766 when he wrote that Smolny allowed girls to "acquire learning, virtue, and morality," and thereby escape the "crudity" of their predecessors. Novikov also praised the school for its part in civilizing young ladies.[46] Prominent noblemen, like V. V. Vigel' and the writer and poet Prince I. M. Dolgorukov, spoke highly of the erudition and humanity displayed by women of their acquaintance who had attended the school.

Dolgorukov was married to two graduates of Smolny and wrote glowingly of them in his recollections. He was friendly with many of their classmates and spoke well of their human and intellectual qualities too. But his definition of an educated woman must be qualified by his description of Katerina Nikolaevna Apochinina, who became the wife of Senator Naryshkin: "She spoke French well, knew music, sang pleasantly, danced with grace, and played roles in the theatre well. In a word, this girl was completely prepared for the world. . . ."[47]

More important, however, was the fact that after 1776 alumnae of the school acted as an informal lobby on its behalf. Levshina became the Baroness Cherkasskaia and a member of the school's Board; Nelidova was long a fixture at court and a very close friend of Paul's. In 1796 she retired to live permanently at Smolny, and Dolgorukov said of her that she was able to intervene with Paul often to save unfortunate victims of his wrath. Two of the Pleshcheev family, who were friends of Karamzin, attended the school. One of the famous Naryshkin family, and the wife of the writer V. V. Kapnist were also

Smolny pupils. Generalissimo A. V. Suvorov sent his daughter there in 1779. Alexander Radishchev's two sisters-in-law were graduates and one of them, Elizabeth Rubanovskaia, lived with him in Siberian exile throughout the 1790s, his first wife having died. Radishchev's descriptions of Elizabeth parallel Dolgorukov's accounts of his second wife and fit in very well with the goodness and light generalizations made by Alymova. Even two of Shcherbatov's daughters completed their education at Smolny.[48]

According to Alymova, who married the very well-educated A. A. Rjewski, "almost all the girls had good morals, and very few were bad, and those rare instances of bad traits were the consequences of laziness, disobedience or stubborness. We had no idea about vices. Everyone was very discreet in spite of the full freedom in which we were educated." She also wrote that all the girls whom she knew at Smolny had excellent character, made "beautiful marriages," and passed on good habits to their own children and to their husbands.[49] If accurate, Catherine and Betskoi's dreams were more than fulfilled, but Dolgorukov mentioned that there were some tragic marriages, one in particular where a friend of his wife was wedded to a merchant of no education and suffered terribly for it. Alymova had had a very unhappy early childhood and was sent to the school by a mother whom she believed did not want her, so the teachers and especially de la Font and Betskoi were her only family. She can hardly be considered an objective witness, but her enthusiasm is striking. At any rate, the fact that by 1796 almost nine hundred girls had graduated from Smolny suggests that the original purpose of the school had at least been partially achieved.[50]

Of all Catherine's institutions, Smolny was the one which demonstrated the greatest resilience, for it continued to flourish throughout the nineteenth century. In 1797, the newly crowned Paul I put the school in the charge of his wife, Maria Fedorovna. De la Font retired and was replaced by a former pupil, Elizabeth Palmenbach (née Baroness Cherkasova), who had graduated from Smolny in 1779 and had been employed there since 1790. The high regard in which de la Font was held by everyone can be illustrated by the fact that of all of Catherine's close associates, she was one of the few whom Paul looked upon favourably. He awarded her an Honour of St. Catherine, 2nd Class, and her retirement was accompanied by a major public ceremony.[51] The new empress became involved in a number of educational enterprises, which she was to maintain after Paul's assassination, and she took special care to see that Smolny was administered according to her dictates. Palmenbach was required to report to her on a weekly basis, and the school curriculum was redirected towards making "good Christians" of its students. Maria took a direct hand in the affairs of the school, placed students in it without much regard to the entrance regulations of the institution, and in her letters to the new headmistress constantly harped upon the need for religious and moral training.[52] Fedorovna brought to Smolny a convent spirit which Catherine had tried to avoid and she put a stop to most of the social affairs which had characterized the school during the 1770s and 1780s. She also changed the class structure of the school, formalizing the predominance of nobility in it. Her hope was to limit enrollment to four hundred, three hundred from nobility and one hundred from the middle class. Paul prevented that and raised the number of bourgeois girls to be recruited to two hundred of a total of five hundred. Forty additional places were left open for pensioners.

Maria did not wish to prevent access to education for girls of non-noble distinction, rather she believed that mixing the classes was harmful to both. Among other things, their academic programmes were different, and so were their future prospects, and she did not wish to see resentment or confusion arise. Eventually she solved the dilemma, to her own satisfaction at least, by opening a separate school for girls from the bourgeoisie in 1797, the Mariansky Institute, and another for noble girls, the St. Catherine's school. Two similar institutions were established in Moscow shortly thereafter. Smolny remained intact, although the bourgeois section was given its own name, the Alexandrov school.[53]

There had already been some expansion of facilities for girls. As Smolny gradually became a preserve of the upper nobility, Catherine had founded a second school for girls in St. Petersburg in 1789. The Mariansky Institute, designed for orphans as well as for regular pupils from the bourgeoisie, included medical facilities along the lines of the Foundling Homes sponsored by Betskoi in the 1760s. In fact, Betskoi's two main orphanages in the capital city and in Moscow still provided education services for both sexes in the 1790s. They served a large number of girls who were given training in skills necessary to make them proficient domestic servants, midwives, nannies, and wives of soldiers.[54] So there had been quite an increase of educational opportunity for girls.

The new empress broke with Betskoi's tradition in another matter as well by having students enter the school at a later age, nobles at eight or nine, bourgeois girls at eleven or twelve. She was not so convinced as he had been that family life was bad for children in Russia. Indeed, she believed that it was very detrimental to the young girls not to have lived with their families long enough to have gained the sense of security and being loved that she assumed only real parents could provide.

There were other agencies for educating women in Catherinian Russia. In general, the *pensions* were dominated by boys, but the report on them made to Catherine in 1785 showed that in the eleven *pensions* of the Moscow region, there were 188 male students and 48 females.[55] A decade before that report, Catherine had already called for elementary schools in Russia's towns and settlements which would admit girls as well as boys.[56] As we have seen, the educative dimension of the provincial project was generally unsuccessful, but it did lead to the opening of a few scattered schools. Information compiled in 1849 by A. S. Voronov shows that forty of the 486 pupils attending church schools of St. Petersburg in 1781 were girls.[57] The Lutheran school which had been founded in that city in 1762 had planned for girls from the beginning, and by 1782 it conducted five classes for boys and three for girls. The main difference between their syllabuses lay in the fact that the girls' sections received no instruction in the sciences. Ten teachers were available for teaching boys, four of them in the science fields, and four were given over to the female division of the school.[58] The Major school begun in 1789 at Kiev started with 58 boys and 18 girls, but within a week grew to 99 boys and 35 girls. A year later the school's enrollment of 210 included 68 girls and that ratio remained more or less the case throughout the nineties.[59] However, the high number of girls in attendance at Kiev was not matched in the other Major schools.

The Major and Minor schools initiated in all the provinces in 1786 were intended as much for girls as they were for boys. It seems, however, that few fathers took advantage of the opportunity to have their daughters educated along with their sons, and some of the public schools had no girls in attendance.[60] Over the entire period from 1782, when the Commission sponsored a few experimental schools in the St. Petersburg district, until Catherine's death, some 176,000 youngsters passed through the imperial public schools. Of those, about 12,600, or almost eight percent were girls. In 1800, the ratio had risen to slightly below ten percent, that is, there were 1,787 girls included in a total enrollment of a little more than eighteen thousand [see Table B].[61] Thus, although female participation in Catherine's public school system was not very substantial, the traditional assumption that there were no educational opportunities for girls in eighteenth-century Russia is not well founded in fact.

One sign that there was a marked change in the presumptions held by men about women as thinkers was the increasing number of printed works that appeared during the final decades of the century with the expressed purpose of directing the feminine mind. One such was *Zhenskaia filosofiia* (*Woman's Philosophy,* 1793) which emphasized the important role that women should be expected to play in keeping the family functioning smoothly. Insisting that women had more sensitive hearts than men, its author urged them to continue to educate themselves even after their school years. He warned women to seek husbands who would be concerned with the well-being of the family as a mutually co-operative unit.

Ivan Pnin's *St. Petersburg Journal* carried an article in 1798 in which he urged that women be granted the same academic opportunities as men, but it was Nicholas Karamzin who best summed up the contemporary rationale for educating women. In 1802, he printed a long eulogy to Catherine which he quite clearly intended as a lesson in rulership for Alexander I. Education is a two-fold procedure, Karamzin wrote, for it involves the moral education of men and the political education of citizens. He went on to single out the Imperial Educational Society for Noble Girls for special attention, and in doing so, he expressed the attitude which had its roots in the early writing of Prokopovich, Saltykov, and Tatishchev: "The Monarch, believing that the good conduct of the delicate sex within the upper class has a strong influence on the good conduct of the state, founded . . . [Smolny] . . . in order to educate women. Morality is its main object; but their minds are enriched by all knowledge, all ideas are necessary for a proper existence, and to make them a delight to their community, a treasure for their husbands, and primary instructors to their children."[63]

Conclusion

The myriad of education projects initiated in Russia between the reigns of Peter I and Alexander I were all influenced by West European pedagogical thought and by Russian circumstances. Just as European educators built schools to produce officers, gentlemen, and loyal citizens, so did Russian ones. But there were certain specifically Russian conditions which prevented any of the Russian plans from becoming systematic and effective. Indeed, none of the eighteenth-century Russian education enterprises ever produced enough graduates to fulfill the other demand made upon schools by West European governments, that is, that they provide the professional expertise essential to the growth of modern state systems.

One of the difficulties faced by those who called for an encompassing plan for instructing Russia's youth was the consistent reluctance on the part of Orthodox leaders to participate in expanding learning facilities. Although a number of individual churchmen saw a need for instruction to defend their faith against the inroads of other forms of Christianity, Orthodoxy did not have an aggressive teaching order to compare with the Jesuits. Even when such enlightened figures as Prokopovich and Platon supported schemes for more schooling, the intransigence of the huge church hierarchy and the rigidity of the clerical caste meant that they could accomplish very little by themselves. The lower order of clergymen were often barely literate, and so not suited to act as teachers. Another difficulty stemmed from the fact that for much of the century Russia was ruled by women, which was an indirect cause of certain inconsistencies in policy-making. While favouritism was common to other nations, the otherwise typical self-serving lobbying and court intrigues at St. Petersburg were more intense than elsewhere because much of it was carried on between professional bureaucrats and courtiers who had to take into account the power of their rulers' lovers. The competition between foreign diplomats was intensified as well insofar as Russian foreign policy had fewer fixed objectives than that of other European states. The rotation of factions in and out of royal favour had its impact on all long-range decision-making, and education suffered along with other dimensions of the administration that needed constant attention.

A pressing problem for schools, however, was the lack of a Russian tradition of institutionalized education. It took a long time to prepare teachers and to build institutions which had a resilience of their own, and it was not until the nineteenth century that Russia had an actual ministry whose purpose it was to deal with education. In fairness, one could refer to Betskoi as a minister of education, but he did not have an administrative staff to keep the affairs of his schools in order. Indeed, he preferred to keep schools out of the hands of government as long as it was possible. At all times too the immediate desires of the monarch overshadowed the fundamental need of the state for a more knowledgeable population.

Peter the Great had demanded above all professional bureaucrats and officers from his schools, and he so desperately wanted his new capital to seem Western that he called for an Academy of scholars without providing a Russian feeder system for it. But Peter was also pragmatic enough (or perhaps iconoclastic in the face of Muscovite tradition) to see the advantages in having children from all ranks learn at least to read, to write and to do simple calculations. He was not able to accomplish that ideal, and it found little favour with his successors. Anna's officialdom of Baltic German military people looked mainly to Cadet academies and garrison schools, and Elizabeth's measures were of a very ad hoc nature. Nevertheless, she provided Russia with the University of Moscow which proved of inestimable value to the evolution of educational thought and practice during the reigns of her successors.

Catherine's efforts on behalf of education were consistent and important. She more than any other monarch was determined at first to use modern pedagogical theory as the basis of a systematic programme of instruction for her subjects. But she was unwaveringly autocratic and whenever a conflict of interest arose, she catered to the factions on whom she assumed her power to depend. The Pugachev rebellion and revolutions in America and France were all important factors in her turn to a more rigidly controlled school administration than that advocated by most of the West Europeans whom she often quoted. However, the overwhelming presence in Russian intellectual life of the tenets of the German *Aufklärung*, the neo-classicist emphasis upon civic responsibilities, and the tradition of absolutism made the likelihood of anything else extremely remote anyway. In short, there were very few teachers or administrators in Russia who were able or willing to put into practice Betskoi's preaching about individualism in schools. His own failure to attend to details and perhaps his age doomed most of his projects to oblivion or to alteration. Furthermore, Betskoi's preference for a relaxed, literary, and aristocratic type of education instead of practical vocational training meant that the empire was to remain short of qualified personnel in its bureaucracy. Even the more suitable public school system which Catherine adopted wholesale from Austria in the 1780s was soon distorted by Russian circumstances because she ignored those operating principles which made Joseph II's schools work.

A full century after Peter I began to employ education as a means for creating useful subjects, Alexander I embarked on a similar undertaking. More inclined than Peter had been to a broad, general enlightenment, but with the same ends in mind, Alexander prefaced a decree of January, 1802, with the statement, "public instruction in the Russian Empire is a special function of the state." As Alexander put it, each of his subjects had to be given a moral education which conformed to the obligations peculiar to his or her station in life.[1] Thus the evolution of state control over its subjects' moral instruction was complete, and the Orthodox Church had lost another of its traditional responsibilities.

Alexander was certainly not alone in this sentiment. The ideological overtones of the French Revolution, which saw the first real participation of public opinion in international affairs, prompted governments everywhere in continental Europe to direct as much as possible the means by which their citizens formed their attitudes. The process of state control over education had begun long before the Revolution, and in Austria, the model for Russia, von Sonnenfels had set as the specific goal of education the task of preparing youth for their place in society as loyal, useful citizens. Francis I, who ruled Austria from 1792 to 1835, went even further than Joseph II had in advocating curriculums designed to mold a complete citizenry, happy with their monarchy and imbued with acceptable religious and moral notions.[2] The clash of ideas in the 1790s prompted other states to sponsor the expansion and systemizing of their educational programmes. But in Russia the old fear of new ideas was more influential than the reasoned pleas from those who saw enlightenment as a foil to revolution, rather than a cause of it. The Russian government remained more afraid of uncontrolled knowledge than it was of ignorance. Even Alexander's quite encompassing educational projects lasted no longer than those of Peter I. Enlightened trappings aside, the purpose of Alexander's school system was to sustain the principles of autocracy and the social status quo. Herein lay the future of education in Imperial Russia.

Alexander's first minister of public instruction was Zavadovsky. Many of his successors would have found Catherinian Russia too enlightened for their liking, and the most important spokesman for Russian conservatives and bureaucrats over the final two decades of the nineteenth century, Konstantin P. Pobedonostsev, represented the epitome of obscurantism in matters of education. Convinced that most people were not capable of absorbing or understanding much knowledge, Pobedonostsev believed that they should be guided in their actions by faith and not by classroom-derived logic. He advocated for most a rudimentary practical education learned from their fathers at home, and he claimed that primary education had as its main function the task of teaching fear of God, patriotism, and love for one's parents.

Reading, writing, arithmetic, and religion were the only necessary forms of learning, Pobedonostsev said, and went on to warn of the dangers to society posed by over-educated intellectuals who were prone to taking up with liberalism and atheism. Schools should produce a passive and strongly religious citizenry, whose males would be content with their lot in life, and whose females would stay at home where they belonged.[3] Pobedonostsev was the ruling force in Russia's cultural life a century and a half after Prokopovich, and a full century after Betskoi, and his views were shaped by quite different circumstances, but his attitude towards education was in many ways less progressive than theirs. While that does not at all mean that Catherinian Russia was a golden age for Russian educators, it does suggest that very little progress was made in imperial sentiments about education after her statute of 1786.

At any rate, it seems that for the highest born of the land, the situation changed very little after Catherine's time. In writing of her own youth, and trying to explain the events of 1917, the Grand Duchess Marie, niece of Alexander III, said with the bitterness of hindsight, "education in the eyes of my teachers was of little importance as compared with religion and moral instruction."[4]

Notes

Introduction

1. Cherniavsky, *Tsar and People: Studies in Russian Myths* (New York, 1969), 91–2.

2. On the subject of absolutism and the ongoing argument about it in the USSR today, see Thomas Esper, "Recent Soviet Views of Russian Absolutism," *Canadian/American Slavic Studies,* VI, no. 4 (1972), 26–30; A. Gerschenkron, "Soviet Marxism and Absolutism," *Slavic Review,* XXX, no. 4 (December, 1971), 853–69; Paul Dukes, "Russia and the Eighteenth-Century Revolution," *History,* 56, (1971), 371–86.

3. On this subject, see Rev. Georges Bissonette, "Peter the Great and the Church as an Educational Institution," in J. S. Curtiss (ed.), *Essays in Russian and Soviet History* (New York, 1965), 3–19.

4. The most recent study of a general nature on education in eighteenth century Russia is the Soviet publication, *Ocherki istorii shkoly i pedagogicheskoi mysli narodov SSSR: XVIII v. – pervaia polovina XIX v.* (ed.) M. F. Shabaeva (Moscow, 1973). The book has a useful bibliography of items in Russian on the theory and practice of education during the last two centuries.

5. Max J. Okenfuss, "Education in Russia during the First Half of the Eighteenth Century," Ph.D. dissertation (Harvard, 1970); George Epp, "The Educational Policies of Catherine II of Russia, 1762–1796," Ph.D. dissertation (University of Manitoba, 1976). There are chapters on education under Peter I and Catherine II in S. R. Tompkins, *The Russian Mind* (Norman, Okla., 1953), 29–52, 76–97, and in Paul Dukes, *Catherine the Great and the Russian Nobility* (Cambridge, 1967), 25–37, 189–217.

6. See G. L. Seidler, "The Reform of the Polish Schools System in the Era of Enlightenment," in James A. Leith (ed.), *Facets of Education in the Eighteenth Century,* Vol. CLXVII of *Studies on Voltaire and the Eighteenth Century* (Oxford, 1977), 337–58.

7. *Dokumenty i materialy po istorii Moskovskogo universiteta vtoroi poloviny XVIII veka,* I (Moscow, 1960), 236–7.

8. See T. E. Willey, "Kant and the German Theory of Education," in Leith, *Facets of Education in the Eighteenth Century,* 543–68. See also Annette Churton, *Kant on Education, A Translation of the Pädagogie* (Trubbner, 1899). In a very interesting recent article, Marc Raeff connects the development of state controlled education in Germany to that in Russia; see his "The Well-Ordered Police State and the Development of Modernity in Seventeenth and Eighteenth Century Europe: An Attempt at a Comparative Approach," *American Historical Review,* 80, no. 5 (December, 1975), 1221–43.

9. See Bruford, *Germany in the Eighteenth Century: The Social Background of the Literary Revival* (Cambridge, 1965), 243. For a general overview of education in the eighteenth century, see Leith, "Unity and Diversity in Education during the Eighteenth Century," in *Facets of Education*, 13–27.

10. Rollin, *Traité des études*, I (Paris, 1845), 9. See also II, 162.

11. See Leith, "The Hope for Moral Regeneration in French Educational Thought, 1750–1789," in P. Fritz, D. Williams (eds.), *City and Society in the 18th Century* (Toronto, 1973), 215–29. See also C. R. Bailey, "Attempts to Institute a 'System' of Secular Education in France, 1762–89," in Leith, *Facets of Education*, 105–24.

12. Locke, *Concerning Human Understanding*, Bk. II, ch. i (Chicago, 1952), 122; Bk. IV, ch. iii, 318; and Stanley E. Ballinger, "Ideals of Social Progress through Education in the French Enlightenment Period: Helvétius and Condorcet," *History of Education Journal*, X (1959), 88–99. See also J. H. Plumb, "The New World of Children in Eighteenth-Century England," *Past and Present*, LXVII (May, 1975).

13. See S. J. Curtiss, *History of Education in Great Britain* (London, 1965).

14. W.A.C. Stewart and W. P. McCann, *The Educational Innovators, 1750–1880* (London, 1970), 23.

15. J. W. Warner, "*Emile* in Eighteenth-Century England," *Publications of the Modern Language Association*, LIX (1944), 773–791.

16. Stewart and McCann, 188.

17. For the question of Habsburg school reforms, Iankovich, and the Serbs, see Philip J. Adler, "Habsburg School Reform among the Orthodox Minorities, 1770–1780," *Slavic Review*, XXXIII, no. 1 (March, 1974), 23–45, and E. V. Povarova, "O Russko-serbiaskikh kul'turnykh sviaziakh v XVIII v.," *Sovetskaia pedagogika*, XXX, no. 11 (1971), 105–13.

18. On von Sonnenfels and Austrian education, see Bärbel Becker-Cantarino, "Joseph von Sonnenfels and the Development of Secular Education in Eighteenth-Century Austria," in Leith, *Facets of Education*, 29–48.

19. Alexander Vucinich, *Science in Russian Culture* (London, 1963), 46, 49; P. P. Pekarsky, *Nauka i literatura pri Petre Velikom*, I (St. Petersburg, 1862), 5; Eugene Schuyler, *Peter the Great: Emperor of Russia*, I (New York, 1884), 267. For Peter's instructions to the scholars whom he sent abroad, see Pekarsky, I, 146.

20. Gladys Scott Thompson, *Catherine the Great and the Expansion of Russia* (London, 1947), 258–59. This writer has not seen a copy of the report on education in England commissioned by Catherine; nor did Thompson cite from it.

21. Nicholas Hans, "Russian Students at Leyden in the 18th Century," *Slavonic and East European Review*, XXXV, no. 85 (June, 1957), 551–61. For the whole question of Russian students in Europe during Peter I's reign, see Max J. Okenfuss, "Russian Students in Europe in the Age of Peter the Great," in J. G. Garrard (ed.), *The Eighteenth-Century in Russia* (Oxford, 1973), 131–48.

22. On Lomonosov at Marburg, see B. N. Menshutkin, *Russia's Lomonosov* (Princeton, 1952), 24–35, and *Zhizni i tvorchestva M. V. Lomonosova* (Moscow-Leningrad, 1961), 35–9, 40–6. Wolff was made an honourary member of the Russian Academy of Sciences.

178   CITIZENS FOR THE FATHERLAND

23. A. H. Brown, "S. E. Desnitsky, Adam Smith, and the *Nakaz* of Catherine II," *Oxford Slavonic Papers*, new series, VII (1974), 42–59.
24. See D. M. Lang, "Student Years in Leipzig," chapter two in his, *The First Russian Radical: Alexander Radishchev, 1749–1802*, (London, 1959), 29–59.
25. *Ibid.*, 53–4; A. McConnell, "Helvétius' Russian Pupils," *Journal of the History of Ideas*, XXIV, no. 3 (1963), 373–86; and Ballinger, in *History of Education Journal*, 88–89.
26. See Okenfuss, in *The Eighteenth Century in Russia*, 131–48, and G. R. Barratt, "Vasily Nikitin: A Note on an Eighteenth-Century Russian Oxonian," *Eighteenth-Century Studies*, VIII, no. 1 (Fall, 1974), 75–99. A much more thorough article is that by A. G. Cross, "Russian Students in Eighteenth-Century Oxford (1766–75)," *Journal of European Studies*, V, no. 2 (June, 1975), 91–110.

Chapter I: The Seventeenth Century

1. *Domostroi* (ed.) I. Glaznov, 2nd edition (St. Petersburg, 1902). There is a French-language version, *Le Domostroi*, translated by M. E. Duchesne (Paris, 1910). It can also be found in *Imperatorskoie obshchestvo istorii i drevnostei rossiiskikh*, II (April/June, 1821), (Moscow, 1881), 1–202. See also N. V. Vodovozov, *Istoriia drevnei russkoi literatury* (Moscow, 1966), 246–48; A. A. Kizevetter, "Istoricheskaia tendentsiia drevnerusskago Domostroia," *Istoricheskie ocherki* (Moscow, 1912), 3–46; V. O. Kliuchevsky, "Dva vospitaniia," *Russkaia mysl'*, XIV, no. 3 (1893), 79–99, which deals with the *Domostroi* and Catherine's *Nakaz* of 1767. For more detailed information on the growth of educational institutions and ideas in Russia before the eighteenth-century, see M. I. Demkov, *Istoriia russkoi pedagogii*, I (Revel', 1895), and the unpublished paper by H. Graham, "Was there institutionalized education in pre-petrine Russia," read at the Banff '74 Conference.
2. *Domostroi*, 9, 29–33, 35–6, 40–46, 62–71.
3. On the Brotherhood schools, see E. E. Medynsky, *Bratskie shkoly Ukrainy i Belorussii v XVI–XVII vv. i ikh rol' vossvedinenii Ukrainy s Rossiei* (Moscow, 1954), and B. N. Mitiurov, *Razvitie pedagogicheskoi mysli na Ukraine v XVI–XVII vv.* (Kiev, 1968), 96–126.
4. Okenfuss, "The Jesuit Origins of Petrine Education," in Garrard (ed.), *The Eighteenth Century in Russia*, 106–30.
5. W.H.E. Johnson, *Russia's Educational Heritage* (New York, 1950), 22–24; Pekarsky, *Nauka i literatura v Rossii. . .*, I, 2.
6. On Comenius in seventeenth-century Russia, see A. A. Chuma, *Ian Amos Komenskii i russkaia shkola (do 70 godov 18 veka)*, (Bratislava, 1970), 9–24. See also, for schools in that century, S. A. Kniaz'kov and N. I. Serbov (eds.), *Ocherk istorii narodnago obrazovaniia v Rossii do epokhi reform Aleksandra II* (Moscow, 1910), 28–9, and Okenfuss, "The Jesuit Origins. . . ," 112–3.
7. On Nikon, see Matthew Spinka, "Patriarch Nikon and the Subjection of the Russian Church to the State," *Church History*, X (December, 1941), 347–66.

8. S. S. Kononovich, "Epifanii Slavinetskii i 'grazhdanstvo obychaev detskikh'," *Sovetskaia pedagogika,* no. 10 (1970), 107–12.

9. Mitiurov, 110–12.

10. Iurii Krizhanich, "Razgovory ob vladatelestvy," in *Russkoe gosudarstvo v polovine XVII veka* (ed.) P. Bezsonov, I (Moscow, 1859). See also M. B. Petrovich, "Jaraj Krishanich. A Precursor of Panslavism," *American Slavic and East European Review,* VI (1947), 75–92. Solov'ev, *Istorii Rossii,* Bk. VII, vol. 13 (Moscow, 1962), 155–62, and *Juraj Križanić (1618–1683) Russophile and Ecumenic Visionary: A Symposium* (eds.) T. Eekman and A. Kadić (The Hague, 1976).

11. On Rostovsky, see I. A. Shliapkin, *Sv. Dimitrii Rostovskii i ego vremia (1651–1709),* (St. Petersburg, 1891), and A. Titov, *Propevedi sviatitelia Dimitriia Rostovskago na Ukrainskom narechii* (Moscow, 1909). Before Rostovsky took Holy Orders and the name Dimitrii, he was Daniel Savvich.

12. For general reference, see Alexander Sydorenko, *The Kievan Academy in the Seventeenth Century* (Ottawa, 1977).

13. See E. N. Medynsky, *Istoriia Russkoi pedagogiki* (Moscow, 1938), 39–43.

Chapter II: Peter I: Ideas and their First Practitioners

1. Even though birth and favouritism soon became the main stimulus for promotion once again, the concept of advancement by merit was a very important one for eighteenth-century Russia, and was a political ideal propagated by Nikita Panin and others in the Catherinian era. In fact, the idea goes back to Muscovite rulers and was basic to Ivan IV's service *ukaz* of 1556. On the fate of the Table of Ranks after Peter's death, see James Hassell, "The Implementation of the Russian Table of Ranks during the Eighteenth Century," *Slavic Review,* 29, no. 2 (June, 1970), 283–95.

2. Johnson, *Russia's Educational Heritage,* and Medynsky, *Istoriia russkoi pedagogiki* (Moscow, 1936), both say that it was the first such school in Europe, but Nicholas Hans has shown quite convincingly that it was modelled after the Royal Mathematical School in London. See his "The Moscow School of Mathematics and Navigation (1701)," *Slavonic and East European Review,* XXXIX, no. 73 (June, 1951), 532–36. See also Okenfuss, "Technical Training in Russia under Peter the Great," *History of Education Quarterly,* XII, no. 4 (Winter, 1973), 325–45.

3. Demkov, *Istoriia,* II, 74–79. On Farquharson, see Hans, "H. Farquharson, Pioneer of Russian Education," *Aberdeen University Review,* XXXVII, 120 (1959), 26–29.

4. Okenfuss, in *History of Education Quarterly,* 327.

5. *Polnoe sobranie zakonov Rossiiskoi imperii* (*PSZR*), V (St. Petersburg, 1830), no. 2979 (18 January, 1714), 189; see also no. 2762 (20 January, 1714), 78, no. 2778 (28 February, 1714), 86.

6. For statistics on enrollment, see Johnson, 34–5, and V. G. Simkhovitch, "History of the School in Russia," *The Educational Review* (May, 1907), 495.

7. *PSZR,* V, no. 2778 (28 February, 1714), 86. See also Marc Raeff, *The Origins of the Russian Intelligentsia: The Eighteenth-Century Nobility* (New York, 1966), 132–3.

8. F. Veselago, *Ocherk istorii Morskago kadetskago korpusa* (St. Petersburg, 1852), 41, 55.

9. See Gregory L. Freeze, *The Russian Levites: Parish Clergy in the Eighteenth Century* (London, 1977), 82–3.

10. See Demkov, *Istoriia,* II, 16; Pekarsky, I, 90–107; *Istoriia russkoi zhurnalistiki XVIII–XIX vekov* (ed.) A. V. Zapadov (Moscow, 1966), 15–33. A decree of 8 March, 1705, called for the preparation of the history of the Swedish Wars, *PSZR,* IV, no. 2040, 298–9.

11. See Kh. Grasgoff, "Iz istorii sviazei Berlinskogo obshchestva nauk s rossiei v 20-x godakh XVIII v.," in *Rol' i znachenie literatury XVIII veka v istorii russkoi kul'tury* (Moscow-Leningrad, 1966), 59–65. Thomas Consett had been the chaplain to the British Factory (as the Russian Company was called in St. Petersburg). In 1729 he published an English version of *Spiritual Regulations.*

12. On Shafirov's book and essay, see S. P. Luppov, *Kniga v Rossii v pervoi chetverti XVIII veka* (Leningrad, 1973), 229, and V. E. Grabar', "Pervaia russkaia kniga po mezhdunarodnomu pravu ('Razsuzhdenie' P. P. Shafirova)," *Vestnik Moskovskogo universiteta,* no. 7 (1950), 101–10. An English translation with an interesting introduction has been published by William E. Butler, Shafirov, *A Discourse Concerning the Just Causes of the War Between Sweden and Russia: 1700-1721* (New York, 1973). It includes a reprint of the original.

13. *PSZR,* IV, no. 2188 (26 January, 1708), 91.

14. On Tessing and his books, see Pekarsky, I, 12–13, 64–5; Demkov, *Istoriia,* I, 12–13, and T. A. Bykova, "Knigoizdatel'skaia deiatel'nosti Il'i Kopievskogo i Iana Tesinga," *Opisanie izdanii, napechatannykh kirillitsei, 1689–ianvar' 1725 g.* (eds.) Bykova and M. M. Gurevich (Moscow-Leningrad, 1958), appendix IV, 318–41.

15. Luppov, *Kniga v Rossii v pervoi chetverti XVIII veka,* 61–2, 126–7.

16. "The Missio Muscovitica [of Antonio Possevino]," translated and edited by Hugh F. Graham, *Canadian/American Slavic Studies,* VI, no. 3 (Fall, 1972), 475. *Of the Russe Commonwealth* (eds.) R. Pipes, John V. A. Fine (Cambridge, 1966), 85–6.

17. *Diary of an Austrian Secretary of Legation at the Court of Czar Peter the Great,* II (London, 1863), 173–4, reprint 1966; *The Travels of Olearius in Seventeenth-Century Russia,* translated and edited by S. H. Baron (Stanford, 1967), 131.

18. John Perry, *The State of Russia* (London, 1716), 209, 211, 220, reprint, 1970; *Vide la Religion ancienne et moderne de Muscovites* (Cologne, 1698), was cited by J. T. Philips, *The Russian Catechism* (London, 1723), 60–62, which was comprised of a translation of Prokopovich's *Pervoe uchenie otrokam* (1720) and a history of the Russian Church.

19. *Spiritual Regulations of Peter the Great* (ed.) A. V. Muller, (Washington, 1972), 31–2.

20. M. Vladimirsky-Budanov, *Gosudarstvo i narodnoe obrazovanie v Rossii XVIII-go veka* (Yaroslavl', 1874), 161–4, 297–301.

21. Muller, 32–9, 40–41. On Prokopovich's educational views, see Demkov, *Istoriia,* II, 68–93, and M. V. Sychev-Mikhailov, *Iz istorii Russkoi shkoly i pedagogiki XVIII veka* (Moscow, 1960), 20–23. The most recent English-language study is that by James Cracraft, "Feofan Prokopovich," in Garrard, *The Eighteenth Century in Russia,* 75–105; see Cracraft's *The Church Reform of Peter the Great* (Bristol, 1971), 262–76.

22. Prokopovich, *Pervoe uchenie otrokam* (St. Petersburg, 1725), 19; third edition of work printed first in 1720.

23. P. N. Tikhanov (ed.), "Propozitsii Fedora Saltykova," in *Pamiatniki drevnei pis'mennosti i iskusstva,* 83, no. 5, series 4, (1891), 23–26. *PSZR,* no. 4624 (December 30, 1724), 394–5.

24. See Jurij Sherech, "Stefan Yavorsky and the Conflict of Ideologies in the Age of Peter I," *Slavonic and East European Review,* XXX, no. 74 (December, 1951), 40–62.

25. Prokopovich, *Pervoe uchenie otrokam,* 10–11.

26. The *O dolzhnosti cheloveka i grazhdanina po zakonu estvestennomu, knigi dve, sochinenyia Samuilom Pufendorfom* (St. Petersburg, 1726), 549 Pp., was printed in 600 copies. It was translated by Krechetovsky and corrected by Gavril Busching.

27. For the various projects, see Demkov, *Istoriia,* II, 18–28, and Pekarsky, I, 25–39, 105–07, 124–39, 478–94.

28. D. E. Mikhal'chi, "I. V. Pauze i ego Slaviano-russkaia grammatika," *Izvestiia AN SSSR:* Literature and Language series, issue no. 1 (1964), 49–57; S. A. Belokurov and A. N. Zertsalov, "O nemetskikh shkolakh v Moskve v pervoi chetverti XVIII v. (1701–1715 gg.)," *Chteniia v imperatorskom obshchestve Istorii i drevnostei Rossiisskikh pri Moskovskom universitete,* Bk. I, no. 1 (1907), ix-xx, 38–9.

29. Saltykov, "Propozitsii," 24–6.

30. *PSZR,* V, no. 3246 (26 November, 1718), 597–8. For one contemporary view of the role played by women in Russian society in 1700, see Korb, *Diary of an Austrian Secretary. . . ,* 207–08.

31. See V. I. Chuchmarev, "G. V. Leibnits i russkaia kul'tura nachala 18 stoletiia," *Vestnik istorii mirovoi kul'tury,* no. 4 (1957), 120–32; Vucinich, *Science in Russian Culture,* 43–8, and V. I. Guerrier, *Sbornik pisem i memorialov Leibnitsa otnosiashchikhsia k Rossii i Petru Velikom* (St. Petersburg, 1873).

32. L. R. Lewitter sees a direct connection between this work and the *Domostroi,* see his "Ivan Tikhonovich Pososhkov (1652–1726) and the 'Spirit of Capitalism'," *Slavonic and East European Review,* LI, no. 125 (October, 1973), 529–31; Pososhkov, *Zaveshchanie otecheskoe k synu* (ed.) A. Popov (Moscow, 1873), 8, 192.

33. Pososhkov, *Zaveshchanie,* 55–56.

34. Pososhkov, *Kniga i skudosti o bogatsve i drugie sochineniia (1724),* (ed.) B. B. Kafengauz (Moscow-Leningrad, 1951), 82–3, 171; Mordukhovich, "Ju. Križanić, W. Petty, and I. Pososhkov (a comparative outline of their economic views)," in Eekman and Kadič, *Križanić,* 223–43.

35. Cited in Plekhanov, *History of Russian Social Thought,* 47.

36. Simkhovitch, in *The Educational Review,* 495–6; the most consistently cited statistics are those from *Sbornik imperatorskago Russkago istoriches-*

kago obshchestva [SIRIO], LVI (1887), no. 159, 133–54. See also Okenfuss, in Garrard, *The Eighteenth Century in Russia*, 124.

37. Pekarsky, *Nauk i literatura v Rossii*, II, 681–94; Luppov, 133–54.

38. A recent article by Walter Gleason, "Political Ideals and Loyalties of Some Russian Writers in the Early 1760's," *Slavic Review*, 34, no. 3 (September, 1975), 560–75, deals with the notions of Wolff and Pufendorf and their pre-eminence in Russian thought at mid-century. See also Sumner Benson, "The Role of Western Political Thought in Petrine Russia," *Canadian/American Slavic Studies*, VIII, no. 2 (1974), 254–73.

39. The "Slovo o vlasti i chesti tsarskoi" was translated by Horace G. Lunt for Marc Raeff (ed.), *Russian Intellectual History: An Anthology* (New York, 1966).

40. There is a huge bibliography on Tatishchev as an historian, a geographer, researcher into mining practices, and as a political thinker. On his educational theories, see Demkov, *Istoriia*, II, 93–107; Sychev-Mikhailov, 17–20; Shabaeva, 51–55; A. A. Burev, "Pervyi ustav russkoi narodnoi shkoly," *Sovetskaia pedagogika*, no. 6 (1960), 119–29; K. N. Bestuzhev-Riumin, *Biografii i kharakteristiki* (St. Petersburg, 1882), 1–176. A recent study in English is that by Rudolph Daniels, *V. N. Tatishchev: Guardian of the Petrine Revolution* (Philadelphia, 1973).

41. Frederick L. Kaplan, "Tatishchev and Kantemir: Two Eighteenth-Century Exponents of a Russian Bureaucratic Style of Thought," *Jahrbücher für Geschichte Osteuropas*, XIII (1965), 503–04, and Daniels, "V. N. Tatishchev and the Succession Crisis of 1730," *Slavonic and East European Review*, no. 4 (1971), 550–59.

42. Tatishchev, *Dukhovnaia moemu synu* (ed.) A. N. Chudinov (St. Petersburg, 1896), 10, 16–17; his son, Evgraf, was educated in a cadet school during the 1730s.

43. *Ibid.*, 8, 11, 16–17, 19.

44. *Ibid.*, 12–16; esp. 16.

45. *Ibid.*, 31, 40. Tatishchev also recommended that seminaries be established in most large cities for the purpose of providing a basic education for girls; see Rozhdestvensky, *Ocherki po istorii sistem narodnago obrazovaniia v Rossii v XVIII–XIX vv.*, I (St. Petersburg, 1912), 98, 101.

46. Tatishchev, *Razgovor o pol'ze nauk i uchilishch* (ed.) N. Popov (Moscow, 1877), 50, 65–6, 96, 100–01; see also M. M. Persits, "'Razgovor dvukh priiatelei o pol'ze nauk i uchilishch' V. N. Tatishcheva, kak pamiatnik russkogo svobodmysliia XVIII v.," *Voprosy istorii, religii i ateizma*, III (Moscow, 1956), 278–310.

47. *Razgovor*, 138–40.

48. *Ibid.*, 76–85.

49. *Ibid.*, 158. Bestuzhev-Riumin, 151–3.

50. Vladimirsky-Budanov, *Gosudarstvo i narodnoe obrazovanie v Rossii XVIII-go veka*, I (Yaroslavl', 1874), 155; *Razgovor*, 126.

51. See N. F. Demidova, "Instruktsia V. N. Tatishcheva o poriadke prepodavaniia v shkolakh pri ural'skikh kazennykh zavodakh," *Istoricheskii arkhiv*, V (Moscow-Leningrad, 1950), 166–78, cited here, 170; and Conrad Grau, *Der Wirtschaftsorganisator, Staatsmann und Wissenschaftler Vasilij N. Tatiščev* (Berlin, 1963), 69. See also N. V. Nechaev, *Shkoly pri gornykh zavodakh Urala v pervoi polovine 18-go stoletiia* (Moscow, 1944).

52. Daniels, *Tatishchev,* 49–57.
53. *Razgovor,* 70.
54. Tatishchev, *Istoriia Rossiiskaia,* I (Moscow-Leningrad, 1962), 79–80.
55. He referred also to Genesis (2.18), St. Peter (2.16), and others; see *Istoriia Rossiiskaia,* I, 359–60. Tatishchev did not include the actual quotations from the scriptures in his manuscript.
56. *Ibid.,* 362–3.
57. *The Dialogues of Plato,* translated by B. Jowett (Chicago, 1952), "Phaedo," 233.
58. See P. P. Epifanov, "'Uchenaia druzhina'i prosvetitelstvo XVIII veka," *Voprosy istorii* (March, 1963), 37–53, and Daniels, *Tatishchev,* 24–33.
59. Plekhanov, *History of Russian Social Thought,* 68, 77.

Chapter III: The Interim Years: 1726–1762

1. *Istoriia akademii nauk SSSR,* I (Moscow-Leningrad, 1958), 142; *Materialy dlia istorii Akademii nauk,* I (St. Petersburg, 1885), 211–18, 714–20; VII, 241, 759–62; IX, 179, 633–38; statistics on this vary slightly, see Dukes, *Catherine the Great and the Russian Nobility,* 26. A short-lived gymnasium was opened in 1704 by Ernst Glück. Foreign languages, rhetoric, philosophy, geography, mathematics, politics, and history were included on its syllabus. But Glück died in 1705 and the school survived him by only six years; see Belokurov and Zertsalov, xxii, 43, 50. The 1726 gymnasium lasted until 1805.
2. *Istoriia akademii nauk SSSR,* I, 145–6; see also D. A. Tolstoi, "Akademicheskaia gimnasiia v XVIII stoletii, po rukopisnye dokumentam Arkhiva Akademii nauk," *Zapiski Imperatorskoi Akademii nauk,* Vol. 51, Bk. 1 (St. Petersburg, 1885), appendix 2, 1–114.
3. On the founding of the Garrison schools, see *PSZR,* VII, no. 6188 (21 September, 1732), 928–30; and Vladimirsky-Budanov, 286–88.
4. See M. T. Beliavsky, "Shkoly i sistema obrazovaniia v Rossii v kontse XVIII v.," *Vestnik Moskovskogo universiteta,* no. 2 (1959), 105–20.
5. K. V. Sivkov, "Iz istorii krepostnoi shkoly vtoroi poloviny XVIII v.," *Istoricheskie zapiski,* III (1938), 269–94; cited here 273.
6. *PSZR,* VIII, no. 5881 (29 July, 1731), 793–4.
7. "Zapiski Danilova," *Russkii arkhiv* (1883), 20–23.
8. *PSZR,* XI, no. 8726 (20 April, 1743), 793–4.
9. For Lomonosov's comment, see "Pis'mo M. V. Lomonosova k I. I. Shuvalovu" (1754), appendix 2, Sychev-Mikhailov, 135–6; see also Lomonosov, *Polnoe sobranie sochinenii,* X (Moscow-Leningrad, 1959), 508–14.
10. Lomonosov, *Polnoe sobranie sochinenii,* X, 403.
11. *Ibid.,* VII, 391; on the lack of professional people, X, 314.
12. *Ibid.,* IX, 481, 513–14.
13. See Vucinich, *Science in Russian Culture,* 131–2, 403; for more on the Kazan gymnasium, see A. Artem'ev, *Kazanskaia gimnasiia v XVIII v.* (St. Petersburg, 1874). For Shuvalov's plan, see *PSZR,* XV, no. 11.144 (15 November, 1760).
15. Derzhavin, "Zapiski," *Sochineniia,* VI (St. Petersburg, 1871), 415–16, 419.
16. Elizabeth's *ukaz* was printed in *Ezhemesiachnye sochineniia (Monthly Essays),* (February, 1755), 98–140. Enrollment at the university remained

No note 14 !

between 80 and 100 students throughout the century; see Simkhovitch in *The Educational Review*, 500–01.

17. *PSZR*, no. 10.724 (5 May, 1757), 765; Elizabeth had already issued this order in April. The minutes of the conference of the University of Moscow carry some accounts of accreditation procedures taking place before them, see *Dokumenty i materialy* . . . *Moskovskogo universiteta*, I, 247 (for attestation of Jean Bazire).

18. *PSZR*, no. 10.718 (11 April, 1757), 758.

19. See Miliukov, *Ocherki po istorii russkoi kul'tury*, II, pt. 2 (Paris, 1931), 740–41.

20. Nicholas Karamzin and Ivan Dmitriev were among the few who reported favourable experiences in their early schooling, and that was in the 1770s, see Dmitriev, *Vzgliad na moiu zhizn'* (St. Petersburg, 1895), 23–4.

21. See Kaplan in *Jahrbücher für Geschichte Osteuropas*, 505–06; Kantemir, "K umu svemu, na khuliashchikh ucheniia" (1729), and "O vospitanii" (1739), in *Russkaia literatura XVIII veka* (ed.) G. P. Makogonenko (Leningrad, 1970), 60–62. On Kantemir's views, see I. V. Shkliar, "Formirovanie mirozzreniia Antiokha Kantemira," *XVIII vek: sbornik 5*, (Moscow-Leningrad, 1962), 129–52.

22. Sychev-Mikhailov, appendix 7, 154–59, and I. Ia. Shchipanov (ed.), *Russkie prosvetitelei ot Radishcheva do Dekabristov* (Moscow, 1966), 95–101. The poem was actually a letter to Shuvalov.

23. Pope's *Essay on Man* was translated for private use already by Prince M. M. Shcherbatov. Locke's *Thoughts*. . . , had been written in 1693. The Russian translation of 1759 was reprinted in 1788. Popovsky's translation of Pope went through nine editions in the eighteenth century, even though a tenth of its lines had to be changed on orders from the censors; see Sychev-Mikhailov, 115–16. *Dokumenty i materialy*. . . *moskovskogo universiteta*, I, 79–83; and N. S. Tikhonravov, "Istoriia izdaniia 'Opyta o cheloveka' v perevoda popovskago," *Sochineniia*, III, pt. 1 (Moscow, 1898), 81–9.

24. Popovsky, "Rech', govorennaia v nachatii filosoficheskikh lektsii pri Moskovskom universitete," *Ezhemesiachnye sochineniia* (August, 1755), 167–76.

25. On Barsov's grammar, see V. I. Chernyshev, "Neskol'ko ukazanii na Moskovskoe narechie v kontse XVIII veka (Iz uchebnika russkoi grammatiki prof. A. A. Barsova, 1780 g.)," *Russkii filologicheskii vestnik*, no. 1/2 (1904), 146–53.

26. Barsov, "Rech' o pol'zu uchrezhdeniia imperatorskogo moskovskogo universiteta pri otkrytii onago 1755 goda aprelia 26 dnia," in Shchipanov, I, 105–07. On Barsov, see M. N. Sukhomlinov, *Istoriia Rossiiskoi akademii*, IV (St. Petersburg, 1874), 186–298. For his 1760 comment, and those of Melissino, see S. P. Shevryev, *Istoriia Moskovskago universiteta (1755–1855)*, (Moscow, 1855), 41, 86.

27. See Catherine's letter to Grimm, 4 August, 1776, *SIRIO*, XXIII (1872), 52.

28. Sychev-Mikhailov, 116–18; for a number of speeches and papers by Anichkov and Desnitsky, see Shchipanov, I, 111–334. See also M. P. Alekseev, "Adam Smith and his Russian Admirers of the Eighteenth Century," in W. R. Scott, *Adam Smith as Student and Professor* (New York, 1955), appendix VII, 424–31; Raeff, "The Empress and the Vinerian Professor: Catherine II's

Projects of Government Reform and Blackstone's *Commentaries*," and A. H. Brown, "S. E. Desnitsky, Adam Smith, and the *Nakaz* of Catherine II," both in *Oxford Slavonic Papers*, new series, VII (1974), 18–41, 42–59.

29. See Walter Gleason, "Political Ideals and Loyalties of Some Russian Writers of the Early 1760s," *Slavic Review*, 34, no. 3 (September, 1975), 563–73. On Schaden, see N. S. Tikhonravov, "Professor I. M. Schaden," in *Sochineniia*, III (Moscow, 1898), 44–59. See L. Krieger, *The Politics of Discretion: Pufendorf and the Acceptance of Natural Law* (London, 1965), 257.

30. "Preduvedomlenie," *Ezhemesiachnye sochineniia*, I (January, 1755), 6.

31. V. A. Miliutin, "Ocherk russkoi zhurnalistiki, preimushchestvenno staroi: I. 'Ezhemesiachnye sochineniia'. Zhurnal, 1755–1784 godov," *Sovremennik*, XXV, section 2 (1851), 3, 15–16. In the third part of his long analysis of the journal, Miliutin listed the contents according to subject matter, *ibid.*, XXVI, 2. For Popovsky's speech, see fn. 24, above.

32. "Pravila vospitaniia detei," *Ezhemesiachnye sochineniia* (May, 1755), 414–20; cited here, 414.

33. "O vospitanii detei v Rimlian," *ibid.*, (August, 1758), 44.

34. "O vospitanii detei v lakedemonian," *ibid.*, (October, 1757), 228–51; "O vospitanii detei v Afinian," *ibid.*, (May, 1758), 166–78; "O detskikh vospitanii drevnikh Persov," *ibid.*, (August, 1763), 157–65.

35. "O vospitanii detei osoblivo kak pri khozhdenii za malymi det'mi postupat dolzhno," translated from a Hanover work of 1751, *ibid.*, (October, 1759), 231–42, especially 239–40.

36. "Pis'mo o vospitanii mal'ykh detei," *ibid.*, (November, 1760), 432–65; cited here 462–3; for the essay against forcing children to learn too soon, "O vred kotoroi proiskhodit ot togo, kogda detei vdrug mnogo prinuzhdaiut uchit'sia," *ibid.*, (January, 1760), 56–74.

37. Shcherbatov, "O nadobnosti i o pol'ze grazhdanskikh zakonov," *ibid.*, (July, 1759), 37–54.

38. *Prazdnoe vremie v pol'zu upotreblennoe* (March, 1759), 163–68; (October, 1759), 233–38; (June, 1760), 369–73.

39. See Demkov, "Kharakter russkago prosveshcheniia i pedagogiki XVIII veka," *Pedagogicheskoi sbornik*, Bk. 367 (August, 1897), 97–114; (September, 1897), 197–215.

40. See V. N. Makeeva, "Ad'iunt Akademii nauk V. E. Adodurov," *Vestnik AN SSSR*, no. 1 (1974), 110–117.

41. *Polnoe sobranie sochinenii D. I. Fonvizina* (St. Petersburg-Moscow, 1888), 848.

42. *Moskovskie vedomosti*, no. 5 (15 January, 1768), 2.

43. See Luppov, *Kniga v Rossii v poslepetrovskoe vremia, 1725–1740* (Leningrad, 1976).

44. See Shabaeva (35–38) who says that over 600 textbooks, both originals and translations, were printed between 1700 and 1725; and Luppov, (1973), 94–112.

45. See Raeff, *Origins*, 139–40. J. G. Garrard makes this point in an interesting introductory essay, "The Emergence of Modern Russian Literature and Thought," to his *The Eighteenth Century in Russia*, 13. See also Vladimirsky-Budanov, 145.

46. Its full title was *Iunost chestnoe zertsalo, ili Pokazanie k zhiteiskomu*

obkhozhdeniiu. Sobrannoe ot raznykh avtorov. There was a second edition in 1718, a third in 1719, and a fourth in 1723, three more in the 1740s and a final one in 1767. See *Svodnyi katalog russkoi knigi grazhdanskoi pechati XVIII veka: 1725–1800,* III (Moscow, 1966), 452–3. The book was still being advertised for sale in St. Petersburg, at 15 kopeks, in 1745 and 1748; see S. M. Solov'ev, *Istoriia Rossii,* Bk. XI, vol. 22 (Moscow, 1963), 578. Demkov suggests that it was an adaptation from Comenius's *Praecepta morum* (1653), but Chuma refutes this; see A. A. Chuma, *Komenskii,* 52.

47. Demkov, *Istoriia,* II, 193; Tatishchev, *Dukhovnaia,* 8.

48. *Nastavlenie o khoroshem povedenii pri gosudarevom dvore takozhde i o drugom sostianii seia zhizni* (n.d.); Demkov, *Istoriia,* II, 201–05, attributes it only to the first half of the century.

49. For a list of such books and short descriptions of them, see Demkov, *ibid.,* 206–17.

50. *Ibid.,* 208–10; the author of "O vospitanii" is unknown; Raeff, *Origins,* 128, 141.

51. Its full title, *Pervoe uchenie otrokam, v nem zhe bukvy i slogi. Takzhe kratkoe tolkovanie zakonnago desiatoslovie Molitvy Gospodni, Simvola very, i deviati blazhenstv.* This author used the third edition, 1725, the location of which at the University of Helsinki library, he was given by James Cracraft. Cracraft's *The Church Reform of Peter the Great* (276–90), provides us with the best analysis of the work to date.

52. E. V. Povarova, "O russko-serbskikh kul'turnykh sviaziakh v XVIII v.," *Sovetskaia pedagogika,* XXX, no. 11 (1971), 108, 111. Cracraft shows the wide extent of the *Primer's* use and says that it had to be memorized by all of Russia's clergy (*The Church Reform of Peter the Great,* 286–7). Prince M. M. Shcherbatov used it in the 1750s, see A. Lentin (ed.), Shcherbatov, *On the Corruption of Morals in Russia* (Cambridge, 1967), 17.

53. The *Raspolozhenie uchenii ego Imperatorskago Velichestva Petra Vtorago Imp. i Samod. Vseross.,* was written by C. B. Bilfinger and translated from the German by Adodurov. On the book's importance, see N. I. Likhareva-Bokii, "Iz istorii pedagogicheskoi mysli. (Voprosy metodiki istorii v Rossii XVIII veka)," *K 25–letiuu ucheno-pedagogicheskoi deiatel'nosti I. M. Grevsa. Sbornik statei* (St. Petersburg, 1911), 446–7.

54. According to Likhareva-Bokii, the title of the text was *Sokrashchenie drevneishei statskoi istorii, ot nachala sveta do srednykh vekov, dlia opotrebleniia Imperatora Petra II,* see 450. The book is not listed in *Svodnye katalog.*

55. P. F. Kapterev, *Istoriia russkoi pedagogiki* (Petrograd, 1915), 218.

56. See Jean Baptiste Morvan de Bellegarde, *Sovershennoe vospitanie detei, soderzhashchee v sebe; molodym znatnago roda, i shliakhetnago dostoinstva liudiam . . .* (St. Petersburg, 1747), 2, 26–7. The 502 rules were on pages 142–308. A second edition appeared in 1759, a third in 1760 and a fourth in 1778. See *Svodnye katalog,* I, 88.

57. Bellegarde, *Sovershennoe* (1747), 79–85, 113–4, 131. Tatishchev's final words to his son can be found in A. Dmitriev, "Predsmertnoe uveshchanie V. N. Tatishcheva synu," *Zhurnal ministerstva narodnago prosveshcheniia,* CCXLIV (1886), 237.

58. For the Academy of Sciences regulations, issued 10 August, 1750, see K. A. Papmehl, *Freedom of Expression in Eighteenth-Century Russia* (The Hague, 1971), 20; Vladimirsky-Budanov, 155; see also 158.

59. See Raeff, *Origins*, 132–69.
60. Jones, *The Emancipation of the Russian Nobility, 1762–1785* (Princeton, 1973), 10–11, 15–16.
61. Hassell, in *Slavic Review*, 284–293.
62. Jones, *The Emancipation of the Russian Nobility*, 29–30, 32; *PSZR*, XV, no. 11.444 (18 February, 1762), 912–15.
63. "Bumag imperatritsy Ekateriny II," *SIRIO*, VII (1871), 86.

Chapter IV: Catherine II and Betskoi to 1775

1. *PSZR*, XV, no. 11.444 (18 February, 1762), 914.
2. *The Memoirs of Catherine the Great* (ed.) D. Maroger (New York, 1961), 72–3.
3. On this general subject, see F. Andrew Brown, "On Education: John Locke, Christian Wolff and the 'Moral Weeklies'," *California University Publications in Modern Philology*, XXXVI (1952), 149–72, and D. A. Tolstoi, "Vzgliad na uchebnuiu chast' v Rossii v XVIII stoletii do 1782 goda," *Zapiski imp. Akademii nauk*, XLVII (1883), appendix 2, 1–100, in which a comparison is drawn between Catherine's instructions to Saltykov in 1784 and Locke's *Some Thoughts Concerning Education* (1693).
4. *Oeuvres choisies de Fénelon*, IV (Paris, 1825), 12.
5. *Ibid.*, 29–31; Locke, *Of the Conduct of the Understanding* (1697) (ed.) F. W. Garforth (New York, 1966), 34–61; *Concerning Human Understanding*, Bk. II, ch. 1 (Chicago, 1952), 122; *Some Thoughts Concerning Education* (London, 1693), exact facsimile reprint (London, 1970), 90.
6. Locke, *Some Thoughts Concerning Education*, 156–7, 173.
7. For the influence of Comenius in Russia, see A. A. Chuma, *Ian Amos Komenskii i Russkaia shkola* (Bratislava, 1970).
8. *The Great Didactic of John Amos Comenius* (Ed. and Translator) M. W. Keatinge (New York, 1967), reprint of 1910 edition, 52, 57–8, 71.
9. See the preface to Comenius, *Izbrannye pedagogicheskiia sochineniia*, pts. I–III (Moscow, 1893).
10. For Panin's views on education, see David L. Ransel, *The Politics of Catherinian Russia: The Panin Party* (New Haven, 1975), 202–11. References to Panin's submission are all from Ransel.
11. On Poroshin in general, see Solov'ev, *Istoriia Rossii*, XXVI, bk. 13, 498–512. Poroshin kept a daily diary for most of the time, 1764–1765; see his *Zapiski* (St. Petersburg, 1844), which was reprinted in *Russkaia starina* (1881).
12. See Demkov, *Istoriia*, II, 340–49.
13. Platon, "Slovo o vospitanii," in Demkov (ed.), *Russkaia pedagogika: v glavneishikh eia predstaviteliakh* (Moscow, 1898), 92–7.
14. "Donesenie arkhiepiskopa Platona" [January, 1786], in Novikov, *Izbrannye sochineniia* (Moscow–Leningrad, 1951), 579–80; *The Great Didactic of John Amos Comenius*, 129; see also his chapter, "The Method of Morals," 211–17.
15. On Betskoi as an educator, see Demkov, *Istoriia*, II, 306–17; A. S. Lappo-Danilevsky, *I. I. Betskoi i ego sistema vospitaniia* (St. Petersburg, 1904); P. M. Maikov, *I. I. Betskoi* (St. Petersburg, 1904); A. A. Kizevetter, "Odin iz reformatorov russkoi shkoly (Betskoi)," *Istoricheskoi ocherki* (St.

Petersburg, 1912), 119–49, and V. O. Kliuchevsky, "Dva vospitaniia," *Russkaia mysl'*, XIV, no. 3 (1893), 79–99.

16. *Correspondence of Catherine the Great when Grand-Duchess with Sir Charles Hanbury-Williams,* (Ed., and translator) Earl of Ilchester, and Mrs. Langford-Brooke (London, 1928), 28–30, 32–3.

17. For scattered information and letters, see "Materialy ob I. I. Betskom," in *Chteniia v obshchestvo i drevnostei rossiiskikh,* IV, no. 5 (1863), 81–156.

18. Betskoi, "General'noe uchrezhdenie o vospitanii oboego pola iunoshestve," *PSZR,* XVI, no. 12.103 (22 March, 1764), 668–71. It was also printed separately and reprinted in Demkov (ed.), *Materialy,* 51–5, cited here, 51.

19. Betskoi, "General'noe uchrezhdenie," 54.

20. Cited in Paul Miliukov, *Ocherki po istorii Russkoi kul'tury,* II, 750.

21. Catherine II to General-Procurator Glebov, 5 September, 1763, *SIRIO,* VII (1871), 318.

22. Catherine to Mme de Bielcke, 13 September, 1770, *ibid.,* XVIII (1874), 37. De Bielcke (Bjelke), née Grothus, was a friend of Catherine's mother. See *SIRIO,* X (1870), 28.

23. Catherine to Geoffrin, *ibid.,* I (1867), 261.

24. Rousseau, *Émile, ou de l'éducation* (Paris, 1904), 14, 458, 339–41.

25. Maikov, *I. I. Betskoi,* 52–5.

26. Poroshin, *Zapiski,* 490.

27. See the as yet unpublished paper prepared by David Ransel, "Ivan Betskoi and the Institutionalization of the Enlightenment in Russia," for *Canadian/American Slavic Studies.*

28. Betskoi, *General'noe plan Imperatorskago Vospitatel'nago doma v Moskve,* pts. I–III (St. Petersburg, 1763), 2nd issue, 1767, 4–6. See also *PSZR,* XVIII, no. 12.957 (11 August, 1767), 292–3. Subsequent information here is taken from the separately published *General'noe plan,* 1767. On the institution in St. Petersburg, see A. P. Piatkovsky, "S.-Peterburgskii Vospitatel'nyi dom' pod upravleniem I. I. Betskago: istoricheskoe izsledovanie," *Russkaia starina,* XII (1875), 146–60, 359–80, 665–81; XIII, 177–253, 532–53; XIV, 421–43.

29. See the interesting paper by David M. Griffiths, "Eighteenth-Century Perceptions of Backwardness: Projects for the Creation of a Third Estate in Catherinian Russia," unpublished paper read at AAASS, Fall, 1977.

30. Betskoi, *Kratkoe nastavlenie vybrannoe iz luchshikh avtorov s nekotorymi fizicheskimi primechaniiami o vospitanii detei ot rozhdeniia ikh do iunoshestva* (St. Petersburg, 1766).

31. *O dolzhnostiakh cheloveka i grazhdanina kniga* (St. Petersburg, 1783), 10th edition, 1811, 113–14. See appendix below.

32. See V. P. Semennikov, *Materialy dlia istorii russkoi literatury i dlia slovaria pisatelei epokha Ekateriny II* (St. Petersburg, 1914), 49–51, which includes a series of letters between Krestinin and Dashkova. Krestinin's essays on education were carried in the 1780s in *Novye ezhemesiachnye sochineniia,* pt. XVII (November, 1787), 3–12; pt. XVIII (December, 1787), 20–49; pt. LII (October, 1790), 27–44.

33. *Istoriia akademii nauk SSSR,* I, 314.

34. Solov'ev, *Istoriia Rossii,* vol. 26, 566.

35. *PSZR,* XIX, no. 13.916 (6 December, 1772), 673–81. For the 1765 proposal, see Shabaeva, 115–16. See also Maikov, *Betskoi,* 402–06.

36. *Catherine the Great's (NAKAZ) Instruction to the Legislative Commission, 1767* (ed.) Paul Dukes (Newtonville, 1977), (no's 348, 356), 90–91.

37. *Ibid.,* (no. 250), 76; (no. 19), 44.

38. See Freeze, "The Disintegration of Traditional Communities: The Parish Clergy in Eighteenth Century Russia," *Journal of Modern History,* 48, no. 1 (March, 1976), 44–45.

39. Robert E. Jones, *The Emancipation of the Russian Nobility, 1762–1785,* 68–71.

40. Dukes, *Catherine the Great and the Russian Nobility,* 195–210; for the plans which were prepared by the School Committee of 1767, see Rozhdestvensky (ed.), *Materialy dlia istorii uchebnyk reform' v Rossii v XVIII–XIX vekakh* (St. Petersburg, 1910), 144–257.

41. Dilthey's and other early proposals can also be found in Rozhdestvensky (ed.), *Materialy,* 1–143. For General-Commissioner A. P. Mel'gunov's report, see *PSZR,* no. 12.099 (22 March, 1764), 667.

42. *Ibid.,* 12. For more on Dilthey and his scheme, see A. Kirpichnikov, "Pedagogi proshlago veka," *Istoricheskii vestnik,* XXI, no. 9 (1885), 436–44.

43. Rozhdestvensky (ed.), *Materialy,* 22.

44. *Ibid.,* 83.

45. *Ibid.,* 1. Italics were those of the anonymous author.

46. Hans, "Dumaresq, Brown, and Some Early Educational Projects under Catherine II," *Slavonic and East European Review,* XL (December, 1961/2), 229–35; Brown, *Sermons on Various Subjects* (London, 1764), 16–17.

47. For a long discussion on La Chalotais, Diderot, and French education in the 1760s, see H. C. Barnard, *The French Tradition in Education* (Cambridge, 1970), 219–40.

48. La Chalotais, *Opyt narodnago vospitaniia ili chertezh nauk,* translated by R. Gvozdikov (St. Petersburg, 1770), 4.

49. See Dukes, *Catherine the Great and the Russian Nobility,* 196–200.

50. See Vladimirsky-Budanov, 159, 202–03.

51. See S. A. Kniaz'kov, and N. I. Serbov, *Ocherk istorii narodnago obrazovaniia v Rossii do epokha reform Aleksandra II* (Moscow, 1910), 61–69.

52. *PSZR,* XVI, no. 12.012 (13 January, 1764), 493–4; no. 12.275 (4 November, 1764), 948–60; no. 11.696 (25 October, 1762), 94–102.

53. *Ibid.,* XVII, no. 12.430 (6 July, 1765), 187–8.

54. See above, chapter VI, on G. S. Skovoroda.

55. V. A. Bil'basov, *Didro v Peterburge* (St. Petersburg, 1884), 137.

56. Betskoi, *Razsuzhdeniia sluzhashchiia rukovodstvom k novomu ustanovleniiu Shliakhetnago kadetskago korpusa* (St. Petersburg, 1766), 2, 8–9, 31, 63. Italics were Betskoi's. He also cited David Hume (53) on the danger of spending too much time on the sciences.

57. *PSZR,* XVII, no. 12.741 (11 September, 1766), 959–92: on "pedantism" (Betskoi's word), see 975; see also *PSZR,* XVII, no. 12.670 (6 June, 1766), 802–03.

58. D. M. Lang, *The First Russian Radical: Alexander Radishchev, 1749–1802* (London, 1959), 27.

59. "Instruktsiia o vospitanii: 1772–1775 gg," *Russkaia starina,* XXXI (1881), 655–64.

60. *SIRIO,* LVIII (1889), 137, 236-7; XIII (1874), 294-97.

61. See E. S. Shumigorsky, "Osnovanie Smol'nago monastyriia," *Russkaia starina,* no. 9 (1914), 306-51.

62. *SIRIO,* XXIII (1878), 19.

63. *Ibid.,* VII (1872), 178-82; letter from Catherine to D'Alembert, 13 November, 1762, and his reply, 17 October, 1763.

64. *Ibid.,* XLIV (1885), 20; Grimm to Catherine, 8 November, 1778.

65. The letters to Diderot's daughter and to Catherine are contained in Bil'basov, *Didro v Peterburge,* appendix III, (no's 27 and 33), 250-56.

66. Diderot, *Mémoires pour Catherine II* (ed.) Paul Vernière (Paris, 1966), 86. All the following information about Diderot in Russia is taken from the Vernière collection of 56 memoranda, ten of which dealt with education. The plan for a university was not included.

67. For Diderot's plan in English, see F. de la Fontainerie (ed. and translator), *French Liberalism and Education in the Eighteenth Century* (New York, 1932), 185-310. See also Allen Wilson, "Diderot in Russia, 1773-1774," in Garrard (ed.), *The Eighteenth Century in Russia,* 166-97.

68. *Dokumenty i materialy po istorii Moskovskogo universiteta vtoroi poloviny XVIII veka,* I (1756-1764), 50, 135, 320.

69. The 1771 and 1790 versions of *Sposob ucheniia* are included as appendices no.'s 8 and 9 in Sychev-Mikhailov, 160-73. Demkov does not mention them.

70. Catherine's "Zapiski kasatel'no rossiiskoi istorii," took up 1348 pages of the total of 2800 pages in *Sobesednik liubitelei rossiiskogo slova,* 1783. It appeared in four books in 1787-90, and in German translation, 1784-85.

71. "Slovo Kh. A. Chebotareva o sposobakh i putiakh, vedushchikh i prosveshcheniiu, govorennoe aprelia 22 dnia, 1779 goda," Sychev-Mikhailov, appendix 15, 208-18.

72. "Pis'ma I. I. Betskago k Imperatritse Ekaterine Vtoroi," *Russkaia starina,* no. 11 (1896), 420.

73. Voltaire to Catherine, October 1775, in *Voltaire and Catherine the Great* (ed.) A. Lentin (Cambridge, 1974), 169-70.

74. Catherine to Grimm, 27 February, 1775, *SIRIO,* XXIII (1878), 19.

75. *PSZR,* XX, no. 14.392 (7 November, 1776), 229-304, article 384.

76. *SIRIO,* XXIII (1878), 183 [24 July, 1780], 193; XLIV (1885), 125-32, 139.

Chapter V: The Intelligentsia and Schools

1. See *Dokumenty i materialy po istorii Moskovskogo universiteta vtoroi poloviny XVIII veka,* I, 301-03; Chuma, 78-79; I. M. Schaden, *Slovo o prave obladatelia v rassuzhdenii vospitaniia i prosveshcheniia naukami i khudozhestvami poddanykh* (Moscow, 1771). See also Tikhonravov, "'Professor' I. M. Schaden," in *Sochineniia,* III (Moscow, 1898), 44-59.

2. *Pervoe polnoe sobranie sochinenii D. I. Fonvizina* (St. Petersburg, 1888), 103-56; for Fonvizin's recollection of his days at Schaden's school see *ibid.,* 857.

3. Fonvizin, "Brigadir," *Russkaia literatura XVIII veka* (Leningrad, 1970), 306. On Fonvizin's questions to Catherine, see Papmehl, "Samuel

Bentham and the *Sobesednik*, 1783," *Slavonic and East European Review*, 46, no. 106 (1968), 210–19. The article contains Bentham's translations of Fonvizin's queries and Catherine's responses to them.

4. See *Satiricheskie zhurnaly N. I. Novikova*, (ed.) P. N. Berkov (Moscow, 1951), 106.

5. For Novikov's extensive writing on education, see his *Izbrannye pedagogicheskie sochineniia* (ed.) N. A. Trushin (Moscow, 1959). Shabaeva (*Ocherki . . .*, 165–76) overstates Novikov's originality.

6. Novikov, "Nravouchenie kak prakticheskoe nastavlenie," *Izbrannye sochineniia* (Moscow–Leningrad, 1951), 379–405; cited here 399, 401.

7. *Utrenii svet*, pt. 1 (1777), viii. See also W. Gareth Jones, "The *Morning Light* Charity Schools, 1777–80," *Slavonic and East European Review*, LVI, no. 1 (January, 1978), 47–67.

8. See In-Ho Ryu, "Moscow Freemasons and the Rosicrucian Order," in Garrard (ed.), *The Eighteenth Century in Russia*, 198–232; and Tikhonravov, "Professor I. G. Shvartz," *Sochineniia*, III, pt. 2 (Moscow, 1895), 60–81.

9. Novikov, "O vospitanii i nastavlenii detei," *Izbrannye sochineniia*, 417–506; cited here 417–18.

10. *Drevniaia rossiiskaia vivliofika*, I (Moscow, 1788), second edition in reprint (1970), "Predislovie."

11. *Detskoe chtenie dlia serdtsa i razuma*, pt. 1 (1785), 2nd edition (1819), 2–3, 4–8.

12. See E. P. Pribalova, "O sotrudnikakh zhurnala 'Detskoe chtenie dlia serdtsa i razuma'," *Russkaia literatura XVIII veka: epokha klassitsizma* (Moscow–Leningrad, 1964), 258–68.

13. For information on the *Dukhovna . . . v nastavlenie ego detiam oboego pola*, see A. A. Kotliarevsky in *Chteniia v istoricheskom obshchestve nestoraletopistsa*, Bk. 2 (Kiev, 1888), 108–11.

14. Lomonosov, *Polnoe sobranie sochineniia*, IX, 252–3.

15. Kurganov, *Rossiiskaia universal'naia grammatika* (St. Petersburg, 1769), "Prinoshenie."

16. On Krechetov's educational views, see B. M. Kobin, "O neizvestnykh pis'makh F. V. Krechetova (1803–1807)," *Vestnik Leningradskogo universiteta*, issue i, no. 5 (1966), 155–58; and K. V. Sivkov, S. V. Paparigopulo, "O vzgliadakh Fedora Krechetova," *Voprosy istorii*, no. 3 (1956), 121–28.

17. Prokopovich-Antonsky, "O vospitanii," in Sychev-Mikhailov, 219–53. On Prokopovich-Antonsky in general, see Demkov, *Istoriia*, II, 477–96.

18. Shcherbatov's, *On the Corruption of Morals in Russia*, was written in the 1780s, but not printed until 1896. It was an extremely unfavourable evaluation of Catherine's reign, her licentiousness, and reliance on favourites.

19. Prokopovich-Antonsky, "O vospitanie," 230.

20. Dashkova, "O smysli slova vospitanie," *Sobesednik liubitelei Rossiiskago slova*, pt. 2 (1783), 12–28.

21. Radishchev, *A Journey from St. Petersburg to Moscow* (ed.) R. P. Thaler (Cambridge, Mass., 1958), 211–12.

22. Kniazhnin, "Chudaki," *Izbrannye proisvedeniia* (Leningrad, 1961), 451–61. On the general subject of foreign tutors and Russian reactions to them, see Clarence Manning, "The French Tutor in Russian Literature," *Romanic Review*, XXVII (June, 1936), 28–32, and L. Ignatieff, "French Emigrés in

Russia after the French Revolution: French Tutors," *Canadian Slavonic Papers,* VIII (1966), 125–31. Lomonosov had accused the French and German instructors at the Academy gymnasium of being "lazy"; see M. Shugurov, "Uchenie i ucheniki v XVIII vek (po povodu biografii A. Ia. Polenova)," *Russkii arkhiv* (1866), 303–24.

23. "Zapiski Messel'era [de la Messelière], *Russkii arkhiv* (1874), 973; letter of Lord Cathcart to the Right Honourable Lord Viscount Weymouth, 26 September, 1768, *SIRIO,* XII (1873), 370; see also W. Richardson, *Anecdotes of the Russian Empire* [1768–1771] (London, 1784), reprint 1972, 25–6.

24. *The Russian Journals of Martha and Catherine Wilmot (1803–1808),* (London, 1935), 194.

25. On Domashnev, see K. S. Veselovsky, "Bor'ba akademikov s direktorom S. G. Domashnevym," *Russkaia starina,* no. 9 (1896), 457–92.

26. Dashkova, *Memoirs,* 203–12, 217–20, 232.

27. N. N. Bolkovitinov, *Stanovlenie russko-amerikanskikh otnoshenii, 1775–1815* (Moscow, 1966), 236–38. Her election was in 1789.

28. On the award to Betskoi, "Materialy ob I. I. Betskom," *Chteniia . . . ,* 90–1, and *PSZR,* XXI, no. 15.515 (22 September, 1782), 671–75. For Dashkova's very unfavourable picture of Betskoi, see *Zapiski kniagini Dashkova* (St. Petersburg, 1907), 70–1. For Diderot's comment about Betskoi as waiting-maid or prime minister, see Janet Aldis, *Madame Geoffrin: Her Salon and Her Times* (London, 1905), 348.

29. Agrippa, *O blagorodstve i preimyshchestve zhenskago pola* (St. Petersburg, 1784). The translator was Peter Alekseevich.

30. See "Instruktsiia kniaziu Nikolaiu Ivanovichu Saltykovu pri naznachenii ego k vospitaniiu velikikh kniazei," *Sochineniia Imperatritsy Ekateriny II,* I (St. Petersburg, 1849), 199–248. It is partially included in Demkov, *Russkaia pedagogika,* 77–90. For Catherine's own textbook writing, see below, fn 50, and chapter VI, fn 10.

31. Helvétius's final book was dedicated to Catherine II. See Reddaway (ed.) *Documents of Catherine the Great,* 186, 189.

32. *SIRIO,* XXIII (1878), 24 (letter of 25 April, 1775); 174 (letter of 2 February, 1780); 201 (letter of 14 April, 1781); 381 (letter of 25 September, 1786). Stéphanie Félicité de Genlis's works were translated into Russian as *Novoe detskoe uchilishch, ili nravstvennago vospitaniia oboego pola . . . ,* I–III (St. Petersburg, 1792).

33. Bestuzhev, "O vospitanii," in *Russkie prosvetiteli,* I, 83, 93–4. Bestuzhev's essay was printed in Pnin's *St. Petersburg Journal.* See also E. M. Medynsky, "Traktat ottsa dekabristov A. F. Bestuzheva 'o vospitanii' (1798)," *Sovietskaia pedagogika,* no. 11 (1955), 76–91.

34. Karamzin, "Nechto o naukakh, iskusstvakh i prosveshchenii," written in 1793 and printed in his journal *Aglaia,* 1794; see *Izbrannye sochineniia,* II (Moscow–Leningrad, 1964), 140.

35. Karamzin, *ibid.,* 132–33, 140–41. On the poem "K milosti," see A. G. Cross, *N. M. Karamzin: A Study of his Literary Career (1783–1803),* (London, 1971), 147, and Karamzin, *Polnoe Sobranie stikhotvorenie* (Moscow–Leningrad, 1966), 110–11.

36. Karamzin, "Moia ispoved" and "Strannosti," *Vestnik evropy,* II (1802), 52–54; VI (1802), 147–63.

37. Karamzin, *Panteon inostrannoi slovestnosti,* II (Moscow, 1798), second edition, 1818, 306–07, 258.

38. On the *Sankt-Peterburgskii zhurnal,* see Cross, "Pnin and the Sanktpeterburgskii zhurnal (1798)," *Canadian/American Slavic Studies,* VII, no. 4 (1973), 78–84. Cross queries convincingly the status of radical attributed to Pnin by Soviet authors, and suggests as well that his overall contribution to the journal has been exaggerated.

39. For Pnin's "Opyt i prosveshchenii otnositel'no k Rossii" (1804), and others of his essays, see *Russkie prosvetiteli,* I, 167–248. His piece on enlightenment is available in English in Raeff (ed.), *Russian Intellectual History: An Anthology,* 125–58.

40. See Samuel Carroll Ramer, "Ivan Pnin and Vasily Popugaev: A Study in Russian Political Thought," unpublished Ph.D. dissertation (Columbia, 1971). See also his "The Traditional and the Modern in the Writings of Ivan Pnin," *Slavic Review,* 34, no. 3 (September, 1975), 539–59. Popugaev's "O blagopoluchi narodnykh tel," can be found in *Russkie prosvetiteli,* I, 323–25.

41. Hobbes, *Nachal'nyia osnovaniia filosoficheskiia o grazhdanine,* translated from the Latin (St. Petersburg–Moscow, 1776).

42. *O nravstvennom vospitanii detei. Vziato iz nravstvennykh nastavlenii pokoinago g. Gellerta,* translated from the French (Moscow, 1787); Karamzin, *Izbrannye sochineniia,* I, 159–60. On the books translated by Catherine's Society for the Translation of Foreign Books, see V. P. Semennikov, *Sobranie staraiushcheesia o perevode inostrannykh knig, uchrezhdennoe Ekaterinoi II (1768-1783),* (St. Petersburg, 1913).

43. B. Svetlov, "'Obshchestvo liubitelei Rossiiskoi uchenosti' pri Moskovskom universitete," *Istoricheskii arkhiv,* V (1950), 300–22; cited here, 304.

44. For the citation about a "little enlightenment," see Shcherbatov, *On the Corruption of Morals in Russia,* (ed.) A. Lentin (Cambridge, 1967), 50. On the *Journey to the Land of Ophir,* see Shcherbatov, *Sochineniia* (St. Petersburg, 1896), I, and Kizevetter, "Russkaia utopiia XVIII stoletiia," *Istoricheskie ocherki,* 29–56; see also Raeff, "State and Nobility in the Ideology of M. M. Shcherbatov," *American Slavic and East European Review,* XIX, no. 3 (October, 1960), 363–79.

45. "Vospominanii Fedora Petrovicha Lubianovskago," *Russkii arkhiv* (1872), 108; Khidzheu, "Grigorij Varsava [sic] Skovoroda," *Teleskop,* pt. 26, no. 5 (1835), 12–15. On Skovoroda, see S. P. Scherer, "The Life and Thought of Russia's First Lay Theologian, Grigorij Savvič Skovoroda (1722–94)," unpublished Ph.D. dissertation, (Ohio State University, 1969).

46. N. I. Petrov, "K biografii ukrainskago filosofa Grigoriia Savvicha Skovorody," *Kievskaia starina,* no. 4 (1903), 14–16. For Catherine's decree of 1765 which called for a wide extension of the curriculum at Kharkov, see *PSZR,* no. 12.430 (6 July, 1765), 187–8.

47. A. A. Artem'ev, *Dobrotetel'naia dysha, ili Nravouchitel'nyiia pravila v pol'zu i nauchenie iunoshestva iz drevnikh i noveishikh mudretsov vybrannyia i na rossiiskoi iazyk perevedennyia podporutchikom A. A.* (St. Petersburg, 1777). It was reprinted in 1782. Barsov, *Azbuka tserkovnaia i grazhdanskaia kratkimi primechaniiami o pravopisannii* (Moscow, 1768); Abbé Bellegarde, *Istinnoi khristianin i chestnoi chelovek. To est' soedinenie dolzhnostei khrist'- tiianskikh s dolzhnost'mi zhitiia grazhdanskago . . . . ,* translated from the

194   CITIZENS FOR THE FATHERLAND

French by Sergei Volkhov (St. Petersburg, 1743). Baibakov wrote textbooks, moralizing tales, stories of the apostles and an historical chronicle. Most of his works were published at Novikov's typography. For Novikov's description of Goodheart, see *Detskoe chtenie*, I, pt. 1 (1785), "Introduction," 7–8.

48. *Zolotoe zerkala dlia detei, sodershashchee v sebe cto nebol'shikh povestei dlia obrazovaniia razuma i serdtsa v iunoshestve . . . ,* Pts. I–IV (St. Petersburg, 1782), 2–3, 13. A second printing appeared in 1787, a third in 1809.

49. Elie Bertrand, *Osnovaniia vseobshchago nravoucheniia, ili kartina dolzhnostei cheloveka, razsmatrivaemago vo vsekh ego otnosheniiakh,* translated from the French by Il'ia Greshishchev (Moscow, 1796); August Witzmann, *Dolzhnosti chestnago cheloveka* (St. Petersburg, 1798), and *Pravila i nravouchitel'nyia izrecheniia. Podarok dlia detei* (St. Petersburg, 1798). On Witzmann, see P. N. Stolpiansky, "Staryi Peterburg (Avgust Vitsman — odin iz byl'nykh peterburgskii pedagogov kontsa XVIII veka)," *Izvestie otdel. russk. iazyka i slovestnosti,* no. 3 (1915), 233–91.

50. *Detskaia kniga, ili obshchiia mneniia i iz'iasnenie veshchei, koim detei obuchat'dolzhno. Ves'ma poleznoe delo dlia tekh, koim vospitanie detei vsereno* (Moscow, 1770); and *Rossiiskaia azbuka dlia obucheniia iunoshestva chteniiu, napechatannaia dlia obshchestvennykh shkol po vysochaishemu poveleniiu* (St. Petersburg, 1781), 47 pp. A second edition came out in 1782, and there were at least two undated issues. For Catherine's letters to Grimm about the text, see *SIRIO,* XXIII (1878), 176, 209.

51. *Detskaia kniga,* 4, 81–3, 150, 198, 201.

52. *Rossiiskaia azbuka,* 35, 31, 46–7.

Chapter VI: Iankovich and the Austrian System for Russia

1. *PSZR,* XXI, no. 15.121 (16 February, 1781), 67–68.

2. Voronov, *Istoriko-statisticheskoe obozrenie,* 11–12.

3. Voronov, *Fedor Ivanovich Iankovich de-Mirievo* (St. Petersburg, 1858), 4, and I. Kiprianovich, "Fedor Ivanovich Iankovich-de-Mirievo, 1741–1891 (po povody 150-letiia so dlia rozhdeniia)," *Gymnaziia,* IV, no. 39 (1891), 2–3. See also on Iankovich, Demkov, *Istoriia,* II, 350–69; L. L. Dodon, "Uchebnaia literatura russkoi narodnoi shkoly vtoroi poloviny XVIII veka i rol' F. I. Iankovicha v ee sozdanii," *Uchenye zapiski L.G.P.I.: kafedra pedagogiki,* CXVIII, (1955), 185–207; Peter Polz, "Theodor Janković und die Schulreform in Russland," in *Die Aufklärung in Ost- und Sudosteuropa* (Cologne, 1972), 119–174; N. A. Konstantinov, "Vydaiushchiisia russkii pedagog F. I. Iankovich (1741–1814)," *Sovetskaia pedagogika,* no. 9 (1945), 38–47.

4. Letters of Catherine to Grimm, 25 May, 24 July, and 23 September, 1780, *SIRIO,* XXIII (1878), 180–81, 183, 193; see also XLIV (1885), 125–32, 139.

5. On Aepinus, see R. W. Home, "Science as a Career in Eighteenth-Century Russia: The Case of F.U.T. Aepinus," *Slavonic and East European Review,* LI, no. 122 (January, 1973), 75–94. Aepinus' memorandum to Catherine can be found in D. Tolstoi, *Gorodskiia uchilishcha v tsarstvovanie Imperatritsy Ekateriny II* (St. Petersburg, 1886), 9–12.

6. See Adler, in *Slavic Review,* 32–3.

10

NOTES

195

7. *PSZR,* XXI, no. 15.507 (7 September, 1782), 663–64. On the history of the Commission's membership and legal status, see Rozhdestvensky, "Kommissia ob uchrezhdenii narodnykh uchilishch (1782–1803), i ministerstva narodnago prosveshcheniia," *ZMNP,* no. 5 (1906), section III, 14–18. For Catherine and Joseph II's correspondence about Iankovich, see *Joseph II und Katharina von Russland: ihr Briefwechsel* (ed.) A. R. von Arneth, 1869 (reprint, Osnabrücke, 1973), 141–3; and *SIRIO,* XXIII (1878), 254; XLIV (1885), 825.

8. Catherine to Grimm, 31 August, 1795, *SIRIO,* XXIII (1878), 644–45. *Sochineniia Derzhavina,* I (St. Petersburg, 1895), 192–3. Betskoi's testament can be found in "Materialy ob I. I. Betskom," *Chteniia . . . ,* 146–50. He left his house to the Ribas family.

9. *PSZR,* XX, no. 15.507, 664.

10. For a list and description of the main items translated or written by the Commission, 1782 to 1802, see Polz, 139–44. On the problems surrounding the preparation of a Russian history textbook, see J. L. Black, "The Search for a Correct Textbook of National History in 18th Century Russia," *The New Review: A Journal of East-European History,* XVI, no. 1 (March, 1976), 1–19.

11. (St. Petersburg, 1783), extracts in Demkov, *Istoriia,* II, 370–82. See also Stolpiansky, "Istoriia odnoi knigi," 189, 193. The book was in its fifth edition by 1818.

12. Shabaeva (*Ocherki istorii shkoly . . . ,* 153–4) insists that the manual was "neither a translation nor a re-worked version of Iankovich's foreign book," but was mainly a product of the "Russian didactic tradition" and was written by "qualified Russian scholars and pedagogues." Certainly Russian educators were the leading contributors to the work of the Commission and this was an important breakthrough, but in this instance Shabaeva's argument is pretty thin. In an otherwise good book, she tries too hard to trace all "progressive" ideas in Russian pedagogy to "traditions" started by Lomonosov and Novikov.

13. (St. Petersburg, 1782), 24 pp. An earlier one by S. G. Zybelin, *Slovo o pravil'nom vospitanii s mladenchestva v razsuzhdenii tela* (Moscow, 1775) was in its eighth edition by 1807, but that was not officially adopted for schools.

14. See Demkov, *Istoriia,* II, 391, and Stolpiansky, "Istoriia odnoi knigi," 194–5.

15. *O dolzhnostiakh cheloveka i grazhdanina kniga, k chteniiu opredelennaia v narodnykh uchilishchakh Rossiiskoi Imperii* (St. Petersburg, 1783), 180 pp., cited here 110. Citations here are from the tenth edition, 1811, which was unchanged from that of 1783, and is included as an appendix to this book. A teachers' edition with questions and answers, some seventy pages longer, appeared in the same year and again in 1786.

16. *O dolzhnostiakh,* 110–41.

17. *Ibid.,* 112–3, and Stolpiansky, "Istoriia odnoi knigi," 198–210.

18. See "Ekaterinskaia kniga v narodnykh uchilishch," *Russkii arkhiv,* no. 2 (1907), 303–04, which is Shishkov's memorandum to Alexander I in 1825 on behalf of the book, which he praised.

19. Voronov, *Istoriko-statisticheskoe obozrenie,* 14. See also E. V. Povarova, "Nauchno-pedagogicheskaia deiatel'nosti professorov i prepodavatelei peterburgskoi uchitel'skoi seminarii v XVIII veke," in M. F. Shabaeva (ed.),

196   CITIZENS FOR THE FATHERLAND

Voprosy istorii pedagogiki (Sbornik nauchnykh trudov), (Moscow, 1973), 112–36, Polz, 134–5, and Voronov, *Fedor Ivanovich Iankovich-de-Mirievo,* 95–6.

20. Voronov, *Istoriko-statisticheskoe obozrenie,* 18–19; and *PSZR,* XXI, no. 15.826 (29 August, 1783), 1006–07.

21. Voronov, *Istoriko-statisticheskoe obozrenie,* 31–2. For the comment about *Normalschulen,* see Catherine to Grimm, 5 April, 1785, *SIRIO,* XXIII (1878), 300–01.

22. See V. Kh. Gensh, *Plan uchilishcha, uchrezhdennago dlia blagorodnago iunoshestva* (Moscow, 1775), 8 pp. For Dimitriev's comment see *Vzgliad na moiu zhizn'* (St. Petersburg, 1895), 2–3.

23. N. V. Sushkov, *Moskovskii universitetskii blagorodnyi pansion* (Moscow, 1858), 28–30; and Sychev-Mikhailov, 87–89.

24. Sychev-Mikhailov, 85.

25. K. V. Sivkov, "Chastnye pansiony i shkoly Moskvi v 80-x godakh XVIII v.," *Istoricheskii arkhiv,* VI (Moscow–Leningrad, 1951), 315–23. The report on each school and the committee's remarks are included. *PSZR,* XXII, no. 16.275 (7 October, 1785), 464–5.

26. By 1783 there were six subscription Charity schools, three in St. Petersburg, one each in Tver (1779), Kremenchug (1782), and Irkutsk (1782); see W. Gareth Jones in *Slavonic and East European Review,* 65.

27. Voronov, *Istoriko-statisticheskoe obozrenie,* 5–8.

28. Dmitriev, *Vzgliad na moiu zhizn',* 23–4.

29. Dodsley's, *The Preceptor, Containing a General Course of Education* (1748), was translated as, *Nastavnik, ili vseobshchaia sistema vospitaniia . . . uchenosti* (St. Petersburg, 1789–92). On Verevkin and the 1792 report on *pensions,* see N. S. Tikhonravov, "Biograficheskie zametki o russkikh pisateliakh XVIII veka (M. L. Verevkin)," *Letopisi rus. literatury i drevnosti,* II, section 3 (1859), 108–116; for his report to Shuvalov, see M. P. Petrovsky, "M. I. Verevkin (Ocherk iz istorii russkago obrazovaniia v polovine XVIII veka)," *Russkoe beseda,* no. 1, section V (1860), 1–21.

30. See Papmehl, "The Regimental School Established in Siberia by Samuel Bentham," *Canadian Slavonic Papers,* VIII (1966), 153–68; Matthew S. Anderson, "Samuel Bentham in Russia, 1779–1791," *American Slavic and East European Review,* XII, no. 2 (1956), 157–58; W.H.G. Armytage, *The Russian Influence on English Education* (London, 1969), 12–14.

31. See Povarova in *Voprosy istorii pedagogiki,* and P. Stolpiansky, "Odin iz nezametnykh deiatelei Ekateriansky epokhi: Iakov Pavlovich Kozel'skii," *Russkii arkhiv,* no. 12 (1906), 567–84.

32. *PSZR,* XXII, no. 16.421 (5 August, 1786), 646–69; cited here 646.

33. *Ibid.,* 649; *Rukovodstvo i chistopisanniu dlia iunoshestva v narodnykh uchilishch v Rossiiskoi imperii* (St. Petersburg, 1782), 305.

34. Rozhdestvensky, *Istoricheskii obzor . . . ,* I, 38–40; Polz, 133.

35. See statistics in G. Fal'bork and V. Charnolutsky, *Narodnoe obrazovanie v Rossii* (St. Petersburg, 1898), 19; Rozhdestvensky, *Istoricheskii obzor . . . ,* 29–30.

36. I. Kiprianovich includes this report in his, "Fedor Ivanovich Iankovich-de-Mirievo: 1741–1891," *Gimnaziia,* IV, no. 3 (1891), 22–3.

37. *PSZR,* XXI, no. 15.523 (27 September, 1782), 685. For the founding of

the Kiev Major school, see "K nachal'noi istorii Kievskago narodnago uchilishcha (1789–1803)," *Kievskaia starina*, no. 10, section II (1900), 1–10; V.
Kallash, "Iz istorii ekaterininskoi shkoly," *Vestnik vospitaniia*, no. 7, section II
(1895), 15–29; cited here, 22–3.
38. *Zapiski Derzhavina*, 379.
39. Beliavsky, "Shkola i sistema obrazovaniia v Rossii v kontsa XVIII v.,"
Vestnik Moskovskogo universiteta, no. 2 (1959), 105–120. On clerical schools,
see tables in Freeze, *The Russian Levites*, 88.
40. M. D. Rabinovich, "K istorii prosveshcheniia v Rossii v kontse XVIII v.
(Saratovskaia soldatskaia garizonnaia shkole v 1793 g.)," *Istoricheskii arkhiv*,
no. 1 (1958), 230–33.
41. V. V. Sipovsky, *Iz istorii russkoi literatury XVIII veka. Opyt statisti-
cheskikh nabliudenii* (St. Petersburg, 1901), 44–46.
42. Novikov, *Izbrannye sochineniia* (Moscow–Leningrad, 1951), 96, 277.
43. On this in general, see M. M. Shtrange, *Russkoe obshchestvo i fran-
tsuzskaia revoliutsiia 1789–1794 gg.* (Moscow, 1956), 24–28.
44. Miliukov, *Ocherki po istorii russkoi kul'tury*, II, 733, 739.

Chapter VII: Educating Woman in Eighteenth-Century Russia

1. Ia. B. Kniazhnin, "Chudaki," *Izbrannye proisvedeniia* (Leningrad,
1961), 457; Fonvizin, "Nedorosl'" (1782), *Sobranie sochinenii*, I, (Moscow-
Leningrad, 1959), 113. A large part of this chapter appeared in my article for
Canadian Slavonic Papers, XX, no. 1 (March, 1978), 23–43.
2. *Domostroi* (ed.) I. Glaznov (St. Petersburg, 1902), 20, 29–34, 40–46.
3. S. A. Belokurov, A. N. Zertsalov, *O nemetskikh shkolakh v Moskve v
pervoi chetverti XVIII veka, 1701–1715 gg.* (Moscow, 1907), 52.
4. *Zapiski kniagina Dashkova*, 8.
5. S. M. Solov'ev, *Istoriia Rossii*, Bk. XIII, vol. 26 (Moscow, 1965), 555–6,
contains a list of several such schools and the requests made by their sponsors
for accreditation.
6. *Ezhemeziachnye sochineniia* (May, 1755), 415.
7. "Izvestie o novouchrezhdaemoi shkole pri Sanktpeterburgskoi nemet-
skoi tser'kvi," *ibid.*, (August, 1762), 140–65. This referred to the school of St.
Peter. A translation of two essays by Mme Thérèse de Lampert, *Avis d'une
mère à son fils* (1726) and *Avis d'une mère à sa fille* (1728) into one book, in
Russian as *Letters of Mme de Lampert to Her Son about Righteousness and
Honour, and to her Daughter about the Virtues that are Proper to the Female
Sex* (*Pis'ma gospozhi de Lampert k eia synu o pravednoi chesti i k docheri o
dobrodeteliakh prolichnykh zhenskomu polu*) in 1761, reflected a similar
opinion.
8. *The Great Didactic of John Amos Comenius*, 66–68.
9. See especially Carolyn C. Lougee, "*Noblesse*, Domesticity, and Social
Reform: The Education of Girls by Fénelon and Saint-Cyr," *History of Education Quarterly*, XIV, no. 1 (Spring, 1974), 87–111.
10. Betskoi, *Sobranie uchrezhdenii i predpisanii kazatel'no vospitaniia, v
Rossii, oboego pola blagorodnago i meshchanskago iunoshestva*, I (St.
Petersburg, 1789), 5. See also 86, 217.
11. *PSZR*, no. 12.099 (22 March, 1764), 655–67, esp. 667.

12. *Ibid.*, no. 12.103 (12 March, 1764), 668–71.

13. N. P. Cherepnin, *Imperatorskoe vospitatel'noe Obshchestvo blagorodnykh devits: Istoricheskii ocherk, 1764–1914*, I (St. Petersburg, 1914), 44–54; Maikov, *Betskoi*, 254–5. Cherepnin's book is based upon the reports and minutes of the Imperial Educational Society, and so contains a wealth of primary information.

14. Catherine to Voltaire, 23 March, 1772, *SIRIO* (1874), 225–56.

15. *PSZR*, no. 12.154 (5 May, 1764), 742–55. All subsequent references to the original regulations of the school are taken from this document.

16. Catherine to Voltaire, 30 January, 1772, *SIRIO*, XIII (1874), 211–12. Diderot, *Mémoires pour Catherine II*, 86–7.

17. In fact, Racine wrote two plays especially for Saint-Cyr, *Esther* and *Athalie*, and they were performed a number of times between 1689 and 1691. Among their carefully selected audiences were Louis XIV and England's exiled James II. But de Maintenon put an end to these entertainments in 1691, and from then on Saint-Cyr became more and more a monastery; see T. Lavallée, *Madame de Maintenon et la maison royale de Saint-Cyr (1686–1793)*, (Paris, 1862), 2nd edition, 79–122.

18. Catherine to Madame Bielcke, 19 November, 1765, *SIRIO*, X (1872), 47; for the appointment of Dolgorukova, see *PSZR, op. cit.*, 742.

19. N. N. Raspopova, *Khronika Smol'nago monastyria v tsarstvovanie imperatritsy Ekateriny II* (St. Petersburg, 1864), 3–4; "Pis'ma I. I. Betskago k imperatritse Ekaterine vtoroi," *Russkaia starina*, LXXXV, no. 11 (1896), 388. On this question in general, see E. S. Shumigorsky, "Osnovanie Smol'nago monastyria," *Russkaia starina*, CLVII, no. 9 (1914), 306–51, esp. 322–23.

20. *PSZR*, no. 12.323 (31 January, 1765), 18–20.

21. Coxe, *Travels into Poland, Russia, Sweden and Denmark*, II (London, 1784), reprint of 2nd edition, 1785 (New York, 1970), 156.

22. *PSZR*, no. 12.957 (11 August, 1767), 290–326.

23. See especially, "Pamiatnyia zapiski Glaviru Ivanovnu Rzhevskoi," *Russkii arkhiv*, no. 1 (1871), 1–53. Rzhevsky (Rjewski), née Alymova, was among the first pupils to graduate from Smolny; "Chetrye pis'ma Imperatritsy Ekateriny II — i k kniagima A. P. Cherkasskoi (Uchrezhd. Levshinoi)," *Russkii arkhiv*, no. 3 (1870), 530–40, and notes on the letters by M. Longinov, *ibid.*, 0868–94. On the first Russian-language teacher, a Mrs. Pakhomova, see Cherepnin, 121.

24. Cherepnin, 86, 171–72, 177–78, 186; Anthony, *Catherine the Great* (New York, 1925), 210–11; Raspopova, *Khronika Smol'nago*, 45–46; E. Likhacheva, *Materialy dlia istorii zhenskago obrazovaniia v Rossii (1086–1796)*, I (St. Petersburg, 1899), 140.

25. Lord Cathcart to the Right Honourable Lord Viscount Weymouth, 26 September, 1768, *SIRIO*, XII (1873), 369–71.

26. Catherine to Voltaire, 30 January, 1772, *SIRIO*, XIII (1874), 211–12.

27. See footnote 22, above, and "E. I. Nelidova," *Russkii arkhiv*, no. 11 (1873), 2160–2202. For more on Nelidova, *Memoirs of Countess Golovina (1766–1821), a Lady at the Court of Catherine II* (London, 1910), 153–6, *et passim*, I. M. Dolgorukov, "Kapishche moego serdtsa," *Chteniia v Imp. obshchestve istorii i drevnostei Rossiiskikh pri Moskovskago universitete*, Bk. I, section 2 (1873), 190–92, and Cherepnin, 386–93.

28. Diderot, *Correspondance,* XIII (Paris, 1964), 76–77; see also 79, 81–2, and Diderot, *Mémoires pour Catherine II,* 84–85; Alymova makes similar comments about her own time as a very young student, "Pamiatnyia Rzhevskoi," 42.

29. Catherine to Grimm, 25 December, 1778, *SIRIO,* XXIII (1878), 216.

30. See "Dnevnik grafa Bobrinskago vedennyi v kadetskom korpuse i vo vremia puteshestviia po Rossii i za granitseiu" (1779), *Russkii arkhiv,* no. 10 (1877), 116–65. This account is filled with stories of dinners at Betskoi's home, and of balls and other fêtes at Smolny, most of which Bobrinsky described as "boring."

31. Catherine to Levshina, 1773, *SIRIO* (1874), 340.

32. Dolgorukov, "Kapishche moego serdtsa," *Russkii arkhiv,* no. 1 (1890), 32–3; for the tale about the girl being sent home, see "Cherty Ekateriny Velikoi," *Russkii arkhiv,* no. 11 (1870), 211–12. The story is recounted from the memoirs of P. I. Sumarokov; "Pamiatnyia Rzhevskoi," 15–16.

33. Coxe, *Travels into Poland, Russia . . . ,* II, 158.

34. The *Razpolozhenie ucheniia v Obshchestve blagorodnykh i meshchanskikh devits po vvedennomu v narodnykh uchilishchakh Rossiiskoi Imperii primeru* is quoted at length in Demkov, *Istoriia,* I, 429–30, and in Cherepnin, 204–06.

35. *SIRIO,* XXIII (1878), 20 September, 1783, 286; Cherepnin, 205; Demkov, *Istoriia,* I, 430. The entire question of moral training for women in eighteenth-century Russia is given careful treatment in A. Levshin, "Zhenskie nravy i vospitanie v proshlago veka," *Kolos'ia,* no. 1, (1887), 155–80; no. 2, 90–112.

36. For Pakhomov's first report to the Commission, which covers the week, 27 November to 3 December, 1783, see "Smol'nyi Monastyr' v 1783," *Russkaia starina,* XXIII (1878), 316–18.

37. V. N. Liadov, *Istoricheskii ocherk 100-letnei zhizni imp. vospitatel'nago obshchestva blagorodnykh devits i S.- Peterburgskago Aleksandrovskago uchilishcha* (St. Petersburg, 1864), 15–17, 23.

38. *O dolzhnostiakh cheloveka,* 111, 117. See also the Pakhomov report, where the text is mentioned several times.

39. *Karmannaia, ili Pamiatnaia knizhka dlia molodykh devits, soderzhashchaia v sebe nastavleniia prekrasnomu polu, s pokazaniem v chem dolzhny sostiat' uprazhneniia ikh* (Moscow, 1784), 11, 16–17.

40. *Ibid.,* 34; *O dolzhnostiakh cheloveka,* 4–5.

41. *Pamiatnaia knizhka,* 35–36, 44–46, 53.

42. "Nastavlenie ot ottsa docheriam," *Moskovskie vedomosti,* supplement no. 52 (1784), 611–12.

43. Shabaeva, *Ocherki istorii shkoly i pedagogicheskoi mysli narodov SSSR: XVIII v. – pervaia polovina XIX v.* (Moscow, 1973), 136–47; Likhacheva, I (1899), 170–71.

44. Shcherbatov, *On the Corruption of Morals in Russia* (ed.) A. Lentin (Cambridge, 1969), 253.

45. *Mémoires ou souvenirs et anecdotes par M. Le Comte de Ségur,* II (Paris, 1825), 235–36. W. Richardson, who was in Russia from mid-1768 to 1771, said much the same thing, see his *Anecdotes of the Russian Empire,* 225.

46. *Satiricheskie zhurnaly N. I. Novikova,* 459–63. For Lukin's comment,

see Semennikov, *Materialy ...*, 64–6. For basic data on the young women who became members of the court in varying capacities, see P. F. Karabanova, "Stats'-damy i frailiny russkago dvora v XVIII i XIX stoletiiakh," *Russkaia starina,* II (1870), 443–73; III (1871), 39–48, 272–82, 457–73; IV, 59–67, 379–405. For Grand Duke Paul's interest in Smolny, see *Zapiski Poroshina,* 436.

47. Dolgorukov, "Kapishche moego serdtse," *Chteniia,* Bk. III, section 2 (1872), 13. On de la Font: "My wife had, as did all the Smolniaks, an unlimited respect for her" (51). On Betskoi, Bk. II, section II (1873), 297.

48. Radishchev, *Polnoe sobranie sochineny,* III (Moscow, 1952), 267–304; Maikov, *Betskoi,* 300–02 and Cherepnin, 287–92, carry general information on both public and individual responses to Smolny. Levshin, in *Kolos'ia* (108–09), describes foreigners' reactions to plays put on at Smolny. For Shcherbatov's daughters, see Dolgorukov, *Chteniia* (1873), 298, and a graduating list contained in Raspopova, appendix 22.

49. "Pamiatnyia Rzhevskoi," 6, 8–10.

50. 1316 girls had attended Smolny 1764–1794; 850 of them graduated, 440 from the nobility and 410 from the bourgeoisie; see Likhacheva, I, 171.

51. The document which made official the award to de la Font is carried in V. T. Timoshchuk, "Imperatritse Mariia Feodorovna v eia zabotakh o Smoln'om monastyre, 1797–1802," *Russkaia starina,* no. 3 (1890), 821; on Palmenbach, see Cherepnin, 339–48.

52. *Ibid.,* 825–28; Raspopova, appendix 31.

53. E. Shumigorsky, "Smolny institut i ego rol' v istorii zhenskago obrazovaniia v Rossii," *Russkaia starina,* no. 8 (1914), 269–80.

54. Shabaeva, *Ocherki istorii shkoly,* 217.

55. Sivkov, in *Istoricheskii arkhiv,* 161.

56. *PSZR,* no. 14.392 (7 November, 1775), 249–51, 271–72.

57. Voronov, *Istoriko-statisticheskoe obozrenie,* 11.

58. *Izvestie o Petrovskom uchilishche* (St. Petersburg, 1782), 4–5.

59. "K nachal'noe istorii Kievskago narodnago uchilishcha (1789–1803)," *Kievskaia starina,* 71, no. 10, section ii (1900), 6, 8.

60. Shabaeva, *Ocherki istorii shkoly,* 141.

61. See chart in Rozhdestvensky, "Ocherki po istorii sistem narodnago prosveshcheniia v Rossii v XVIII–XIX vekakh," in *Zapiski istoriko filologicheskago Fakul'teta Imperatorskago S. Peterburgskago universiteta,* 54 (St. Petersburg, 1912), 605.

62. Andrei Briantsov, *Zhenskaia filosofiia* (Moscow, 1793), 12, 18–19, 75. See also *Zhenskoe serdechko* (St. Petersburg, 1789).

63. Karamzin, "Istoricheskoe pokhval'noe Ekaterine II," *Sochineniia Karamzina,* II (ed.) A. Smirdin (St. Petersburg, 1848), 276–77.

Conclusion

1. *PSZR,* no. 20.597 (26 January, 1802), 437–42; cited here 437–8.

2. See R. John Rath, "Training for Citizenship in the Austrian Elementary Schools during the Reign of Francis I," *Journal of Central European Affairs,* IV, no. 2 (1944), 147–64.

3. On Pobedonostsev's ideas about education and his general philosophy,

see Robert F. Byrnes, *Pobedonostsev: His Life and Thoughts* (Bloomington, Indiana, 1968). See also Pobedonostsev's *Reflections of a Russian Statesman* (London, 1898) in which, among other things, he insists that young Russians should not be educated to have ambitions beyond their station in life and that schools should be designed to instruct, rather than impart the means whereby children would learn to think for themselves.

4. Marie, Grand Duchess of Russia, *Education of a Princess: A Memoir* (New York, 1930), 3-4.

Select Bibliography

The following bibliography is limited to items concerned directly with education in eighteenth-century Russia, and is selective within that category. Special attention is given to English-language titles. Many more sources are referred to in the footnotes, among them titles of eighteenth-century texts, official documents, memoirs, and general works on pedagogy. For further sources of information, the reader of Russian could turn to the reasonably inclusive bibliography contained in M. F. Shabaeva (ed.), *Ocherki istorii shkoly i pedagogicheskoi mysli narodov SSSR: XVIII v. - pervaia polovina XIX v.* (Moscow, 1973), the sections on pedagogy and schools in P. Stepanov, Iu. V. Stennik (compilers), *Istoriia russkoi literatury XVIII veka: Bibliograficheskii ukazatel'* (Leningrad, 1968), and the useful bibliographical serial, *Literatura po pedagogicheskim naukam i narodnomu obrazovaniiu,* "Pedagogika" (Moscow), the first issue of which appeared in 1970. Complete titles, edition listing, translators and even numbers of copies printed of eighteenth-century works can be found in *Svodnyi katalog russkoi knigi grazhdanskoi pechati XVIII veka, 1725-1800,* I-IV (Moscow, 1963-67). A supplementary volume appeared in 1975.

Documentary Collections and Works

[Betskoi, I. I.], *Sobranie uchrezhdenii i predpisanii, kasatel'no vospitaniia, v Rossii, oboego pola blagorodnago i meshchanskago iunoshestva,* I-III (St. Petersburg, 1789-1791).
———, "Pis'ma I. I. Betskago k Imperatritse Ekaterine vtoroi," *Russkaia starina,* no. 11 (1896), 351-420.
Catherine the Great's Instruction (NAKAZ) to the Legislative Commission, 1767 (ed.) Paul Dukes (Newtonville, Mass., 1977).
Dokumenty i materialy po istorii Moskovskogo universiteta vtoroi poloviny XVIII veka, I (Moscow, 1960).
Ezhemesiachnye sochineniia, I-IX (1755-1763): journal.
Izbrannye proizvedeniia russkikh myslitelei vtoroi poloviny XVIII veka, I-II (ed.) I. Ia. Shchipanov (Moscow, 1952).
Khrestomatiia po istorii pedagogiki, I-IV, (ed.) N. A. Zhelvakov (Moscow, 1936).
Prazdnoe vremie v pol'zu upotreblennoe, (1759-1760): journal.
[PSZR], Polnoe sobranie zakonov Rossiiskoi imperii, IV-XLIV (St. Petersburg, 1830).
Materialy dlia istorii uchebnykh reform' v Rossii v XVIII-XIX vv., (ed.) S. V. Rozhdestvensky (St. Petersburg, 1910).

Russkie prosvetiteli (ot Radishcheva do Dekabristov): Sobranie proisvedenii v dvykh tomakh, I–II (ed.) I. Ia. Shchipanov (Moscow, 1966).

Semennikov, V. P., *Materialy dlia istorii russkoi literatury i dlia slovaria pisatelei epokha Ekateriny II* (St. Petersburg, 1914).

[SIRIO], Sbornik imp. Russkago Istoricheskago obshchestva, I–CXLVIII (1867–1916).

Sbornik materialov dlia istorii prosveshcheniia v Rossii, I–III (St. Petersburg, 1893).

[ZMNP], Zhurnal Ministerstva Narodnago Prosveshcheniia, I–CXLVIII (St. Petersburg, 1867–1917).

General Works: Education in Eighteenth-Century Russia:

Aleshintsev, I., *Istoriia gimnazicheskago obrazovaniia v Rossii (XVIII i XIX veka),* (St. Petersburg, 1912).

Andreev, V. V., *Ocherki po istorii obrazovaniia i literatury v Rossii* (St. Petersburg, 1872).

Chekhov, N. V., *Tipy russkoi shkoly* (Moscow, 1932).

Darlington, T., *Education in Russia* (London, 1909).

Demkov, M. I., *Istoriia russkoi pedagogiki,* I–II (Revel' and St. Petersburg, 1895, 1898).

———, *Russkaia pedagogika v glavneishikh ee predstaviteliakh* (St. Petersburg, 1898).

Epp, George, "The Educational Policies of Catherine II of Russia, 1762–1796," Ph.D. dissertation, University of Manitoba, 1976.

Fal'bork, G., and V. Charnolusky, *Narodnoe obrazovanie v Rossii* (St. Petersburg, 1893).

Freeze, Gregory L., *The Russian Levites: Parish Clergy in the Eighteenth Century* (Cambridge, Mass., 1977). See chapter on seminaries.

Grigor'ev, V. V., *Istoricheskii ocherk Russkoi shkoly* (Moscow, 1900).

Hans, Nicholas, *The Russian Tradition in Education* (London, 1963).

———, *History of Russian Educational Policy, 1701–1917* (New York, 1964).

Hassell, James, "The Implementation of the Russian Table of Ranks during the Eighteenth Century," *Slavic Review,* 29, no. 2 (June, 1970), 283–95.

Istoriia akademii nauk SSSR [1724–1803], I (Moscow-Leningrad, 1958).

Johnson, W.H.E., *Russia's Educational Heritage* (New York, 1950).

Kapterev, P. F., *Istoriia russkoi pedagogiki* (Petrograd, 1915).

Kniaz'kov, S. A., and N. I. Serbov, *Ocherk istorii narodnago obrazovaniia v Rossii do epokhi reform Aleksandra I* (Moscow, 1910).

Konstantinov, N. A., and V. Z. Smirnov, *Istoriia pedagogiki: uchebnik dlia pedagogicheskikh uchilishch* (Moscow, 1959).

Krasnobaev, B. I., *Ocherki istorii russkoi kul'tury XVIII veka* (Moscow, 1972).

Luppov, S. P., *Kniga v Rossii v pervoi chetverti XVIII veka* (Leningrad, 1973).

———, *Kniga v Rossii v poslepetrovskoe vremia, 1725–1740* (Leningrad, 1976).

Medynsky, E. N., *Istoriia russkoi pedagogiki* (Moscow, 1936).

———, "Development of Educational Ideas in Russia," *Soviet War News* (London), no. 802 (3 March, 1944).

no Alston!

Miliukov, P. N., *Ocherki po istorii Russkoi kul'tury,* II (Paris, 1931).
Moleva, N., and E. Beliutin, *Pedagogicheskaia sistema Akademii Khudozhestv XVIII veka* (Moscow, 1956).
Okenfuss, Max J., "Education in Russia in the First Half of the Eighteenth Century," Ph.D. dissertation, Harvard, 1970.
✓ Papmehl, K., *Freedom of Expression in 18th Century Russia* (The Hague, 1971).
Pekarsky, P., *Nauka i literatura v Rossii pri Petre Velikom,* I–II (St. Petersburg, 1862).
Raeff, Marc, *Origins of the Russian Intelligentsia: The Eighteenth Century Nobility* (New York, 1966).
✓ Roucek, J. S., "Education Within the Czarist Framework," *Pedagogica Historica,* IV (1964), 392–443.
Rozhdestvensky, S. V., *Ocherki po istorii sistem narodnago obrazovaniia v Rossii v XVIII–XIX vv.,* I (St. Petersburg, 1912).
Shabaeva, M. F., *Ocherki istorii shkoly i pedagogicheskoi mysli narodov SSSR: XVIII v. – pervaia polovina XIX v.* (Moscow, 1973).
Shevryev, S. P., *Istoriia moskovskago universiteta (1755–1855)* (Moscow, 1855).
Simkovitch, V. G., "History of the School in Russia," *The Educational Review* (May, 1907), 486–522.
Stoiunin, V. Ia., *Pedagogicheskie sochineniia* (St. Petersburg, 1903), 2nd edition.
Sychev-Mikhailov, M. V., *Iz istorii Russkoi shkoly i pedagogiki XVIII veka* (Moscow, 1960).
Tolstoi, D. A., *Vzgliad na uchebnuiu chast' v Rossii v XVIII stoletii do 1782 g.* (St. Petersburg, 1883).
———, *Akademicheskii universitet v XVIII stoletii* (St. Petersburg, 1885).
———, "Akademicheskaia gimnasiia v XVIII stoletii, po rukopisnym dokumentam Arkhiva Akademii nauk," *Zapiski Imperatorskoi Akademii nauk,* vol. 51, bk. 1 (St. Petersburg, 1885), appendix 2, 1–114.
Tompkins, S. R., *The Russian Mind* (Norman, Okla., 1953), Chapters three and five.
Vladimirsky-Budanov, M., *Gosudarstvo i narodnoe obrazovanie v Rossii XVIII-go veka,* Pt. I (Yaroslavl', 1874).
Voronov, A. S., *Istoriko-statisticheskoe obozrenie uchebnykh zavedenii S. Petersburgskago uchebnago okruga s 1715 po 1828 g. vkliuchitel'no* (St. Petersburg, 1849).
Vucinich, Alexander, *Science in Russian Culture: A History to 1860* (London, 1963).
Zeiliger-Rubinshtein, E., *Ocherki po istorii pedagogiki* (Leningrad, 1975).

Topical Works: Education in 18th Century Russia:

Anderson, M. S., "Samuel Bentham in Russia, 1779–1791," *American Slavic and East European Review,* XII, no. 2 (1956), 157–68.
Adler, Philip J., "Habsburg School Reform among the Orthodox Minorities, 1770–1780," *Slavic Review,* XXXIII, no. 1 (March, 1974), 23–45. Information on Iankovich de Mirievo.

Artem'ev, A., *Kazanskaia gimnaziia v XVIII v.* (St. Petersburg, 1874).
Barbashev, N. I., *K istorii morekhodnogo obrazovaniia v Rossii* (Moscow, 1959).
Barratt, G.R.V., "Vasily Nikitin: A Note on an Eighteenth-Century Russian Oxonian," *Eighteenth-Century Studies,* VIII, no. 1 (Fall, 1974), 75–99.
Beliavsky, M. T., "Shkola i sistema obrazovaniia v Rossii v kontse XVIII v.," *Vestnik Moskovskogo universiteta: istoriko-filologicheskaia,* no. 2 (1959), 105–20.
Belokurov, S. A., and A. N. Zertsalov, *O nemetskikh shkolakh v Moskve v pervoi chetverti XVIII veka (1701–1715 gg.)* (Moscow, 1907).
Bissonnette, Rev. Georges, "Peter the Great and the Church as an Educational Institution," in J. S. Curtiss (ed.), *Essays in Russian and Soviet History* (New York, 1965), 3–19.
✓ Black, J. L., "The Search for a 'Correct' Textbook of National History for 18th Century Russian Schools," *New Review of East European History,* XVI, no. 1 (March, 1976), 1–19.
✓ _____, "Citizenship Training and Moral Regeneration as the Mainstays of Russian Schools," *Studies on Voltaire and the Eighteenth Century,* CLXVII (1977), 427–51.
_____, "Educating Russia's Women in the Eighteenth Century: Myths and Realities," *Canadian Slavonic Papers,* XX, no. 1 (March, 1978), 23–43.
Boss, Valentin, *Newton and Russia: The Early Influence, 1698–1796* (Cambridge, 1972).
Brown, A. H., "S. E. Desnitsky, Adam Smith, and the *Nakaz* of Catherine II," *Oxford Slavonic Papers,* new series, VII (1974), 42–59.
Burov, A. A., "Pervyi ustav russkoi narodnoi shkoly" [Tatishchev], *Sovietskaia pedagogiki,* no. 6 (1960), 119–29.
Cherepnin, N. P., *Imperatorskoe vospitatel'noe Obshchestvo blagorodnykh devits: Istoricheskii ocherk, 1764–1914,* I (St. Petersburg, 1914).
✓ Chuchmarev, V. I., "G. V. Leibnits i russkaia kul'tura nachala 18 stoletiia," *Vestnik istorii mirovoi kul'tury,* no. 4 (1957), 120–32.
Chuma, A. A., *Ian Amos Komenskii i russkaia shkola (do 70 godov 18 veka)* (Bratislava, 1970).
Chuvashev, I. V., "I. I. Betskoi o pervonachal'nom vospitanii detei," *Doshkol'noe vospitanie,* no. 2 (1944), 30–40.
Cracraft, James, *The Church Reform of Peter the Great* (Bristol, 1971).
Cross, A. G., "Russian Students in Eighteenth-Century Oxford (1766–75)," *Journal of European Studies,* V, no. 2 (June, 1975), 91–110.
_____, "Russian Students at Edinburgh University, 1774–87," *Study Group on Eighteenth-Century Russia: Newsletter,* no. 5 (1977), 5–7.
Demkov, M. I., "Kharakter russkago prosveshcheniia i pedagogiki XVIII veka," *Pedagogicheskoi sbornik,* Bk. 367 (August, 1897), 97–114; (September, 1897), 197–215.
Demidova, N. F., "Instruktsiia V. N. Tatishcheva o poriadke prepodavaniia v shkolakh pri ural'skikh kazennykh zavodakh," *Istoricheskii arkhiv,* V (Moscow–Leningrad, 1950), 166–78.
Derevtsov, I. A., "K otsenke roli shkol'nogo ustava 1786 goda v razvitii shkol'noi sistemy i prosveshcheniia v Rossii v kontse XVIII veka," *Uchenye zapiski. Krasnodarskii pedagogicheskii institut,* XVI (1956), 94–110.

Dodon, L. L., "Uchebnaia literatura russkoi narodnoi shkoly vtoroi poloviny XVIII veka i rol' F. I. Iankovicha v ee sozdanii," *Uchenye zapiski LGPI im. A. I. Gertsena,* CXVIII (1955), 185–207.

———, "Nachalo pedagogicheskoi obrazovanosti v Rossii," *Uchenye zapiski LGPI im. A. I. Gertsena,* CXXXIX (1957), 167–86.

Dukes, Paul, *Catherine the Great and the Russian Nobility* (Cambridge, 1967).

Eingorn, V., "Moskovskoe Glavnoe narodnoe uchilishche v kontse XVIII veka," *ZMNP* (April, 1910), 129–68.

———, "Prepodavanie istorii v Moskovskom glavnom narodnom uchilishche (1786–1802)," *Sbornik statei posviashchennykh V. O. Kliuchevskomu* (Moscow, 1909), 765–90.

———, "Vospitatel'noe zavedenie pri moskovskom Glavnom narodnom uchilishche," *Sbornik statei v chest' M. K. Liubavskago* (Petrograd, 1917), 497–523.

Epifanov, P. P., "'Uchenaia druzhina' i prosvetitelstvo XVIII veka," *Voprosy istorii* (March, 1963), 37–53.

Ewal'd, V., *Materialy dlia istorii prosveshcheniia v Rossii v XVIII stoletii. Fedor Ivanovich Iankovich de Mirievo* (St. Petersburg, 1858).

Gleason, Walter, "Political Ideals and Loyalties of Some Russian Writers of the Early 1760s," *Slavic Review,* 34, no. 3 (September, 1975), 563–73.

Hans, Nicholas, "The Moscow School of Mathematics and Navigation (1701)," *Slavonic and East European Review,* XXXIX, no. 73 (June, 1951), 532–36.

———, "Russian Students at Leyden in the 18th Century," *Slavonic and East European Review,* XXV, no. 85 (June, 1957), 551–61.

———, "H. Farquharson, Pioneer of Russian Education," *Aberdeen University Review,* XXXVIII, 120 (1959), 26–29.

Home, R. W., "Science as a Career in Eighteenth-Century Russia: The Case of F.U.T. Aepinus," *Slavonic and East European Review,* LI, no. 122 (January, 1973), 75–94.

Ignatieff, L. "French Emigrés in Russia after the French Revolution: French Tutors," *Canadian Slavonic Papers,* VIII (1966), 125–31.

"Instruktsiia o vospitanii: 1722–1775 gg.," *Russkaia starina,* 31 (1881), 655–664 [M. G. Lebedev for his son].

Jones, Robert E., *The Emancipation of the Russian Nobility, 1762–1785* (Princeton, 1973).

Jones, W. Gareth, "The *Morning Light* Charity Schools, 1777–80," *Slavonic and East European Review,* LVI, no. 1 (January, 1978), 47–67.

Kallash, V., "Iz istorii ekaterinskoi shkoly," *Vestnik vospitaniia,* no. 7, section 2 (1895), 15–29.

Kaplan, Frederick L., "Tatishchev and Kantemir: Two Eighteenth-Century Exponents of a Russian Bureaucratic Style of Thought," *Jahrbücher für Geschichte Osteuropas,* XIII (1965), 503–20.

Kiprianovich, I., "Fedor Ivanovich Iankovich-de-Mirievo," *Gimnazii,* IV, no. 3 (1891), 1–24.

Kirpichnikov, A. I., "Pedagogi proshlago veka," *Istoricheskie vestnik,* no. 9 (1885), 433–43 [Dilthey's Plan of 1764].

Kizevetter, A. A., "Odin iz reformatorov russkoi shkoly (Betskoi)," *Istoricheskoi ocherki* (St. Petersburg, 1912), 119–49.

_____, "Shkol'nye voprosy nashego vremeni v dokumentakh XVIII st.," *Istoricheskie ocherki* (St. Petersburg, 1912), 91–118.

Kliuchevsky, V. O., "Dva vospitaniia," *Russkaia mysl'*, XIV, no. 3 (1893), 79–99. [Betskoi, *Domostroi, Nakaz*].

Kolybel' *flota: Navigatskaia shkola — Morskoi korpus: 1701–1951* (Paris, 1951).

Lappo-Danilevsky, A. S., *I. I. Betskoi i ego sisteme vospitaniia* (St. Petersburg, 1904).

Lepskaia, L. A., "Sostav uchashchikhsia narodnykh uchilishch Moskvy v kontse XVIII v.," *Vestnik Moskovskogo universiteta,* no. 5 (1973), 88–96.

Levshin, A., "Zhenskie nravy i vospitanie proshlago veka," *Kolos'ia,* no's 1 & 2 (1887), 155–80, 90–112.

Liadov, V. N., *Istoricheskii ocherk 100-letnei zhizni imp. vospitatel'nago obshchestva blagorodnykh devits i S.-Peterburgskago Aleksandrovskago uchilishcha* (St. Petersburg, 1864).

Likhacheva, E., *Materialy dlia istorii zhenskago obrazovaniia v Rossii (1086–1796),* I–II (St. Petersburg, 1899).

Likhareva-Boky, N. I., "Iz istorii pedagogicheskoi mysli. (Voprosy metodiki istorii v Rossii XVIII veka)," *K 25-letiiu uchenopedagogicheskoi deiatel'-nosti I. M. Grevsa. Sbornik statei* (St. Petersburg, 1911), 445–76.

Lipski, A., "The Beginnings of General Secondary Education in Russia," *History of Education Journal,* VI, no. 3 (1955), 210–20.

Maikov, P. M., *I. I. Betskoi: opyt ego biografii* (St. Petersburg, 1904).

Makeeva, V. N., "Ad'iunt akademii nauk V. E. Adodurov," *Akademii nauk SSSR: Vestnik,* no. 1 (1974), 110–17.

Manning, Clarence, "The French Tutor in Russian Literature," *Romanic Review,* XXVII (June, 1936), 28–32.

McConnell, A., "Helvétius' Russian Pupils," *Journal of the History of Ideas,* XXIV, no. 3 (1963), 373–86.

Mikhnevich, V., *Russkaia zhenshchina XVIII stoletii* (Kiev, 1895).

Nechaev, N. V., *Shkoly pri gornykh zavodakh Urala v pervoi polovine 18-go stoletiia* (Moscow, 1944).

Okenfuss, Max J., "Technical Training in Russia under Peter the Great," *History of Education Quarterly,* XIII (1973), 325–45.

_____, "The Jesuit Origins of Petrine Education," in J. G. Garrard (ed.), *The Eighteenth Century in Russia* (Oxford, 1973), 106–30.

_____, "Russian Students in Europe in the Age of Peter the Great," in J. G. Garrard (ed.), *The Eighteenth Century in Russia* (Oxford, 1973), 131–48.

Papmehl, K. A., "The Regimental Schools Established in Siberia by Samuel Bentham," *Canadian Slavonic Papers,* VIII (1966), 153–68.

Persits, M. M., "'Razgovor dvukh priitelei o pol'zu nauk i uchilishch' V. N. Tatishcheva, kak pamiatnik russkogo svobodmysliia XVIII v.," *Voprosy istorii, religii i ateizma,* III (Moscow, 1956), 278–310.

Piatkovsky, A. P., "S.-Peterburgskii Vospitatel'nyi dom' pod upravleniem I. I. Betskago: Istoricheskoe izsledovanie," *Russkaia starina,* XII (1875), 146–60, 359–80, 665–81; XIII (1875), 177–253, 532–53; XIV (1875), 421–43.

no Rogger!

Polz, Peter, "Theodor Janković und die Schulreform in Russland," in *Die Aufklärung in Ost- und Sudosteuropas* (Cologne, 1972), 119–74.

Povarova, E. V., "Rol' 'Kommissii ob uchrezhdenii narodnykh uchilishch' i razvitii russkoi shkoly i pedagogiki XVIII v.," *Novye issledovaniia v pedagogicheskikh naukakh,* XVII, no. 4 (1971), 17–22.

———, "Nauchno-pedagogicheskaia deiatel'nosti professorov i prepodavatelei peterburgskoi uchitel'skoi seminarii v XVIII veke," in M. F. Shabaeva (ed.), *Voprosy istorii pedagogiki (Sbornik nauchnykh trudov)* (Moscow, 1973), 112–36.

Rabinovich, M. D., "K istorii prosveshcheniia v Rossii v kontse XVIII v. (Saratovskaia soldatskaia garizonnaia shkola v 1793 g.)," *Istoricheskii arkhiv,* no. 1 (1958), 230–33.

Raeff, Marc, "Home, School and Service in the Life of the 18th Century Russian Nobleman," *Slavonic and East European Review,* XL, no. 95 (June, 1962), 295–307.

Ransel, David L., *The Politics of Catherinian Russia: The Panin Party* (New Haven, 1975).

Raspopova, N. N., *Khronika Smol'nago monastyria v tsarstvovanie Imperatritsy Ekateriny II* (St. Petersburg, 1864).

Rozhdestvensky, S. V., "Kommissiia ob uchrezhdenii narodnykh uchilishch (1782–1803) i Ministerstvo narodnago prosveshcheniia," *ZMNP,* no. 5, section iii (1906), 14–18.

———, "Proekty uchebnykh reform v tsarstvovanie Imperatritsy Ekateriny I do uchrezhdeniia Kommissiia i narodnykh uchilishchakh," *ZMNP,* no. 1, section iii (1907), 175–86.

Shugurov, M., "Uchenie i ucheniki v XVIII vek (po povodu biografii A. Ia. Polenova)," *Russkii arkhiv* (1866), 303–24.

Sivkov, K. V., "Iz istorii krepostnoi shkoly vtoroi poloviny XVIII v.," *Istoricheskie zapiski:* AN SSSR institut istorii, III (1938), 270–94.

———, "Chastnye pansiony o shkoly Moskvy v 80-x godakh XVIII v.," *Istoricheskii arkhiv,* VI (1951), 315–23.

Stoiunin, V. Ia., "Razvitie pedagogicheskikh idei v Rossii v XVIII st.," *Pedagogicheskie sochineniia* (St. Petersburg, 1903), 2nd edition, 91–175.

Stolpiansky, P., "Odin iz nezametnykh deiatelei Ekateriansky epokhi: Iakov Pavlovich Kozels'kii," *Russkii arkhiv* (1906), 567–84.

Veselago, F., *Ocherk istorii Morskago kadetskago korpusa* (St. Petersburg, 1852).

Voronov, A. S., *Fedor Ivanovich Iankovich de-Mirievo ili narodnyia uchilishcha v Rossii pri imp. Ekaterine II* (St. Petersburg, 1858).

Znamensky, P., *Dukhovnye shkola v Rossii do reformy 1808 goda* (Kazan, 1881).

BOOK ON THE DUTIES OF MAN AND CITIZEN

Designated for reading in the Public Schools of the
Russian Empire, and published by Royal Command

(St. Petersburg, 1783)

Translated by ELIZABETH GORKY,
Laurentian University, Sudbury, from the
tenth printing, 1811

Edited by J. L. Black

Table of Contents*

*Page numbers listed here refer to those from the Russian text, which are marked in parentheses in the translation. All the original footnotes, which were references to appropriate places in the Bible, have been excluded from this translation.

Introduction

On well-being in general.

1. Every man wishes well-being for himself, and it does not suffice
   that others might think that we are prosperous, but everyone
   wants in fact to be prosperous and wishes this prosperity not only
   for a short time, but forever and for eternity.
2. In any occupation one can be prosperous. Often people think that
   only Tsars, princes, noblemen and aristocrats have a prosperous
   life. This, however, is not true: God's grace does not exclude anyone from prosperity; citizens, tradesmen, settlers and /2/ slaves
   and hirelings can be prosperous people.
3. It is possible for one to lack well-being regardless of his occupation. One should not think of people of the lower and poor classes
   as unhappy, because often noblemen and the wealthy are much
   more unhappy than simple and poor people.
4. Of course, in every occupation there is something pleasant which
   other occupations lack, but on the other hand every occupation
   has its own hardships. The very nature of things in this world
   brings such things to pass and God himself caused it to be.

   Theefore whoever chooses a given occupation for himself, or
   whomever is designated to a given occupation by God, must
   accept the hardship of that position and patiently endure them.
   /3/
   We should never wish for something that is unsuited to our
   occupation because we can never attain it: wishing in vain would
   only cause our heart to suffer, and we can be happy according to
   our status even though we lack what others in higher positions
   possess.
5. People would not be tormented by many vain wishes if they knew
   that happiness is not contained in the material things which sur-
   round them. It does not consist in wealth, that is: land, expensive
   clothing, splendid ornaments, and other things which we see and
   have around us. The rich can very easily obtain such things for
   themselves, but that does not mean that they are happy because of

that, and this proves that happiness does not /4/ consist merely in the possession of such things.

6. True happiness lies within ourselves. When our soul is well, free of unruly desires, and the body is healthy, then man is happy. Therefore, the only people in the world who are completely happy are those who are satisfied with their possessions, because without satisfaction, a clean conscience, decency and wisdom the richest and most distinguished person can be just as unhappy as a person of lowest rank.

   To acquire a good conscience, health and contentment we must:
   a. forge our soul with virtue.
   b. take proper care of our body. /5/
   c. fulfill our duties to which we are appointed by God.
   d. know the rules of housekeeping.

Part I
ON THE FORMATION OF THE SOUL
Preface

1. Man is composed not only of his visible body. Something that we do not see resides in that body. Whoever does not want to believe this can persuade himself scientifically by recalling many things that he long ago saw, heard, touched, tasted and smelled. For there is no part of the human body that could recall the past. The bodily senses perceive the present, but not the past and since man recalls also the past, there is /6/ in him something separate from the body, which knows past sensations. And this being within us which experiences other things, is called the *soul*.

2. The soul can recall the past; therefore it has:
   a. *Memory.* An attentive man can retain in his memory a great deal; because he listens attentively to many things he perfectly remembers all things and circumstances which he intently saw and heard. The more and longer man uses attentiveness, the stronger his memory becomes: On the other hand, a light-minded and unattentive man recalls nothing or very little because for the most part he notices /7/ only half of what is going on, or misperceives it.

b. The soul meditates further on the impression it made on the memory; one thought produces another and thus the soul reasons and draws conclusions; and if the soul can think and reason about what is instilled in its memory, then it has *intelligence* or *wisdom*. If one has correctly noticed a certain thing and if he can correctly fix it in his memory, he can reason about it correctly. One can easily see that there is a great necessity for the soul to reason correctly. Almost all things in the world have something in them that can be useful or harmful to us. Often evil seems quite pleasant, and good /8/ often has within it something unpleasant for us. He who does not fix this in his memory well enough and only thinks about what seems pleasant or unpleasant to him, forgets what is truly evil or good; and he reasons incorrectly, mistaking sometimes evil for good and good for evil, and often causes himself unspeakable harm.

c. Those things that please us, we want and desire and if we do not receive them soon, we undertake such actions by which we could get what we desire. This action of the soul is called *will*. Wishes and intentions are sometimes so strong that man spares neither his energy, nor possessions, nor health, nor life in order to obtain what he desires. Therefore one can clearly see how important it is to know whether /9/ those things we desire are really good or harmful, or if they only seem to be good. He who reasons about things incorrectly, wishes and does evil, thinking at the time to himself that he wishes and does good. *Memory, intelligence* or *reason, will, wishes* and *intentions* are called *powers of the soul.*

3. When these powers of the soul are not being refined by frequent practice, are not governed, and are not guided by good instructions then ideas which man has about worldly things and about well-being often are false and incorrect. He does not learn then to distinguish correctly good from evil, takes as good only those things which can appease his wishes and the inclinations of his heart. And therefore it is a great advantage / 10/ to a man when he is taught to reason correctly, and consequently to act properly.

Chapter One

On virtues of men.

1. *On righteousness.*

He who acts according to what he has recognized as right is a righteous man. A righteous man does not act on the basis of what is compatible with his inclinations and desires, rather he does that which is right.

Therefore, righteousness is the inclination and endeavour to fulfill not only the duties of one's occupation but also one's duties to God and people. We must not think that this world was created for our sake only; just as /11/ we want to live and be happy, so others want and desire the same.

But these other people with whom we have to live are not always kind and intelligent; therefore we have to learn how to live among people of all classes, [to live] among kind and evil people happily and safely; and we will achieve this when we try to fulfill not only the duties of our occupation but also our obligations to neighbours. Because not only kind people have benevolence towards righteous people, but also those who do not make an effort or try to fulfill their duties through some affection slowly come closer to them. Virtue has such an intrinsic attractiveness that it is revered even by its enemies. /12/

2. *On Love of Honour.*

The love of honour is the inclination to make oneself worthy of honour, and the very effort to do that by which true honour is acquired. We have an obligation to undertake that which will make us worthy of honour in the eyes of others, that is, to act in order to acquire respect. Therefore, we have the right to rejoice when others respect us. But one must not set his heart merely to seeking fame, or think about it excessively when others do not recognize the good that is in us. It may be that others sometimes have well-founded reasons which prevent them from thinking about our good deeds in the way we would like them to. We must not seek honour by illegal means, nor /13/ place honour alone as the only goal of our activities: let the fulfillment of our obligations be their own reward. The former sets fallacious rules, and the latter causes vanity. Honour is not in the power of the one who wishes to be honoured, rather it lies in the hands of those who honour us. Only reasonable people can truthfully honour us. A scoundrel does nothing without reward or compulsion, while the man who loves honour and desires to reap the praises of reasonable men does good without personal advantage and compulsion.

3. *On tranquility of the spirit.*

Tranquility of the spirit is the inclination and effort to endure evil circumstances and injury patiently and without complaint. By tranquility of the spirit we lessen dissatisfaction and sorrows which arise from poverty and misfortune /14/ in life. There are misfortunes which can not be averted by reasoning or by any power and these we must patiently endure, all the more because intolerance and complaints can not in any way relieve us of such misfortunes, but rather make them more unbearable. A reasoning man always chooses the most effective means from all those possible in order, if not to completely relieve his condition then at least to make it as bearable as he can. And for this purpose we must often remind ourselves about the impermanence and transience of material goods, and seek such small permissible diversions, as can be afforded by people of any class, in order thus to reinforce the tranquility of our spirit. In order /15/ to maintain our tranquility let us believe that everything that happens on the earth contains good and serves, if not each person in particular, then at least the general well-being of the human race. With such a belief one can always be content and happy and protect his soul from unnecessary grief. Let us dedicate ourselves only to God's will and let us place our hopes on His providence.

4. *On love of knowledge.*

The love of knowledge is the inclination and the effort to acquire useful knowledge and to willingly follow good instructions, examples, and admonitions of others. We must try to soundly understand our duties, because in this way we learn clearly and thoroughly the reasons for performing them, and /16/ are more inclined to fulfill them. After acquiring a sound knowledge of our duties we must seclude ourselves from delusions, that is from fallacious opinions; because a man who is possessed by fallacious opinions is unable to recognize the real good and can not choose what is useful for him. From our early childhood we must learn to know ourselves and others, to imitate good and honest people, to receive instructions from the wise willingly but carefully avoid evil, and plan wisely ahead of time our actions for every day and at the end of the day ask ourselves of what sort were our deeds and in what way on that day did we expand our knowledge /17/.

5. *On truthfulness.*

Truthfulness is the nature of honest man which makes him never to speak in any other way than the way he thinks and knows, and which restrains him from falsehood, makes that vice truly distasteful to him and which never allows him to use any evil means.

Chapter Two

On duties to God.

Duties which we must render to God are offered in detail in the catechism. Here we will say only that an honest man must be pious and that true piety consists not only in the careful observance of the Holy worship and in the perfect knowledge of laws and its duties, but /18/ more so in the wholehearted love and reverence for God, to obey His will, always live according to it and all this because we are all created by God.

Chapter Three

On duties to our neighbour.

1. *On Friendliness*

Friendliness is the inclination and effort to treat others kindly without spite and without aversion. At times even the smallest things can make us amiable in the eyes of others.

Only a greeting, or a visit when someone we know is ill, and sometimes only a kind look is enough to earn the benevolence and friendship of our neighbours. For those people who always have /19/ a gloomy face filled with spite it is usually quite difficult to acquire friends. Even though many of them have commendable qualities, a sad and sullen person does not attract friends.

2. *On the love of peace.*

The love of peace consists in the ability to live in harmony with anyone, to forego quarrelling and even to concede when one is not obligated to do so.

3. *On obligingness.*

Obligingness is the inclination and attempt to do willingly what is pleasing, useful and necessary to others.

When people see that we are inclined to help them whenever this can be done without detriment to us, when /20/ they see that we protect them from real harm, or at the beginning of some undertaking we give them good advice, or if they find in our treatment of them something pleasant, then they will do for us just as much and often even more, than we are willing to do for them. Therefore we should not miss any opportunity to serve our neighbour.

The world would be in a very happy state if all people on such occasions would fulfill their duties. If each man would love all others as [he loves] himself we would wish nothing but to see them happy, and if each man had sincere benevolence for others, then each would /21/ apply all his energies to help others be happy. In word and deed people not only help one another wholeheartedly and zealously but would also be happy that they had correctly guessed the wishes of others and had anticipated [those wishes] by helping and serving.

Of course not all people are so obliging, but nevertheless we should not be lazy in the performance of our duties, nor wait for others to perform them before us.

4. *On sincerity.*

Sincerity is the inclination and effort to tell others without hesitation what is useful to them and safeguard them from what is harmful to them.

He who treats people insincerely will soon be hated by all. /22/ It is impossible to know all intentions and wishes of your neighbour just as it is generally impossible for people to know everything. Therefore one must rely often on what others say. But when people do not tell the whole truth then by our ignorance we might do many things which would do us real harm. Therefore all liars are always hated by all people, but people believe a sincere man who is known as a lover of truth and hates falsehood and flattery in his words without oaths and vows. Everyone to whom he gives promises relies firmly on his word, just as if one had received from him a written obligation. Sincere people generally have the weakness /23/ (if one can call it a weakness) that they judge all people by their example, and expect the same sincerity from others. And since they are often forced to have business with insincere people, so it sometimes happens that they are taken advantage of and cheated. Therefore, we must be very careful not to seem untrusting on one hand, and on the other hand to safeguard ourselves from the danger of deceit. We can offend a sincere man by not trusting him, on the other hand, it would be madness to trust someone whose sincerity was not yet proven. /24/

5. *On honesty.*

Honesty is the inclination and effort to promote the well-being of others with sincerity, especially if we are bound to do so by a promise or otherwise. One must demonstrate honesty more by his deeds and feelings than by his words or facial expression. One acts cunningly and dishonestly if he is friendly in word, but scheming and wicked in heart. But he who is benevolent to others, while forgetting his own interests, acts unreasonably.

6. *On respectfulness.*

Respectfulness consists in thinking only good things of others and showing our respect to them at every occasion in word and deed. /25/

Chapter Four

On one's duties to himself.

1. *On order.*

Order is the inclination and effort to arrange and carry out one's affairs in such a way as their nature demands, and to place one's belongings in a certain place and to keep them there, so that one might find them intact quickly, when they are needed.

The person who at night puts his clothing, footwear etc. at a certain familiar place does not need to look for one thing here and another somewhere else in the morning; at the end of play one should put everything away in its usual place. /26/

In a home where there is no order, everything comes to confusion; in such a home things that should have been done in the morning are done only at noon or towards evening. Nobody knows who is the master and who is the servant, who is the mistress or servant-girl, who is the cook or custodian.

2. *On love of labour.*

One who performs work which he is obligated to do by his position or his duties is called industrious.

The love of labour is the inclination and effort to acquire honestly for oneself or for one's family the means suitable to one's occupation, and to preserve righteously what one has acquired. Labour and work are not /27/ only for the acquisition of life's necessities, but also for providing the exercise essential for health of the mind and body, and consequently for the preservation of one's well-being.

And since both the former and the latter further the attainment of man's perfection, it is our duty to work.

Every activity we undertake for our sake or for the sake of others we call labour or work.

In a country there is nothing more useful and more necessary than subjects who love to work diligently. And there is nothing more harmful than laziness and idleness. Laziness deprives one even of health. He who has overslept, does not go to work happily; food and drink are never so pleasant /28/ as [they are] after sufficient activity. One who loves work is diligent, one that does not is lazy. Labour is our duty and our strongest shield against vice. A lazy and idle man is a useless burden on the earth and a rotten member of society.

3. *On contentment.*

Contentment is the inclination and effort to be satisfied with what was honestly acquired. A poor man who is satisfied with what he has, is much happier than a rich man who always wants more and is never satisfied.

There are in the world many examples which show that people never had more problems than when their possessions were multiplied. /29/

What is granted by God is ours to enjoy;
We must not grieve over what we cannot have,
In every walk of life there is a pleasant part,
So too every walk of life has its misfortunes.
O, mere mortal! Don't ever be deluded in your thoughts
That somehow God's grace has passed you by.
God grants us more than we deserve;
And always protects us from harm.

A content man does not desire much for himself and since he desires little, he often receives more than he hopes for; and therefore he often has reason for unexpected joy.

4.   *On housekeeping.*

The inclination and effort to allocate one's income in such a way that one's home has everything it needs is called housekeeping.

In housekeeping it is not enough to try to acquire wealth honestly, /30/ one must also think about how to keep one's accumulated wealth and not to waste money on non-necessities.

No matter how large one's inheritance is, it can be squandered in a short time, if one does not save it.

5.   *On thriftiness.*

Thriftiness is the inclination and effort to allocate one's estate and profit in such a way that after all necessary expenses one can save something and put it away for future needs.

Since we cannot foresee what events might befall us in the future, which may cause us to lose our possessions or make us unfit to earn what we need, it is our duty /31/ to think about such eventualities and save part of our present possessions so that in such a case we might not suffer need.

The thrifty man shuns squandering as much as he does hideous stinginess. The squanderer spends more than is necessary and this is a vice; and the stingy man always wants to amass more than he can save without damage to his status and to his decency; and that too is a vice. By squandering we arouse the suspicion in others that we are foolish; for our stinginess we shall be considered mean, and then too we shall have to answer to God himself for not making sensible use of the gifts we have derived from His great goodness. /32/

Chapter Five

On things that the virtuous man should avoid.

1. *Excessive egotism.*

    One who cares only about his own peace and profit, even though they might bring harm to others, or one who thinks in such a way will have few friends.

    Since we cannot achieve complete happiness by ourselves alone and we are destined to be happy only through union with others, we must treat other men the same way we expect to be treated ourselves. People love each other, and therefore they will love us too if they see that we respect their interests and help satisfy their desires. /33/ But if they notice that we do not hesitate to insult them, they will consider us enemies and will repay us in kind. Therefore, in our every deed we must take careful note of what reaction that deed can evoke in the heart of our neighbour, so that we might earnestly prevent any evil consequence.

2. *Pride and conceit.*

    Out of pride and conceit we imagine to ourselves that we are better than others and think that others owe much to us, while we owe them less or nothing at all.

    Pride leads us to the false opinion that we are exceedingly wise, rich, beautiful and virtuous, or at least /34/ that we are in such a privileged position that others must therefore pay honour to us and that we have the right to demand it from them. Pride before all others is abominable, it does not achieve its goal and prevents the real acquisition of imagined privileges.

    The best remedy against pride is to know oneself. If we only realize that we appear more perfect to ourselves than we do to others, that others have much greater gifts and that they already have proved this with much more evidence than we have, then we shall not have reason to consider ourselves better than others. /35/

3. *Vanity.*

    Vanity is the excessive yearning for honour and the desire to have more honours than one deserves or can receive. He who honours us undeservingly is mistaken or does not know us. Even though we ought to behave in such a way that others might recognize our good qualities; when people do not recognize those qualities in us, we should not feel insulted and hate them for this, least of all be angered by this, because such is not the way to make our merits known.

Titles and plaudits are usually empty affectations. The wise man does not pay regard to the title that one wears, but only to one's merits themselves. When he notices merits /36/ in a man without any title he respects him more than one who has a title he does deserve.

The same is true of the praises we receive from ordinary people. The praises of one wise man are better than those from a thousand fools. Many people are greedy for money, because they see that simple people pay special honour to those who are rich. One is not exalted by his possessions, if he did not acquire them through his own merits. Often poverty itself is commendable when one surpasses others in reason and virtue. He who seeks honour in expensive clothing is highly praised for the most part only by merchants and artisans /37/ since he gives them a large profit. The wise man does not respect us more for the clothing which distinguishes us from others but rather ridicules us for seeking honour in such an idle pursuit.

4. *Meanness and neglect of honour.*

Meanness is found in people who do not derive pleasure from real honour, act indecently or who are inclined to such behaviour as might evoke despisal in reasonable people. A man has mean thoughts if he likes deeds which deserve to be despised in others, if he talks about such deeds eagerly and if he himself is inclined to perform them, /38/ to talk with pleasure about the sins of others, to divulge their shortcomings, to initiate squabbles, disturbances and other unfitting acts for which we are despised by others. A young man who is eager to do such things or praises his friends for doing them and loves them for this is mean and will in most cases agree to do evil things without any hesitation and through this will earn disrespect of all reasonable people.

5. *Dissoluteness.*

A dissolute person is one who is given to vice and violence.

He who lives a dissolute life, falls into disgrace and becomes a laughing-stock, weakens his body, makes himself worthy of God's punishment and causes himself to be reviled by others. When Christians /39/ wanted to curse their enemies, they would wish them to be overcome by lawless passions or, what is just the same, wished that [their enemies] might plunge themselves into misfortune and disgrace.

6.   *Crudeness.*

Crudeness is doing something that insults others or is disgusting and unpleasant to them. There is a kind of crudeness which is unforgivable even for people of the lowest rank and is contrary to Christianity, which orders us to honour one another — namely because it signifies a heart deprived of any love. That language is crude if in it one can clearly discern contempt for one's neighbour, or if in it all kinds of abusive and sarcastic names are used even in the guise of a joke. /40/ This vice gives rise to indignation in our neighbour, because everyone to whom our crudeness is directed or whom we refuse even little favors, can discern in this our ill-will.

7.   *Impoliteness.*

One who does not care to be respectful and kind and who does not do what well-behaved people of equal condition are used to do, is impolite.

Of course we cannot demand refined manners from people who are not familiar with them from childhood; nevertheless we must always be at least as polite as other people of our station. /41/

One must treat with respect all people according to their rank, age and occupation and not treat anyone in a contemptuous way. One must not speak about things that others do not wish to hear or understand. One must rather try to be in accord with others, not demand that others agree with us about everything. In this way, when we begin to do this, not only shall we be regarded as polite, but also our neighbours will come to love and honour us.

8.   *Contradiction, contempt, finding fault, mockery, nonindulgent condemnation and slander.*

There are some people who cannot say anything good about anyone. As soon as they learn about somebody's error /42/ they report it everywhere, publicly, laugh and are glad that their neighbour has erred. They often lie and themselves invent rumours.

Such people are in fact harmful to themselves, because they cause others to avoid them, since no one wants to help them, nor even to have anything to do with them. Nobody is pleased when someone else speaks ill of him and everyone dislikes a person who in this way has made him despised or even unhappy.

Similarly we are sometimes obliged out of necessary politeness to others to pretend that we are retreating from our opinion so long as this is in accord with the truth and love of others, because otherwise we shall be thought inconsiderate, stubborn and arrogant, and thus /43/ shall lose the good-will which we received from people of high station. One never ought to entertain companions with tales of other people's sins. When one speaks ill of someone else these reports are either truthful or doubtful. If they are doubtful one should try to divert the conversation in a reasonable manner away from that person; if they are truthful, one should show regret that this person committed such errors. At the same time one should try to minimize these faults as much as possible. Keeping in mind human weakness in general and trying to recall one's own shortcomings.

9.   *Self-praise and boasting.*

Since one seldom and possibly never believes in bragging /44/ and since as soon as it is recognized in us, we become ridiculous and despicable, we must avoid this sin. By boasting we insult reasonable people, because we show that we take them for fools as if they are incapable of recognizing in us the absence of the good qualities whose presence we are trying to convince them.

10.   *Lying, curses and vows.*

If all people were reasonable and good, then they could avoid the ill consequences of this sin. But there are many people who are foolish enough to become furiously drunk, even though they know that in this way they do harm to their own health and lose their own possessions; or those who are so lazy that they do not want to do anything even though they know that /45/ in this way they become poor and needy; similarly there are many people who speak untruths even though they know that through lying they lose the credence and trust of others, and upon discovery of their lie they are likely to be persecuted and hated.

Curses and vows are very often used by people to no purpose.

Some people, especially cab drivers think that animals obey curses more, but the reason for this is not in the curses, but in the [cab driver's] harsh voice. Curses do nothing except show others how angry and fierce we are and that in our hearts we would like to accomplish more than we are able. Swearing by one's soul and the like are /46/ foolish and sinful words. Christian law does not allow us to swear not even by one hair on our head and so much the less should we dare to pledge our soul for the pettiest of trifles.

11. *One should not talk about things one does not understand.*

When there is a conversation about things of which we know either nothing or very little, it is best to be silent, and if we are asked about them we should confess honestly our ignorance, because such a confession is never so harmful to us, as trying to enter conversation in which we understand nothing and from which we realize with shame and humiliation that it would have been wiser to keep silent. /47/

12. *Not to interrupt others.*

It is extremely impolite to interrupt the speech of someone who is talking, especially if he is older or of higher station than us. If your matter is not of great importance and can wait, you should never begin to talk until the other is finished.

13. *Avoid Unintelligibility in conversation, shouting, etc.*

We ought to pronounce words neither too quickly, nor too slowly, not singing but speaking, adjusting the voice to suit the subject and pronouncing all words clearly. But if we do not complete our statement because we do not care enough to give a comprehensible and intelligent answer, then such behaviour can fairly be called rudeness. /48/

Part II
ON THE CARE OF THE BODY
Chapter One

On health.

1. The good health of our body is the condition in which our body is free of all defects and illnesses.
    The good health of our body fills our soul with happiness and makes our relations with true, intelligent friends joyful and the

execution of our duties pleasant. Sickness, on the other hand, makes us sad, hinders our relations with good friends, deprives us of the opportunity to enjoy /49/ ourselves and delight in the various creations of nature in different seasons, causes us to be despised by others when our sickness is from our own doing and our own immoderation, and it finally plunges us along with our family into poverty, misery and death. And so it follows from this that we ought to safeguard the health of our bodies.

2. The human body is subject to many attacks as a result of which physical defects, infirmities and illnesses arise. People are born with some of these, these are therefore hereditary. Others, on the other hand, befall a man during his life and these therefore are *accidental.* /50/

3. *Accidental physical defects, infirmities and illnesses which affect us originate:*
   a. Partly from other people.
   b. Partly from ourselves.
   c. Partly also from unexpected misfortunes.

4. *The causes of diseases which we contract from others are as follows:*
   a. Carelessness and negligence on the part of mothers, midwives, wet-nurses and nannies.
   b. Spoiling during upbringing: if children are given freedom in everything, if their wishes and caprices are appeased and if they receive no punishment at all or insufficient punishment for disobedience and stubbornness. /51/
   c. *Infection from others: when any kind of disease is introduced into us from others.*
   d. Improper treatment of illness; for example: when a patient with a fever is given hot drinks, as a result of which he can go mad and be subjected to extreme danger for his life.
   e. Thoughtlessness: when people frighten children with devils, house demons and with other horrifying fancies; because this can be the origin of all kinds of dangerous attacks such as childhood convulsions and epilepsy.
   f. Bad examples and temptations at parties or at illicit places and gatherings. /52/

5. The causes of diseases which we contract by ourselves are as follows:
   a. Excess in food and drink.

b. Consuming unripened vegetables, fruits and foods which are unhealthful and difficult to digest.

c. Inattention to heat and cold.

d. Sitting or standing in a draft, especially when we are overheated.

e. Dampness and stuffiness in living quarters.

f. Severe passions: like anger, sorrow, anxiety, etc.

g. Any uncleanness of the flesh, which causes terrible contagious diseases that are passed on from generation to generation. /53/

h. Careless use of firearms and tools.

i. Carlessness in climbing, wrestling, jumping, lifting heavy objects, etc.

j. Neglecting useful remedies.

k. Careless use of good medicines and indiscriminate use of superstitious remedies.

6. Serious illnesses are also often caused by unforseeable accidents such as sudden fright, unexpected shame, a blow, a fall, infectious air, etc. In such cases courage is necessary.

7. *Rules for abstinence during extreme fever.*

If someone feels he has any illness whatsoever and /54/ especially if he has a high fever he should only rest and scrupulously avoid all extremes no matter what kind they may be and by what name they might be known; most of all one must make sure to stay away from very warm and soft beds and hot houses because fresh and moderate air is the first medicine in such cases. If the patient is not hungry he should not force himself to eat, because foods, especially meat, are likely to be poisonous to him at that time and may nourish his sickness; his stomach is unable to digest it and therefore the food causes nausea and in a few hours becomes rotten.

8. *Rules of abstinence during fever.*

During illness, especially inflammatory illness like /55/ fever, one must take medicine which cools and cleans the blood such as clear fresh water, not too cold, especially if it is mixed with some vinegar or boiled with barley or oats, buttermilk and the ripest juicy fruits, such as cranberries and the like. On the contrary, if we love life, we must be careful not to consume food which is tough, fatty and indigestable for the stomach, such as meat, especially smoked meat, ham, etc.

9. *Rules of abstinence in the case of constipation and indigestion.*

If one feels extreme weakness, now fever, now chills, thirst, nausea, headache, belching, /56/ a foul taste in the mouth and on the tongue, this is a sure sign that his stomach is constipated and is suffering from indigestion and therefore can no longer digest food properly. It is useless for one to seek relief and comfort in hot steambaths, ointments, binding his head and wrapping up his body; it is useless for him to try to quench his thirst with wine and vodka. He can help himself better by:

a. Taking beforehand the proper emetic or laxative which will clean out his stomach.

b. Abstain for some time from all food, especially from hard and indigestable food, and instead satisfying himself with small amounts of thin soup. /57/

c. Drinking pure and fresh water thus helping his body to rectify itself sooner and purge him of the foulness.

10. *Rules on small-pox.*

Small-pox is an illness which can befall any man, not only in the younger years but at any age. It is the most dangerous illness because it not only disfigures people horribly, but often makes them partially blind, and sometimes completely blind. Parents are inconsolably distressed over the condition of their children, when they see their eyes blinded by small-pox, their lips and tongue hardly able to speak. And the children suffer unbearable torment and often lose their life as a result [of the disease]. /58/

But if one wants to save his children such torment and not let them suffer the terribly consequences of small-pox, he should call the doctor ahead of time. The doctor will vaccinate still healthy children and save their good health and the beauty of their faces and avert the danger of untimely death. An example worthy of great and immortal glory for the good of mankind was shown by the Sovereign, Empress Catherine II, blessed be her memory, who during her reign used on herself as well as on her heir the life-saving vaccine which since has been adopted for use all over the Russian Empire. /59/

11. *General rules for the ailing.*

When one notices he is ill, he must avoid everything that would contribute to that sickness and seek help and advice from a skilled physician. In such cases, God acts through people he has created, as He does in most other cases. When we are ill He wants us to appeal to Him, to ask Him to free us from our sins, and to make use of physicians and medicine. Witchcraft and other superstitious remedies such as conjuring, putting on spells, lavations /60/ amulets — should not be used because they are repugnant to God and violate His commandment; God himself guides physicians to a cure for the sick.

12. *Rules for the use of medicines.*

All medicines which God offers us through a skilled physician, must be used in /61/ the proper way and the instructions of your physician must be obeyed exactly, because:
a. The physician understands our illness and knows what is good and what is harmful for us.
b. He knows herbs, flowers, roots and other medications, he knows how and when to use them so that they would have the proper effect.
c. The druggist prepares medicine only on a doctor's prescription and therefore one should not be misled by the guide of a cheap liar, who shamelessly gives himself many names by which he can dupe only fools. /62/

Chapter Two

On Decency.

The Roman consul Cicero, among many instructions he gave to his son who was studying in Athens, gave the following one *on decency:* "While standing, walking, sitting, at the table, in the movements of the face, eyes and arms one must have the proper appearance and especially that appearance which nature itself teaches us. In this one must be careful to avoid two faults: first, a too delicate and unmanly appearance, and second, a lewd and rude [appearance]."

1. *On walking.*

We walk decently when we turn our legs slightly outwards in a natural and not excessive manner.
When we take steps which are neither too small nor too big. /63/
When in stepping we lift our feet so that they don't drag on the

ground and when we raise our soles not too high while constantly
stretching out our toes slightly towards the ground.

When we step first on the forepart of our foot, not on our heels
and then slowly lower our heels to a standing position. This way
we avoid stamping on our feet and the noise some people make
with their heels.

We walk indecently when we twist our feet slightly outward and
lazily drag them along on the ground.

When we walk on our toes or with our feet turned inward or
crosswise.

When we sway from side to side, walk with bent knees or bend
our body first to the right then to the left as we walk. This is called
swaying. /64/

When we bend head and body forward and walk as if we were
looking for something we had lost.

When we stamp and take hard steps so that every step makes a
loud noise.

2. *On standing.*

One must get used to standing freely and straight without leaning on anything and to straighten one's knees and hold them
steady, to plant one's feet neither too close nor too far apart and
turned slightly outward, to lift one's head up from the shoulders
and to look with respect at the person to whom one is talking. If
one is asked about something, he should answer modestly, intelligently, succinctly and well; and not to start twaddling especially in
the presence of nobility. /65/

3. *On sitting.*

One must sit quietly without dangling his legs, crossing them or
putting one leg on top of the other. While sitting at the table one
should not lean against the table or his neighbour, and above all
one must not prop oneself against the table or put his elbows on
the table. One may put his hands on the table sometimes but never
the elbows, except when we write. One must get used to holding
the back and the head straight and upright.

4. *On kneeling.*

When we kneel to pray, we should not lean on anything, but
rather hold our bodies free, straight and not hunched. The knees
should be together with the shins touching, the front part /66/ of

one foot should not be on the sole of the other. The heels should be put together at the back, and one should be specially careful not to sit on his shins while kneeling.

5. *On bows.*

   a. *To common people.*

   Courtesy demands that we bow amiably when we meet an acquaintance and especially if he is of noble birth. Men should always greet people by taking off their hat or cap, if they are not carrying anything in both hands and if they are not otherwise prevented from doing so, and women only by bowing their head. Such courtesy is not at all difficult and therefore one should offer it even to people of the lowest station because the rules of courtesy demand this /67/ and through this one may deserve to be called a courteous person.

   b. *To noble people.*

   When we encounter noble people we must bow to them more or less according to their station and dignity and cover our head only after they have passed us completely. If one has business with such persons and he has not been announced by a servant, one should knock at the door or wait in the entrance hall and bow upon entering the room.

6. *On decency of the face.*

   Decency also consists to a considerable degree on the appearance of the face. Both a kind as well as an evil heart is often manifested in one's face. Therefore the best way of improving one's external appearance /68/ is to improve the heart. Although the differences between people's faces seem to be not without purpose and they can in some ways serve as a mirror for learning about the soul, nevertheless one should not depend on that exclusively because often under a kind and pleasant exterior hides a cunning flatterer and under a dark and gloomy appearance a noble soul often is concealed.

   In facial expressions one should avoid any kind of indecency. Such indecencies are: frequent winking, that is raising and lowering one's eyelashes, frivolous and mocking glances in all directions, sticking one's tongue out or putting one's fingers into the mouth, pursing one's lips or staring, coughing rather loudly or yawning without /69/ covering one's mouth, making an impertinent, shameless or roguish face, picking one's nose and taking on a contemptuous, arrogant or angry appearance.

7.   *On decency in clothing and other things.*

Although the clothing that covers our body does not measure our merits, nevertheless it is true too that indecent clothing sometimes gives us a bad reputation. Conventions in clothing are in themselves unimportant, but in as much as they become general and accepted we have to follow them and it is sufficient to be neither ahead of the fashion nor behind it.

Tidiness is also a part of it. One should wash his face and hands, cut his nails /70/ and not bite them off, keep one's head clean, and comb his hair. Common people should at least cut their hair so that it does not hang over their eyes, and best of all braid the hair or tie it back. Clothing and footwear, as much as time allows, should always be kept clean. In short, one should dress in such a way that everyone who knows us would notice our good demeanour. We must also keep everything else around us tidy because tidiness is a necessary quality of well-being, and it promotes good health too; even in poverty one can be tidy. Everything that makes our body foul damages our health as well: underclothing which is dirty from sweat causes clotting and rotting in our blood, while clean underclothing /71/ is not only pleasant to the eye but also makes our body fresher and stronger. Just as the cold water we use to wash ourselves strengthens our veins and invigorates the life forces within us, just as stale and stuffy air in the room is repugnant to our noses, so it damages and weakens our lungs. The effort we make to get our teeth white and our breath fresh also protects our mouth from putrefaction and unhealthy phlegm. There are a great many sicknesses which develop from the lack of body hygiene and therefore one must bathe often, especially in the summer, let fresh air into the room often, wipe up dust so as not to breathe it in. Also one ought not to eat and drink carelessly without examining the food and drink first to see that it is clean and wholesome. /72/

Part III
ON PUBLIC DUTIES TO WHICH WE ARE APPOINTED BY GOD
Chapter One

On public unity in general.

1. Every man should love his neighbour, that is, other people, and do as many good deeds as he can under the circumstances because every man desires the same from others.

2. The condition in which one can easily get all that is necessary for human life and its advantages and can own and enjoy confidently is called *material well-being.* /73/

3. Because of many obstacles people can not acquire for themselves all the necessities and advantages of life without the help of others, and as a consequence they cannot attain a condition of material well-being by themselves but need the assistance of others. This is the reason why many people united in one society with the purpose of helping one another to acquire the essentials of life.

4. It follows from this that we ought to love those who help us achieve the condition of material well-being or those who help us or are able to help us directly. In other words, we must, whenever possible, do a good turn and be useful to others and thus seek their well-being together with them. Therefore *love of fellow-men* is the basis of society. /74/

Chapter Two

On marital union.   .

1. The first union is the marital union. This union is the oldest because God himself established it in Heaven. The purpose and the end of it is the continuation of the human race.

2. Only one husband and only one wife form this union. They must

love each other and be faithful to each other. [They must] be together /75/ until death do them part.

3. The husband is the head of the family and the wife is his helper; she has to honour and obey him, be subordinate to him and help him in the home building.

4. The husband should not treat his wife strictly, nor use his power over her maliciously, but should treat her /76/ with love; he is obliged to try his utmost to provide food and other necessities.

Chapter Three

On Union of parents and children.

From the first or marital union when children are born begins another, namely: *the union between parents and children.*

1. Parents, generally speaking, should care for their children. As long as the children are small and still incapable of helping themselves, parents should /77/ feed them, bring them up and point out what they should do, because children do not know yet what is good and what is really useful for them and because they would be subjected to want and great harm without the parent's care and guidance since children are helpless. This care of children by their parents should be in the upbringing and upbringing is the guidance of children towards good; [upbringing is] teaching them or through others everything that is necessary in their situation /78/ especially the scriptures, providing good examples to deter the evil in them at its inception, and when admonition does not help, not missing the opportunity to punish them without doing them any harm, so that they might not become irritable and /79/ embittered from excessive strictness. Parents must also make an effort to acquire and pass on to their children some inheritance. Negligence by the parents in anything mentioned here is a serious violation of their duties.

2. Children also have quite a large responsibility to their parents: since they received their life from their parents, they have to be very grateful to them. They are obliged to honour their parents not only in words but /80/ also in heart and deed and they receive for that God's blessing. They must obey [their parents] and show obedience still more by heeding their parents' admonitions and

following their precepts. Children should not distress their parents, /81/ but try to make them happy; they should not grieve, annoy or insult them, nor despise or ridicule them, nor curse them, or much worse lift an impertinent hand against them; nor gloat at their /82/ misfortunes; rather [children] should patiently bear their [parents'] weaknesses, especially in old age and treat them kindly. They must try to earn their parents' blessing; and to avert their execration.

Chapter Four

On the union between masters and servants.

1. The third union is the *union between masters and servants*. It exists between master and slaves, landlord and servants /83/ of both sexes. Such unions without doubt date back to the beginning of time, because Abraham had men and women slaves in Egypt.

2. This society of masters and servants is by no means contrary to God, because there are God's commandments, which instruct masters, free servants and slaves of their duties. Paul in his First Epistle to the Corinthians (7:21, 22, 24) clearly mentions slaves and free servants, and instructs all members of both stations, saying: *Wast thou a slave when called? Let it not trouble thee . . . Brethren, in the state in which he was when called, let every man remain in God.*

3. Masters and landlords should not burden their slaves and domestic servants with work that is beyond their strength, nor demand from them more /84/ than they are obliged to do. They must prevent any evil from happening to their slaves and domestics and enduce them to do all that is good and especially to do service to God. [Masters] must treat their servants humanely, give them their usual or /85/ promised pay and bread at the proper time without reducing [their earnings].

4. Slaves and servants must love and honour their masters and landlords, and obey them according to their rank /86/ not only outwardly but sincerely and wholeheartedly also. They must perform their duties willingly and faithfully and painstakingly at the proper time, so that they might be really useful to their masters and landlords; and they are obliged to do this not only for kind [masters] but also for those they dislike. They must also [strive to] please

their masters and landlords, seeking /87/ advantages for them as well as they can and protecting them from any harm. [They must] be content with the agreed and fixed pay and under no circumstances expropriate anything for themselves furtively even though they may feel they deserve more and [they must] not keep or conceal any money that is left after an expense for the master.

Chapter Five

On civic union.

Unit I

On civic union in general.

1. The fourth kind of union is one in which many families /88/ unite and live together under one state and under the same laws. Such unions or societies are called *civic unions* or *nations*.

    Such societies arose in different ways but were established identically: sometimes the chieftain of a large tribe subjugated the weak one by force; sometimes the extraordinary qualities of one man induced the others to submit to him and entrust to him the institution of their common welfare or the management of their defense either for a short time or until his death, or even to his descendants either with or without certain restrictions. There were nations and some of them still exist today, in which many persons care for the welfare of their fellow-citizens and have the same power /89/ as the Sovereign in a sovereign state. Such societies are called *Republics*.

2. However the government of any country is established, in each one there is one person or several persons who govern and whom the others must obey.

3. Those who govern must set as their purpose in all their institutions the general well-being of all their subjects. They order or prohibit what every subject would himself do or not do, if he could comprehend the totality of all circumstances and if at the same time he had enough intelligence to choose to do what would insure his well-being.

4. Consequently those who are under someone's command /90/

must obey their superiors, that is: subjects must have absolute trust in the superior intellect of their supreme authorities, rely on their kindness and firmly believe that those who govern know what is good for the state, their subjects and all civic society in general, and that they desire nothing except what they recognize as good for the society.

5. Every subject must beware of disobedience of the Law as the greatest evil in society, because thence arise obstacles to that common good which the supreme authorities try to maintain.

6. No ruler or supreme authority would be what he is now /91/ and even less could he remain so, if God, who governs everything in the world, had not designed it. The Holy scriptures tell us that authorities are established by God, that they are established for the benefit of those who are governed by them.

Unit II

On the title and authority of The Ruler.

1. For the well-being and security of their subjects, Rulers have the duty and authority to make *laws and regulations, and to take care that they are enforced; to preserve and administer justice and jurisprudence, to punish criminals and* /92/ *wrongdoers, to protect the life and possessions of citizens against unjust offense and resist attacks by a foreign enemy.*

2. Rulers derive their authority from God and make an effort to see *that subjects are taught and instructed in such duties which Divine Law obligates us* and without fulfillment of which one can not receive everlasting happiness because to be temporarily happy is not enough and man, in whose body /93/ lives an immortal soul, has to think about everlasting happiness.

3. *Rulers create the well-being of their subjects in various ways: They give them laws,* that is, precepts composed by Supreme power and properly published which define what to do and what not to do. They indicate what is just and what is not, they define the duties of every subject to his country and of each citizen to the other and they do not allow anyone to harm another and secure everyone's possessions. The life, honour, property and possessions of every

person are defended by law. Possible offences are averted by laws and the offended /94/ is given justice and satisfaction.

Since the country is so large and it is made up of so many people, no Sovereign can judge everyone and consider all complaints by himself. Therefore it was necessary to appoint many others to manage State affairs. The large distance between the Sovereign and most of his subjects requires that in many locations authorities be established who would be subordinated to each other as well as being generally subordinate to the Sovereign, partly in order to make more objective judgements by considering many different opinions. /95/

Rulers defend their subjects from enemies.

4. Those that are more vigorous, younger, taller and stronger are selected from society so that they can serve to defend others and preserve all the state's institutions against any enemy; and so that in time of peace they might practice what they have to do in time of war, and this is the origin of today's *soldiers.*

Thanks to such an institution all other members of society may peacefully continue their trade and plough their fields even in time of war. Therefore all those good institutions will be kept in order and allowed to continue functioning at least in those places /96/ which the enemy troops have not invaded.

5. The concern of someone who governs extends beyond just defending his subjects from foreign enemies and from harm inflicted by their fellow citizens. [It goes beyond just] preserving their property in conformity with laws and [the right] to peaceful possession. [Someone who governs] *strives to insure the well-being of* [the subjects] *in many other ways.*

By calling upon all the efforts of society and by availing himself of valuable resources and talented persons, the Sovereign can do what his subjects are unable to do by themselves separately: building dams across large rivers in order to prevent floods; laying convenient roads; constructing wharfs for the merchant marine, filling emergency /97/ storehouses in case of famine and need; running enterprises which require great expense in order to give his subjects a profit for their work and give the fruit of the earth a decent price; promoting the flourishing of science, art and any kind of craft; and doing innumerable other things which are beneficial to the state. Only Sovereigns are able to do this and good Sovereigns have always taken great pain in this regard.

Unit III

On the obligations of subjects in general.

1. *Subjects* are all people in the State who are subordinate to the Sovereign or rulers. /98/

2. There are subjects of different status. Some of them are of the *nobility,* others are of the *lower class.*
    Within the *lower class* there are free people. There are also those who are obliged to their lords in service, in taxes, or in various other ways, and some are so owned that neither they, nor their children can move from the place they live to another without the permission of their lords.

3. *Noble subjects* of the state are those who differ from others by their property, education or talent, and they are distinguished not only by lofty titles but also by the fact that they perform a service to the state in various ways.

4. All subjects, or members of society, must honour /99/ their rulers for their good deeds and the protection they provide. [All subjects must] pray to God for them, obey their laws and regulations, willingly and diligently give taxes and services without which the rulers can not maintain the general well-being and safety. [One must do this] not out of fear /100/ of punishment but because it is their moral obligation before God. Every subject must show honour, love, obedience and loyalty not only to the Sovereign but also to those lesser authorities who are appointed and designated by Him.

5. In general it is the duty of every subject to be obedient, to act according to established laws and honour them highly. /101/ [It is the duty of every subject] not to take revenge by himself or to act according to his own whim when he is insulted by another or in quarrel with another, but rather (as long as it is not done from malice) to seek help from the authorities, and to voice one's complaints through the established order; and, while waiting for judgement, to be calm and ready to accept the judge's verdict.

6. Just as private people and subjects of the state can quarrel among themselves, so whole nations or their rulers for various reasons, have disputes. And these disputes cannot be resolved by ordinary judges, because there is no man who can judge whole nations. In

such cases there is war. Quarrelling nations act against one another as enemies. /102/ They attack each other's land, besiege and capture cities, set fire to places, take harvests from local inhabitants, take people and cattle into captivity, do battle with one another and cause each other as much harm as possible.

7. When such a misfortune or war occurs, it demands from all citizens that they try with all their energy to give resistance, defend their society, and zealously assist the Sovereign in His plans for defense.

8. In ancient times in such cases everyone took up arms. There are still some nations today where all subjects are soldiers. And there are others where the nobility is obligated to take up arms, go against the enemy and serve /103/ a certain length of time in a campaign at his own expense.

9. When an enemy was not expelled quickly and war went on for a long time, the state suffered from it. Fields were not plowed, crafts and other activities were neglected, and the damage [from war] was so great that it was felt for centuries.

10. As states became larger and stronger with time the number of occupations and ranks in society also increased. With time [people of] different occupations provided each other more and more benefits, and therefore a military campaign seemed all the more difficult, the more accustomed people became to these benefits. And people had to abandon these advantages when necessity forced them to do battle with an enemy. /104/

11. All the above-mentioned circumstances gave cause to establish a special class of people, who would always be armed and defend the fatherland. They were given the necessary support and encouraged by the possibility of honour and reward.

12. Such an institution of military personnel, created for the security of the state, requires at the same time considerable expense, because a soldier must receive pay, clothing, arms, living quarters and food. In addition, war calls for other expenses, for example: carriages, delivery of supplies, etc. It is only fair for those who profit from this defense to pay the expenses and assist in various other ways /105/ in order not to be forced to come to their own defense.

13. And therefore lords as well as private families of rural dwellers

must comply when the Sovereign enlists some of their people into military service. And those who are drafted in such a way, must get accustomed to their new circumstances, be loyal and faithful in this service and willingly give their lives. They must regard themselves as fellow members of a society of citizens of that country for whose defense they are appointed, act decorously and not do them any harm. And during war they must not consider it permissible to do anything they please to the inhabitants of the enemy's land, that is, to private citizens, who have /106/ already suffered enough from war. Nor must they do any harm to them personally or to their property as they are instructed by their appointed military superiors.

The military must restrain from violence for the purpose of revenge or greed, and from other excesses. They must be content with their allotted salary. Those who act contrary to their regulations sin gravely before God and before their neighbour, because neither their rank nor war gives them the right to be savage and brutal.

14. For the subject's further well-being, which the Sovereign maintains on various methods and institutions, great expense and considerable support is needed from subjects. In fairness they must /107/ assist in the maintenance [of the state] and also give willingly things that are needed for that maintenance and service, because they benefit from this. And therefore they ought to pay eagerly a fixed assessment and taxes according to their occupation. These taxes are always levied on each individual in keeping with the needs of the state.

15. Those subjects who are appointed by the Sovereign to collect taxes must act with loyalty according to given instructions and not demand from anyone more than one should pay. And they should not keep anything for themselves from the money collected but rather submit everything honestly to its proper place.

16. Those subjects whom the Sovereign appoints to other duties must also act in a similar manner. /108/ They must carry out their duties faithfully and conscientiously as is required of them. It is unforgivable to neglect one's entrusted duties out of self-interest, excessive love for peace or for any other reason.

17. All members of civil society must do their utmost for society's well-being, assist willingly in whatever the supreme authority instructs, and honour all its institutions, even if one is to incur a

certain loss as a result and even if one does not see how the common good is promoted by one's [compliance]. One must believe that the higher authorities understand everything better, since they know the circumstances better and that they intend by their laws and institutions /109/ only to achieve what is best for the entire society. Therefore it is unjust and worthy of punishment to grumble about institutions of high authorities or to misinterpret them maliciously.

If any subject has any useful intention or suggestion by which the society can profit or [by which] harm can be avoided, then he ought to submit his suggestion to the high authorities, wait for a response from them, stay calm in the meantime and not be offended if his suggestion is not accepted. Subjects who think and act in this way, rejoice in the well-being of the fatherland, recognize its advantages and good institutions, honour and try as much as possible /110/ to preserve and increase them, are called *true sons of the fatherland.*

Unit IV

On love for the fatherland.

Article 1

On love for the fatherland in general.

1. Among the virtuous inclinations and deeds of a good citizen, love for one's fatherland and the deeds [which this love engenders] take a special place. Most of the great deeds of the ancient Greeks and Romans — actions which still amaze us and which we offer each other as models to be emulated — were a consequence and result of love for the fatherland. In history books one can find well-known and almost unbelievable deeds wrought by virtuous sons /111/ of the fatherland. This name is given to people of both sexes and all ranks who honour their fatherland, who care about its well-being, who derive genuine satisfaction from seeing it prosper, and who are not indifferent in times of misfortune and danger, but rather promote the well-being and salvation of the fatherland as much as possible.

2. Those people who have had the honour to be called sons of father-

land showed their love for the fatherland in different ways. Some undertook useful though very difficult tasks for the good of the fatherland, and strove to accomplish those tasks regardless of all obstacles. Others constantly and graciously endured all misfortune and injury for the common benefit and well-being of their fatherland. For some there could be nothing so /112/ dear and pleasing that they would not sacrifice it for the fatherland. Many were undaunted by any danger and even marched courageously to their death, calmly bearing the death of comrades who had sacrificed their lives for their beloved fatherland.

3. There are many people whom it is almost impossible to convince of this, because in our times such cases either occur not so often or are not as numerous as they were in ancient times. Some believe that love for the fatherland is a civic virtue more characteristic of a free society or *Republic,** than of a monarchy, /113/ or that in a Republic there are at least more reasons and motives for [such love]. But all this is quite unjust because if one finds less love for the fatherland in our time than in ancient times, then the cause of this lies not in the form of government, but in an inadequate education. As soon as this [cause] is destroyed there will be a great number of true sons of the fatherland in our time too.

4. And [to achieve] this one must do as the Romans and particularly the ancient Greeks did. The Greeks considered education of children a matter for the state. The supreme /114/ leaders were concerned with them and conducted their education. They never left this to the discretion of the parents alone, despite the fact that many of them understood very well their responsibility to educate their children not only for themselves and their families, but also for the society. Those who were entrusted by the government with the task of education strove to arouse in young people an attentiveness to the advantages of the fatherland. They explained to them the usefulness of state institutions, taught the young people to notice their excellence, honour and get the feeling of all the

---

* A republic is the name given to a state in which many people, selected either from the nobility or from the common folk, govern. Such a state is called *free* because it is free from autocracy and because the supreme authority is shared by many. A land in which the supreme authority is in the hands of a single Sovereign is called a *monarchial state.*

advantages which everyone in the fatherland can enjoy. [The teachers] did not forget to tell them about glorious deeds performed by the sons of the fatherland and by giving examples to arouse their passion for emulation. /115/ All this made a strong impression on young people. They were inspired by [stories of] good, useful as well as honourable deeds, and they felt pleasure and could not help but love and do what they considered to be honourable and useful.

5. If in our times young people will be treated in such a manner, then they will be inspired by the example of the ancients to love the fatherland. Then subjects of the Monarchy will do what we marvel at in the sons of the fatherland in ancient free states.

Article 2

What is the fatherland and what is love for the fatherland.

1. People have misconceptions about what we generally call the fatherland. /116/ Almost never or at least very seldom do people understand the true meaning of this word when they speak about love for the fatherland.

2. In its true meaning the *FATHERLAND* is a large society of which one is a fellow citizen, i.e. the state whose subject one is either by place of birth or by resettlement and residence.

3. Such a large society which sometimes extends over many regions is called the fatherland because the well-being of all inhabitants and fellow citizens is maintained and supported by the same authority and laws, just as the well-being of children in the home is secured by the father's care. Therefore all those who are subjects of one /117/ or one supreme power are sons of the fatherland.

4. As members and residents of one state everyone has the same right to the benefits given to people of all occupations by laws and form of government. Likewise the people must have, on their part, the same honourable feelings and zealous affection for the fatherland.

5. The true son of the fatherland must be dedicated to the state, its own form of government, its leaders and its laws. *LOVE FOR THE FATHERLAND* consists in showing esteem and gratitude to the government, in obeying the laws, institutions and just rights of society in which we live, in respecting the advantages of society

and using them /118/ for the general good, and in striving as much as possible to perfect these things so that we might partake of the glory of the society to which we belong and might do our utmost [to promote] its well-being.

Article 3

The origins of love for one's fatherland.

1. If love for one's fatherland consists in our earnest obedience to the Sovereign, the authorities and the laws of the society in which we live, then we must take note of what that love produces in our hearts.

2. It is true that love for the fatherland is based on love for our neighbour as it is prescribed most forcefully in the Holy Scriptures themselves. But just as the Holy Scriptures obliges us without violating [the commandments of] general love /119/ for our neighbour, to take care for our relatives more than for others, and [just as] children are naturally inclined to love their parents and brothers more than others because of their close union, so members of one country are obliged to love their Sovereign and countrymen, with whom they are bound by the closest ties, more than foreign Sovereigns and their subjects.

3. Everyone knows that a parent tries to protect his children from all dangers. So the Sovereign provides security from foreign enemies to the whole country, like a father who loves his children. A parent keeps order and harmony between his children. Similarly the Sovereign maintains justice and /120/ defends every subject who is offended unjustly by his fellow-countrymen. A parent provides his children with various necessities and benefits. The Sovereign too extends order, prosperity and benefits befitting every rank all over [his realm].

4. A parent chooses people to teach his children all that is good and does not leave them helpless, rather he furthers their well-being even if [in doing so] he forfeits his own rest and amusements. So too the Sovereign employs a great variety of able persons to accomplish major projects useful to the whole country. He heeds the appeals of his subjects and does not become bored with his work. He orders that these [appeals] be submitted to him orally or in written form, and to the limit of his ability he leaves none /121/

helpless while forfeiting his own rest, amusement and interests so that he can provide peace and [other] benefits to his subjects.

5. Just as a parent is dearly loved by his children for providing all the aforementioned benefits, so the Sovereign deserves the love of his subjects even more so because of the importance of His good deeds.

Article 4

How should one demonstrate love for his fatherland in general.

1. The general well-being of a country's citizens is the aim of all government. Citizens lose this well-being if their government is in disorder or not respected; /122/ it follows therefore, that the *first duty* of a son of the fatherland is *not to say or do anything reprehensible in the eyes of the government,* such as the following disgraceful acts: complaining, malicious conversations, defamatory or impertinent remarks [aimed] at a state institution and the government. [These] are crimes against the fatherland and warrant harsh punishment.

2. Laws are institutions by which the government defines what it considers useful for the well-being of the country. Therefore the *second duty* of sons of the fatherland is *compliance* [with the laws]. Everyone is obligated to obey [laws] even when obedience seems difficult and when one thinks that the laws ought to be different. /123/

3. Often the general well-being can not be achieved except by having some people feel some kind of an encumbrance. Yet the common good must be preferred to the personal [good]. Private individuals cannot see everything in the state and learn enough about the condition in it to determine correctly how one or another law contributes to the general and personal good. Those who govern can and must know all this better and more reliably. For this reason *trust in the foresight and jurisprudence of those who govern* is the *third duty* of sons of the fatherland.

4. The obedience of sons of the fatherland must be active. That is, every son of the fatherland /124/ must really use all his abilities and property for the good of the state, especially when they are needed by those who govern. *Doing this* is the *fourth duty* of a son

of the fatherland. The needs of the state are varied; they cannot be known to every citizen; they can be greater or less according to circumstances. Not everyone can determine the needs [of the state], or their [relative] importance, or what is required, [to supply these needs] because sometimes they must be kept secret for legal reasons. Therefore a son of the fatherland must show his willingness to serve his country with his abilities and possessions not according to his own reasoning and volition, but rather /125/ according to what his government demands from him, and he is obligated to fulfill that demand willingly in all situations.

Article 5

How common people and the middle class ought to show their love for the fatherland.

1. Love for the fatherland is the obligation of every member of the state and of every citizen. But there are cases where each class must show that love in its own particular and characteristic way.

2. Common people, that is, those who live by cultivating the land and working with their hands, comprise the lowest level of the citizenry. They must show their love for the fatherland /126/ by obedience and activity, especially by industriousness. They have many various opportunities to do so, namely: when soldiers, defenders of the fatherland against foreign enemies, are chosen, when the government instructs farmers to give part of what is obtained by farming either in order to help the government in need or in order to provide the army with food, or [when the government instructs them to] provide transportation or keep billets.

3. A common person must show his diligence and industriousness not only in performing willingly the tasks imposed on him by the government, but also in working to support himself. This is always useful to the state /127/ because through industriousness the fruits of the earth are multiplied and members of the state are provided with all necessities, advantages and affluence. Quite to the contrary, those who are lazy, inactive and idle are always a burden to the state because they harm and hinder its well-being.

4. Common people show themselves to be sons of the fatherland when they do not cling to old-fashioned habits, but try as much as

possible to borrow whatever is useful from other countries and use it for the benefit of the fatherland, or when they plant and cultivate foreign products on their own fields, or when they imitate their neighbour's manner of farming [in order to increase their own income] or when they /128/ are as diligent as their neighbour in manufacturing their own products, [they should do this] so that there would be no need for foreign produce and manufacturers and so that the money paid out [to foreign countries] for [these products] might be kept in their own fatherland.

5. Love for the fatherland demands the same from artists, who, strictly speaking, belong to the second level of state subjects. Along with some writers they can be called *well-bred citizens.* Besides artists and merchants to this level belong also those who, because they are gifted and knowledgeable, contribute to the well-being of their country in various ways. In this category are also those men who teach other citizens their duties. /129/ From this group the Sovereign appoints those who are occupied in jurisprudence and other government positions. This category also includes those who make an effort to improve people's manners.

6. As the diligence of common persons is shown in the application of their physical strength and in handcrafts, so must well-bred citizens show their diligence by using kindly and willingly their mental power. The main rule that people of this category must keep before them is to consider it their duty to be useful to the fatherland through the very occupation to which they are devoted or to which they are appointed. They ought to /130/ know that only those who bring real advantages to the fatherland render true services to it, and that every class can render such services even though they may not be noticed by everyone and may not be recognized by all [as services to the state]; nevertheless they are quite essential to the country.

7. When someone wishes to avert some kind of evil, he must consider whether the consequences of the means he employs [to do so] will not produce more harm than the evil which he intended to eradicate [originally].

8. Suggestions whose implementation would be useful only to certain persons or to a certain group of people /131/ are not good if they are harmful to most people or to most categories of people. In a state [people] must give heed primarily to the general well-being or at least the well-being of a majority.

Well bred citizens are obligated to be obedient no less than the common people are. They must not only obey the laws in general but also carry out the orders of the government [even if the government] does not consider useful what in their opinion seems to be useful. They must exert all their spiritual effort to benefit the fatherland in such a way as is required of them by the government. /132/

Article 6

How the clergy, nobility and military must show their love for the fatherland.

1. There is a class in the state which is called *the clergy,* and it includes: archbishops, bishops, archimandrites, fathers superior, presbyters, clergymen and deacons. Their duty is to enlighten people with the true knowledge of God, to improve their hearts and will with the Scriptures and to prepare their way to the bliss of the future life by strengthening them [along the paths of] virtue and in the performance of good deeds during this life.

2. Their love for the fatherland is shown all the more when they perform their duties in such a way as the salutary intentions of the civic society /133/ demand. This includes evoking in people loyalty and love for the Sovereign through their admonitions, directing them away from harmful misconceptions and superstitious opinions by [showing them an example of] spiritual humility; enlightening their soul with true rules which promote their well-being, so that they might be useful and productive members of society, and so that they might serve the fatherland effectively, be rich in virtue, good qualities and good thoughts.

3. Another class of people is called the *nobility.* It has many levels but all of them in general have the advantages over the lower class: they hold high positions in the government and /134/ in the army; they are the people closest to the person of the Monarch and consequently are known mainly to Him, employed by Him and they live and work before His very eyes. The nobility, therefore, is the class which can and must do most for the fatherland.

4. Nobility is actually a reward for great and useful service performed either by the noble himself or by his parents and ancestors who are supposed to be a model to be emulated by their children and grandchildren: for those who have earned the rank of nobility

by themselves, their services and the advantages received through [such services] must act as an incentive for them to distinguish themselves even more; they must preserve the distinction they have received by honourable behaviour and not /135/ bring vilification either upon themselves or upon their descendants by any despicable behaviour.

5. The nobility, just like people of other stations, must demonstrate their obedience, diligence and love for the fatherland. The diligence of nobles must be incomparably greater than that of people in other stations. They are faced with the most difficult tasks to perform. Their vigor and perseverance must be incomparably greater and commensurate with the importance of the responsibility placed upon them. Noblemen must discharge their responsibilities in the most difficult circumstances, in the face of the greatest dangers and even where there is a possibility of losing one's life. Honour and the desire to preserve their acquired privileges without any suspicion ought to be the incentive for all the noblemen's deeds. /136/

6. Love for the Sovereign and unshakable loyalty to him is the most important duty of a nobleman. He has more occasions to show them than people of other stations who are more removed from the Person of the Monarch.

   Love for the fatherland demands from noblemen that they respect their countrymen and people of lower stations and not despise or insult them. Noblemen must remember that every class of citizens in a country promotes the general good, and people of every station have the right to partake of the benefits offered all society by the state. And just as nobles profit in various ways from people of lower stations, so must /137/ they try to be useful to them in turn.

7. Besides the aforementioned three classes, there is a fourth one, namely, the *military*. It is quite unjust for some people to see this class with regard to the aristocracy as a refuge for poor people of noble birth, with regard to the well-bred as punishment for debauched children, and with regard to common people as a state of slavery.

8. The military is actually a group which acts in lieu of most members of other stations in defending the fatherland. Soldiers do themselves what the rest of the people would have to do during an attack on the state by an enemy.

9. It is the duty of the Sovereign to protect his subjects from enemy attacks. He has /138/ the right to recruit and use every subject for his defense. Harm done to the state in one area or only to some of the subjects always has harmful consequences for the whole country; the danger can spread to others. That is why all members of the state must assist in its defense even if only one part of it is attacked by the enemy. It is unnecessary and would [even] be very harmful at the present day to bring all citizens out into the battlefield to defend the country from an enemy attack as was often done in ancient times.

10. That is why Sovereigns by virtue of their authority have the right to command, establish and determine who and how many subjects /139/ must appear for military service. This authority is all the more important since without it very few people would enlist voluntarily. Even though everyone is convinced that an army is needed by the state, without conscription by the Sovereign and [other] authorities private individuals would not be willing to agree that they themselves or their relatives must take arms.

11. Subjects conscripted to defend the country must obey unquestioningly and discharge loyally the duties of their rank. A soldier must show his love to the fatherland by obedience and bravery. This is more costly to him than to others because he must actually sacrifice his peace, good health, freedom and life itself, or at least be ready /140/ to do so for the good of society at any time. For this he deserves to receive honour and gratitude.

12. It is true that obedience and loyalty in the execution of his duties is a most difficult task, but disobedience and negligence could have the most dire consequences for him himself and for the whole country.

    A soldier must blindly obey the orders of his superiors without pondering the purpose and efficiency of those orders. Those who might have any doubt about an order, must rest assured in the trust which the Sovereign, the commander and the other officers deserve according to their station and rank. Every soldier is obliged to have such /141/ trust in his superiors and therefore it is his duty to believe that whatever order he receives, it is the best one under present circumstances and that it is needed to protect or to save the country. He has to remember that it is impossible and even undesirable for the superior to account for his actions to his subordinates.

13. The recollection of his duties enables a soldier to show love for the fatherland by obedience and bravery, and inevitably makes a soldier resilient in all difficulties, courageous and determined in all dangers and unshakable in battle.

14. It is a soldier's duty as John the Baptist [The Predecessor to Christ] said to soldiers of his time, to be content with his pay and not to mistreat anyone (that is, anyone who is not an enemy of the fatherland) /142/ and even to the enemy himself do no more harm than was ordered by superiors. Humanity in general obliges us to treat even subjects of an enemy country kindly, especially if they do not take arms.

Unit V

On sciences, arts, crafts and handwork which serve the mutual benefit of citizens.

Introduction

1. There are large and small communities in a state, namely cities and villages.

   There are members of the gentry who require the help of other people of different ranks with various education and skills to serve /143/ their needs. There are also always people who willingly offer their services and thus earn a living not only for themselves but also for their families. It is the obligation of these people to serve loyally, according to the requirements of quality in the work entrusted to them and according to the wish and interest of the person they serve.

2. *Members of the society serve one another without being servants, so to speak.*

   A person's needs are so great, that he cannot do everything for himself alone, no matter how small these needs may seem to be. Every person needs the work of others and everyone who does his job and from it tries to make his living serves /144/ others by doing so. And one who needs a service pays the worker and gets what he needs for the money. It is a great advantage to know how many different ways there are by which people can help one another, or, to say it differently, can serve one another without being servants.

Article 1

On sciences.

1. Some dedicate themselves to science and thus serve others either through instructions or through application of [science] to the various needs of human life. These people comprise the so called class of scientists.

2. In general all sciences no matter how many there are today, may be divided into four main categories: /145/
    a) Some sciences are concerned only with our soul, the strengthening of it, especially that science which teaches us what God created, commanded and demands for the salvation of humanity and this science is called *Theology.*
    b) There is a science which consists in learning the characteristics of our body and all of its parts whether they are healthy or ailing, in order to help in the case of bodily infirmity and to prepare remedies. This is called the *Science of Medicine.*
    c) There is another science which deals with the peaceful ownership of property. It is called the *Science of Rights and Laws,* because it investigates and determines what is just and fair as regards things and people and protects people's possessions. /146/
    d) The fourth category of sciences is comprised of *philosophical, mathematical, historical and philological knowledge,* which are not only useful by themselves, but also assist in making great achievements in all the aforementioned main sciences.

Article 2

On arts.

1. Some people are occupied with the arts, which help in various ways to benefit our lives and [increase] our enjoyment. The arts are:
    a) *Painting.* It represents things we apprehend by our senses on a flat surface in one or more colours. The methods of representation and the colours used for that are very varied. /147/
    b) *Carving,* represents the same thing on copper with carved lines and dots filled with colours or imprinted on paper or on anything else suitable for that.
    c) *Sculpture* represents things apprehended by our senses in many different mediums (wood, stone and the like) with raised outlines.

d) *Architecture,* designs and erects buildings which are not only strong and safe, but also beautiful.

e) *Music* pleases the ear with well measured tones produced in quite various ways. /148/

Article 3

On labour and crafts.

1. Some people occupy themselves with handwork and crafts, which are sometimes essential to us and sometimes needed only because of our accepted way of life and customs.

The number of such crafts is tremendous and it multiplies almost every day, not only because from time to time new crafts are invented, but also because art has perfected some of them which were previously counted among handcrafts to the status of art. We shall mention handwork and arts here under crafts and attach to them an incomplete list only to show what various benefits they bring. /149/

a) Some of them provide us with sustenance, and such trades are performed by:

1) *Farmers,* who sow wheat and other grains and raise the cattle we need for food.

2) *Millers,* who grind wheat on wind or water mills.

3) *Bakers,* who bake bread for us from flour.

4) *Butchers,* who sell meat.

5) *Vegetable and fruit gardeners,* who supply us with various vegetables and greens.

6) *Cooks,* who cook food for us.

7) *Sugar manufacturers* and *candy makers,* who make all kinds of sweet jams and appetizers.

8) *Vineyard gardeners* cultivate vineyards. /150/

9) *Brewers,* who brew beer; and

10) *Distillers* make hard beverages.

The last three professions supply us with drinks.

b) Other crafts provide us with clothing, namely: weavers prepare linen, cotton, wool and silk and other useful fabrics; *dyers* dye them, *tailors* make clothing out of them; and other craftsmen assist, such as *buttonmakers,* and, primarily for nobles *gold braid makers* and *gold embroidery makers.*

To cover one's hands, feet and head there are *glovemakers, shoemakers, stockingmakers, hatmakers* and *hairdressers.* The materials necessary for this are supplied again by others. Wool

/151/ from which cloth and other wool materials are made, and leather from which so many things are made are supplied by cattle-raising. All this is fashioned for various uses by leather workers and suede makers.

c) For building our dwellings we need *brickmakers, quarry-workers, stone cutters, limestone miners, masons, carpenters, roofmakers, black-smiths, wiremakers, metal workers, cabinet makers, window makers and many* others.

d) For making things needed for the house, many other tradesmen are required: *hoopmakers, turners, potters, sheet-metal workers, tinsmiths, coppersmiths and smelters.*

e) For various other necessities: *watchmakers, ropemakers, harness-makers and comb makers.* /152/

f) Many others who work for our benefit too, for example: *coachbuilders, saddlers* and others.

g) Our luxuries are provided by those who deal *in diamonds, goldsmiths, silversmiths, mirror makers, guilders and upholsterers.*

2. To all these must be added *merchants,* tradesmen, whose occupation consists in buying and selling things that are manufactured by others, transporting them great distances and receiving cash for them or exchanging them for other useful items.

Article 4

On the usefulness and necessity of various occupations.

1. The earth bears an innumerable variety of plants and /153/ other things which serve our different needs and which are useful for people's interest, pleasure and enjoyment. Everywhere there are people with quite different inclinations and abilities. There are many who prepare the fruit of the earth [for consumption] in different ways and many others who gladly use the skills of these people for their own needs.

2. Nowadays one can make use of almost all things, even out of their smallest parts. As a result, people use the powers given them by God at the time of creation, and insofar as people /154/ use and make things out of these materials they carry out exactly what God said to Adam, that is, that people receive their living from the earth with great effort, even though not everyone plows it.

3. Herewith we must be amazed at the wisdom, kindness and Providence of God and be grateful that He created all creatures, spread

them all over the earth with a generous hand and made all of them for human use. When we realize that we can make [what God created] useful to us by applying some effort, we cannot have any doubt, that at the very time of creation His intention was to give people various occupations. /155/

4. After the population multiplied it became impossible for all to plow the earth like farmers, and make their living directly from this. Many thousands of people would not be able to acquire anything and would not be able to support themselves, if we were to live nowadays like our ancestors, and be content with bare necessities. Therefore when some members of the elite and the rich employ a large number of people for their benefit and comfort, then many thousands of families make their living as a result and assist the elite and the rich not only by [providing] their necessities, but also by [increasing] their luxury and enjoyment. They have the opportunity to work and the things created for the sake of man are put to good use as a result. /156/

5. Native human talents and the inclinations towards different occupations and various activities born out of [these talents] are, without contradiction, the act of Him who created human souls in which such talents and inclinations can be found. Many qualities are applicable [to the pursuit of] some sciences and arts, and these, as it is correctly said, can not be acquired: they must be native or, to say it better, innate to the human soul.

6. Those natural talents and inclinations usually determine to what occupation, craft, art or science a person who possesses them will devote himself. Often these native talents induce those in authority to use /157/ their subordinates according to their recognized abilities.

7. Reason as well as experience teaches us very important truths related to this, namely:
    a) That everyone may choose and remain in any occupation and any class in which he can honestly and in a lawful manner make a living for himself.
    b) That everyone is obliged to act in such a way as is demanded by the duties and qualities of the occupation he has.
    c) That once one has chosen an occupation he must not /158/ abandon it foolishly. It follows from this, that a man must be content with the occupation which he chose for himself or to

which he was appointed in some other way. And he must try as much as possible to be useful to himself and to others [as long as he remains in that occupation].

8. Every occupation, every craft, every art and every science contributes to human society: and therefore every occupation and everyone who devotes himself to any occupation deserves respect. To despise something useful is unjust. Everything that provides a genuine benefit is important and worthy / 159/ of respect. Therefore one ought not despise any trade or any means of earning an honest living. Everyone can not be in the same occupation; therefore one occupation or one trade ought not despise another, because all of them are quite useful to society.

9. We ought to be amazed and thank God for His kindness and wisdom, for He not only created different things and commanded the earth to bring forth [these things] from which much can be made many things, but He also gave people inclinations and talents to occupy themselves in various ways and by this serve one another. / 160/

Part IV

On housekeeping.

Chapter One

A definition of housekeeping, its purpose and variety.

1. Knowing how to acquire possessions for oneself by honest means, keep the acquired possessions and use them intelligently for the benefit of one's own household is called *housekeeping.*

People who err in one of these three, that is, in acquiring, in keeping and in using their possessions are poor housekeepers.*

---

*A peasant, no matter how well he cultivated his land, and [no matter] how plentiful his harvest seems to be, is a poor housekeeper if he does not reap the rye at the proper time, if he lets it rot from bad weather or brings it into the granary wet and does not scatter it in the granary, if he lets it become mouldy or lets it be eaten by mice or worms, or if he misses an opportune time to sell his surplus. He should not be surprised when he does not receive the profit he could have had.

And therefore a housekeeper must /161/ think not only about acquiring, but also about protecting and putting to good use all that he has acquired.

2. Everyone needs an understanding of housekeeping because people of all stations must work and manage their homes to provide the essentials of life for themselves and their families.

By what one needs and must try to provide we mean *food, drink, clothing* and *lodging.*

Since every member of society must to some degree help provide for [society] needs and since the head of the household is a member of society; then /162/ he should not be content just to earn his own living; he should keep in mind what he must give to the supreme government for the well-being of society. The head of the household must also try to be in a position to be able to give something to his children, friends and the poor.

He must also save something so that he can improve his condition and so that in case of unforeseen misfortunes, during illness or in old age might be able to take care of himself.

3. Although the goal of acquiring possessions and providing the necessities for oneself and for one's family by work is identical in every occupation, nevertheless the means of realizing this goal are different for people of different stations because /163/ a rich and noble man must manage his household differently from the poor or common person. A peasant keeps his household differently from an artist or tradesman, and a merchant and civil servant manage their households differently also. Nevertheless there are some common rules which a man of any occupation follows and these [rules] are listed below.

Chapter Two

What is necessary for good housekeeping and economy.

1. For housekeeping one needs property, the prudent use and wise management of which help him obtain the necessities of life. Property can be of various kinds. Villages, fields, money /164/ personal possessions, sciences, arts and handwork are [property] and are also means of acquiring what one needs.

2. No matter what kind of property we own or what means of

support we have, *knowledge* is essential to every head of a household.

Man is not given knowledge by nature. He must try to acquire it in various ways. One can acquire knowledge by his own reasoning and various experiences, but this is difficult and dangerous for most people. Not everyone likes to ponder things at length and many are not even capable of doing so; when experiments fail, they suffer losses which are quite painful for people of moderate means. /165/

One can also acquire knowledge by [heeding] the oral or written instructions of experienced people.

Finally, by noticing what other wise people do or have done we acquire knowledge through examples.

He who wants to acquire knowledge through oral or written instructions or through examples must look to experienced people who have had success in those things about which he wants to know.

One must carefully note and understand what is most useful in the ideas and instructions of such people, and especially in their system of housekeeping, so that he might be able to follow their example.

3. From a good housekeeper we require a *strong and good will to do* /166/ *immediately, without procrastinating, whatever he considers right*. The best knowledge is useless if one does not have the strong will to do what he has recognized as right. Though people always wish and do what is really good for them or what seems [good] to them, if the good itself contradicts their inclinations or [upsets] their peace, or if something else attracts them more, then often they do not care about [doing] things which they themselves consider good. Such people must convince themselves that whatever they ought to do is not only really good, but deserves to be preferred over anything else.

4. For housekeeping one needs great diligence. One who is industrious and constantly /167/ tries to acquire as much as possible by lawful and honest means is diligent, but one who does not like to work and avoids it is lazy and unconscientious. Such a man spends his best time in vain, and when he does do something, he does not get so great a benefit as he would have if he had used his time and energy more prudently.

5. One man cannot do everything in the house by himself. *The wife,*

children and servants must help the head of the household, and in order to receive such help the head of the household must organize everything that is needed and see that his instructions are carried out. He must explain clearly to each of his subordinates what must be done, and if any of them errs he must correct them with seriousness and at the same time / 168/ with gentleness. He must provide them with the necessary material support, pay all hired hands the promised wage at the proper time, treat all in the household not cruelly and savagely but kindly, and induce them to decency without which all our efforts are vain and useless. Most of all, the head of the household must take care in the upbringing of his children and not think only about feeding them and teaching them to work to the limit of their strength. Rather he should, either by himself or through others, give them advice from which they might learn to understand and do what is necessary for their well-being at present and in the future.

Everyone in the household, that is, the lady of the house, the children and the servants must love the head of the household or master / 169/ as a benefactor and guardian. They should honour him as their superior and obey him in everything, unless his orders are in conflict with the Holy Commandments or regulations of government authorities. In short, they should act in the interest of the household in every way possible and to avert all misfortunes.

6. In every household there must be *order.* The head of the household, if he wants to be orderly, must undertake only those deeds which offer a real possibility of making him prosperous under existing circumstances. Order in the household also entails doing everything at the proper time, not at /170/ the wrong time and doing everything properly. The head of the household must prescribe what members of the household are to do beforehand, not at the time something is to be done. A proper place must be assigned for everything and he should see that everything is returned to its original place after it is used.

7. The head of the household should *keep a careful account of income and expenses,* note everything precisely and keep an inventory of everything he owns, review it often and check his possessions with it. Without recording [this information] and making notes he will never know exactly how much he has received and spent, how much he owns at present or whether his financial situation has become better or worse. /171/

8. *Economy* is an essential quality for a housekeeper. It consists in wisdom as regards expenses and every use of one's possessions in general.

One who can not save what he has acquired will have nothing even if he has a large income.

A good housekeeper must spend and pay out from what he has only what is necessary to provide necessities or some innocent pleasure, and sometimes in the interests of simple decency. Another reason he ought not spend everything he earns is in order to have something left over for a time of need, so that with [his savings] he can earn more, or give to the poor, or leave something for his family. One who spends everything he earns /172/ can not save anything for the above mentioned needs. He who spends more than he earns is a squanderer and in time will become a beggar or swindler.

There are examples everywhere of people who earned for themselves considerable prosperity without having a large income at the beginning. Wise and orderly management of what was necessary to spend and self-restraint from [acquiring] superfluous things have been the means by which many have become rich.

Some people have earned their wealth through the zealousness with which they saved their possessions from damage. [Such possessions] are needed for [various] exigencies for one's comfort, and purchase or repair of them is a great expense, if /173/ they are not zealously saved or taken care of. And how many belongings are there in each house? No matter how insignificant they may seem, their great number and their daily use makes them quite indispensable.

Chapter Three

Deficiencies and errors in housekeeping.

1. It is equally detrimental for a housekeeper to think either too much or too little about what he must do. The first makes him indecisive and this is of no help to him; the second deprives him even of that advantage he might otherwise have had. A wise man reasons and deliberates about the most fitting means /174/ to acquire property, about how to keep what he has acquired, and about what useful purpose he can put it to. He does not, however, stop at deliberation, but [rather] sets about realizing what he

found to be most useful. He prepares himself accordingly and diligently tries to achieve [that which he set out to do].

2. The good housekeeper must consider diligently how to manage his business in the best and most useful way. He must think whether what he does is really good, whether it is in accordance with the rules of good housekeeping, whether there is some other way to do it better. Such thoughts are helpful to the housekeeper if he acts according to them and conducts his housekeeping accordingly. /175/

3. There are things that are good by themselves, but under certain circumstances actually cause harm. The housekeeper must diligently consider those circumstances so that he might not suffer loss or for the sake of a small profit lose a large one.*

4. A housekeeper should not be negligent, but remain firm and tireless in his labours even though this is sometimes burdensome and difficult. *One should not interfere* in the business of other occupations, lest he undertake something beyond his abilities. It is also impossible for one man to undertake very varied tasks profitably because he loses his primary business by occupying himself with secondary concerns, and people of other stations are hurt. Every man can find enough to do in his own occupation and very often he does not even have enough strength to perform the function of his own occupation.

5. One must be careful in his work not to forget his duties *to God, to himself and to his neighbour.*
    We sin before God when we covet what we have acquired, give our whole heart to temporal well-being and forget God, use our possessions for sinful [purposes] and without extreme /177/ need work on days which have been designated as holidays.
    One violates his obligations to himself if he does not care about eternal bliss while acquiring temporal goods and spends his wealth parsimoniously or not at all out of stinginess in order to save more;

---

*A peasant who owns horses can make money by being a carrier. But if he realizes that his housekeeping and working the fields (which have to be plowed at the proper time) will suffer from doing so, that the manure which enriches [his land] is being wasted and consequently the harvest will be smaller, then he will see that he ought to give the proper working of his fields priority over the profit he would get from being a carrier. /176/

or if he forces himself to work so [much] that he harms his health and shortens his life.

One violates his obligation to his neighbour if he tries to enrich himself by harming others. This is done generally by actual taking or withholding. Actual taking is when someone obtains something from his neighbour either by force or by insidiousness, by false measure or weight, fraudulent goods, /178/ by deceitful trading and excessive interest, or by begging alone when one is able to make a living by working. By withholding one violates his duty to his neighbour, by borrowing and not returning, by forcing his family or servants to do more than is possible or normal, by treating them cruelly and savagely, and retaining what was promised them.

6. As much as it is indecent to multiply one's possessions in such a manner, it is equally indecent for the head of the household to fail to apply himself and not try to obtain everything he can honestly obtain under the circumstances, or for him to fail to take good care of his property so that it can be very easily stolen or damaged. /179/

Chapter Four

Several reminders to housekeepers.

1. The head of the household can be happy and calm at his work only if he believes that God consigned us to toil, and toil and work serve our interest and health, and that God blesses our toil.

2. Very often we see that some people do not succeed in anything even though they work with all their strength. Various adversities befall them without any fault of theirs, such as fires, floods, hail, bad weather, unfaithful servants and many other things which render efforts of the most diligent housekeeper useless. Those to whom this happens /180/ as it is said, have neither good luck, nor God's blessing.

3. Christian law teaches us that God governs the world, that except for this will not a single hair would fall from our head and that God blesses our good intentions. But we often lose His blessing as punishment for our sins and for disobedience of His commandments.

It follows from this that every householder must ask God's blessings in prayer and seek true piety, that is, he must restrain himself from sin and obey God in order not to make himself unworthy of God's blessing.

Index